WORLD WAR I

PEOPLE, POLITICS, AND POWER

AMERICA AT WAR

WORLD WAR I

PEOPLE, POLITICS, AND POWER

EDITED BY WILLIAM L. HOSCH, ASSOCIATE EDITOR, SCIENCE AND TECHNOLOGY

Britannica®
Educational Publishing

IN ASSOCIATION WITH

ROSEN
EDUCATIONAL SERVICES

Published in 2010 by Britannica Educational Publishing
(a trademark of Encyclopædia Britannica, Inc.)
in association with Rosen Educational Services, LLC
29 East 21st Street, New York, NY 10010.

Distributed exclusively by Rosen Educational Services.
For a listing of additional Britannica Educational Publishing titles, call toll free (800) 237-9932.

First Edition

Britannica Educational Publishing
Michael I. Levy: Executive Editor
Marilyn L. Barton: Senior Coordinator, Production Control
Steven Bosco: Director, Editorial Technologies
Lisa S. Braucher: Senior Producer and Data Editor
Yvette Charboneau: Senior Copy Editor
Kathy Nakamura: Manager, Media Acquisition
William L. Hosch: Associate Editor, Science and Technology

Rosen Educational Services
Hope Lourie Killcoyne: Senior Editor and Project Manager
Maggie Murphy: Editor
Nelson Sá: Art Director
Matthew Cauli: Designer
Introduction by Julie Smith

Library of Congress Cataloging-in-Publication Data

World War I: people, politics, and power / edited by William L. Hosch.
    p. cm.—(America at war)
"In association with Britannica Educational Publishing, Rosen Educational Services."
Includes bibliographical references.
ISBN 978-1-61530-013-6 (library binding)
1. World War, 1914–1918—Juvenile literature. I. Hosch, William L. II. Title: World War 1.
III. Title: World War One.
D522.7.W68 2010
940.3—dc22

                                                                        2009033707

Manufactured in the United States of America

On the cover: Trench warfare, in which opposing forces sacrifice mobility for some degree
of protection, reached its highest development on the Western Front during World War I.
In this 1916 photo, British troops "go over the top" during the First Battle of the Somme.
Popperfoto/Getty Images

CONTENTS

43

88

115

179

196

221

INTRODUCTION

A four-year war, running from 1914 to 1918, World War I left 10 million people dead, 21 million people wounded, and nearly 8 million missing or imprisoned. While it was neither the biggest nor the most deadly war in history, this war, sometimes referred to as the Great War, is still being researched and written about nearly 100 years later. Beyond the 39 million people directly affected by this epic struggle, empires were toppled, revolutions incited, and the seeds of another global war sewn.

The effects of the Great War were felt far and wide and lasted years after the fighting had stopped. Some scholars argue that these effects—notably what Germans viewed as the financially punitive aspects of the Versailles Treaty—led to the beginnings of World War II. Within the pages of this book, readers will find a robust scholarship surrounding the roots of World War I, the strategic battles and alliances, the key political and military leaders, the all-important introduction of technology onto the battlefield, and the geopolitical ramifications of the Great War.

Early in 1914, the advent of industrialization and increasingly complex trade issues made international politics tense for the imperial governments involved, but war was not considered inevitable. The spark that lit the fuse of the Great War was the assassination of one man,

Archduke Francis Ferdinand of Austria. On June 28, 1914, the Archduke, heir to the Austrian throne, and his wife, Sophie, duchess of Hohenberg, were shot and killed in the Bosnian capital of Sarajevo by a 19-year-old Bosnian Serb, Gavrilo Princip.

The assassination of the Archduke changed everything, moving Austria-Hungary toward all-out war. Initially, the Austrian government ordered only an investigation into the assassination, but behind the scenes the Habsburg monarchy obtained German support for retaliation against Serbia. Though the assassin and his companions were residents of Bosnia and therefore subjects of the Habsburgs, the Austrian government alleged that the assassination plot was conceived in Belgrade with the assistance of Serbian officials.

Less than a month later, the Habsburg officials presented Serbia with an ultimatum, to which Serbian officials responded within 48 hours. They accepted all but one demand. Austrian leaders broke off relations and declared war on July 28, 1914.

Austro-Hungarian forces began to attack Belgrade the next day, which led Russia to order a mobilization against Austria-Hungary. This action led Germany, Austria-Hungary's ally, to issue ultimatums. Germany demanded that Russia halt mobilization, and that France remain neutral, should war be declared

German soldiers, wearing their distinctive Pickelhaube helmets, practice maneuvers as they prepare for war in June 1914. Topical Press Agency/Hulton Archive/Getty Images

between Germany and Russia. France and Russia ignored the German demands, which brought about both Germany's order for mobilization against Russia as well as France's initial mobilization against Germany. Germany then threatened Belgium, demanding free passage through that country to France.

The conflict that would embroil the world began in the first week of August 1914, when Germany declared war on France, and well-trained and disciplined German troops invaded Belgium. Great Britain, which had no reason to support Serbia, Russia, or France, was obligated to defend Belgium, which led them to declare war on Germany that same week. With lightning-fast speed, Austria-Hungary declared war against Russia, Japan, and Belgium; Serbia and Japan declared war against Germany; Montenegro declared war against Austria-Hungary and Germany; and France and Great Britain declared war against Austria-Hungary. This rush to war all happened by the end of the month.

As alliances were solidified, the war was divided into the Central Powers: mainly Austria-Hungary, Germany, and Turkey; and the Allies: mainly France, Great Britain, Russia, Italy, and Japan (later joined by the United States).

Patriotic fervour was running high at the outset of the war, creating an intense feeling of "right against might" that propelled Europeans to support their home countries through the war's infancy. No one could have known in the summer of 1914 that this conflict would grow from a clash among Europeans to a long, drawn-out total war involving belligerents from six of the seven continents, inflicting carnage and devastation on a scale the world had never seen.

In the initial stages of the Great War, the Allies had clear advantages—industrially, demographically, and militarily. And though the United States was still neutral at this point, the young nation supported the Allies.

But the Allies' advantages notwithstanding, there was no denying the superior training of the German army, long feared by many other nations. German military leaders were considered some of the best in the world at the beginning of the 20th century. In an effort to ally themselves against the perceived threat of the German army, in 1904 France and Britain had signed the Entente Cordiale. The two countries then began to include Russia in negotiations, which became known as the Triple Entente. Once the negotiations began with Russia, Germany began to fear attack from the three allied countries, prompting them to plan for that military eventuality. In 1904, in answer to the German government's concern surrounding the Triple Entente, German Army Chief of Staff Alfred von Schlieffen was tasked with developing a plan to counter a joint attack.

His plan, known as the Schlieffen Plan, became the key German strategy for the

German infantrymen stream through a field as they invade France in November 1914.
Popperfoto/Getty Images

beginning of World War I. The Schlieffen Plan revolved around the swift defeat of France, which would give Great Britain and Russia pause, especially given the prolonged period of time Germany believed it would take the Russians to organize their large army. The strategy called for France's surrender before Russian mobilization could take place.

During the first days of August 1914, the Schlieffen Plan was put into operation, with Germany rushing into Belgium, a neutral country. Much to their surprise though, the Germans were held up by the Belgian army, and were further stunned by the speedy Russian advance into East Prussia. Germany was also taken aback by the quick arrival of the British into France and Belgium.

The First Battle of the Marne, the first major battle of the Western Front of the war, was fought in September 1914. It established the trench warfare with which World War I would become indelibly linked. As the Germans advanced into France, coming within 30 miles of Paris, the French army commander, Joseph Joffre, decided that the best form of defense for his troops would be to attack the advancing Germans. On Sept. 6, 1914, France's Sixth Army attacked the Germans with 150,000 French soldiers.

The attack caused the German army to split, and August von Moltke, German chief of staff ordered a retreat to the Aisne River. There they dug trenches and waited for the Allied army to advance. It was then that the Germans discovered the fatal flaw in the Schlieffen Plan: there was no contingency plan for the French fighting back. The costs of the battle were high on all sides, with the French and the Germans each losing nearly a quarter of a million soldiers, and the British Expeditionary Force (BEF) losing over 10,000.

The trench warfare employed by the Germans in this first battle set the stage for numerous stalemates, on all fronts, through the next three years of war. By the end of 1914, the Germans had replaced von Moltke with Erich von Falkenhayn, who decided that his army would be best served by focusing on the Eastern Front until the impasse created by the trenches could be overcome. He also worked to develop German economic organization and management of resources, which prepared them well for the British blockade.

The Allies were divided on how to break the deadlock. The French wished to continue their assault on the Germans entrenched in their homeland. The British were of two minds: some were with the French, others wished to move against the Central Powers either in the Balkans or by landing on the German Baltic Coast.

The British stayed true to the adage "necessity is the mother of invention," devising a plan to build a device that could withstand machine gun fire and break through the trenches. Conceived by Col. Ernest Swinton and guided through the development process by its champion, Winston Churchill, at that time first lord of the Admiralty, the weapon that came into being in 1916 was none other than the tank.

But the tank was not the only innovative technology devised during the Great War that would change the face of warfare. The burgeoning industries throughout the world were able to develop machines and technologies that strengthened the offensive and defensive military operations. These innovations included weaponry such as bolt-action rifles, long-range artillery, machine guns, a more effective hand grenade, and high-explosive shells.

Another technological advance—if such a term can be used—was the

France's Gen. Joseph Jacques Joffre (surrounded by, left to right, British Gens. John French and Douglas Haig) plans the Allies' next move near the front lines early in 1915. Time & Life Pictures/Getty Images

development of chemical weapons. In 1915, the German Army first used a windborn chemical cloud of chlorine gas in Ypres, France. Soon, both sides sent choking agents such as phosgene gas and blistering agents such as mustard gas across enemy lines. This in turn led to the development of gas masks and protective overgear. Though deadly, these weapons ultimately had little impact on the course of the war.

Transportation technology developments also added heretofore unimaginable advantages in warfare. Railways allowed armies to move men and materials to the front at an unprecedented rate. Aircraft, initially used as spotters, were eventually transformed into deadly weapons when machine guns were mounted behind the propeller. Manned observation balloons were used to reconnoiter troop positions and direct artillery fire.

As far as naval warfare was concerned, World War I became the breeding ground for submarine development. Indeed, the Great War was the first time submarines were seriously depended upon in combat. The development of torpedoes during World War I had more of an effect than just sinking ships, though. In 1915, when Germany sank the British passenger ship the *Lusitania*, Americans were outraged. The killing of the 1,198 passengers was one of the major reasons that the United States joined forces with the Allies. President Woodrow Wilson had been opposed to war from

the beginning, but public outcry was drummed up by several factors. One was Germany's plan for unlimited submarine warfare. Another was news that the U.S. had decoded a secret German telegram promising Mexico parts of the American southwest if it entered the war on Germany's side. These and other factors prompted the United States to declare on Germany, two years later on April 6, 1917.

The battle lines on the Western Front had barely moved from 1914 to 1917, but the entry of the United States into the war was a turning point. Not only was America's weapons production able to arm its own fighting forces as well as those belonging to France and Great Britain, its entry into battle inspired other Western Hemisphere countries such as Brazil, Costa Rica, and Honduras to declare war on Germany as well. These developments made the defeat of Germany a possibility in the eyes of the Allies, and, most important, they weakened the Central Powers' resolve. The economic contributions of the Americans also kept the Allies afloat, because by April 1917, the Allies had exhausted their finances.

The long-running war destabilized Russia to the point of anarchy, and in March 1917, the Russian Revolution overthrew the Russian monarchy. A provisional government launched an offensive against the Austrians in July, but the Germans stopped the Russians in a spectacular defeat that rocked the provisional government and gave the Bolsheviks an opening to take control. Lenin and the Marxist soviets seized power in November and ended Russian involvement in the war, signing an armistice on Dec. 15, 1917.

Although Russia's withdrawal from the war was a clear advantage to Germany, its effects were cancelled out by America's entry into the fight. The British blockade had all but starved Germany, and the 100 days' offensive that started on Aug. 8, 1918, spelled the end. An armistice was signed at 11:00 AM on Nov. 11, 1918—the 11th hour of the 11th day of the 11th month—though the Treaty of Versailles, which formally ended hostilities, was not signed until June 28, 1919.

Although the fighting had ended, the consequences of the Great War would not be fully realized for decades, as this book will illustrate. Events of history do not occur in a vacuum of time or space. Rather, they unfurl over the years, impacting politics and global relationships as time moves forward, bringing the past with it.

CHAPTER 1

THE ROOTS OF WORLD WAR I

After forty-three years of peace among the Great Powers of Europe, an act of political terrorism on June 28, 1914 provoked two great alliance systems into mortal combat. The South Slav campaign against Austrian rule in Bosnia, culminating in the assassination of Archduke Francis Ferdinand—the Habsburg heir apparent—at Sarajevo, catalyzed a rapid chain reaction leading to War. This local crisis quickly engulfed all the powers of Europe through the mechanisms of the Triple Alliance and the Triple Entente, diplomatic arrangements meant precisely to enhance the security of their members and to deter potential aggressors. The long-term causes of the war can therefore be traced to the factors that impelled the formation of those alliances, increased tensions among the Great Powers, and made at least some European leaders desperate enough to seek their objectives even at the risk of a general war. These factors include the forces of militarism and mass mobilization, instability in domestic and international politics occasioned by rapid industrial growth, global imperialism, popular nationalism, and the rise of a social Darwinist worldview. However, the question of why World War I broke out should be considered together with two further questions: why did this period of peace between the Great Powers of Europe finally end, and why did it end in 1914 rather than before or after?

A portrait of Otto Eduard Leopold von Bismarck, the first chancellor of the German Empire, c. 1880. Hulton Archive/Getty Images

INDUSTRIALISM AND IMPERIALISM

PATTERNS OF POPULATION

In the 19th century, both demographic and industrial growth in Europe were frantic and uneven, with both qualities contributing to growing misperceptions and paranoia in international affairs. The European population grew at the rate of 1 percent per year in the century following 1815, an increase that would have been disastrous had it not been for the outlet of emigration and the new prospects of employment in the rapidly expanding cities. However, as the distribution of Europe's peoples changed radically, the military balance among the Great Powers also shifted. In the days of Louis XIV, France was the wealthiest and most populous kingdom in Europe, numbering 25,000,000 to Britain's 14,500,000 as late as 1789. When the French Revolution unleashed this national power through rationalized central administration, meritocracy, and a national draft predicated on patriotism, it achieved unprecedented organization of force in the form of armies of millions of men.

The size of the French population was greatly diminished after the loss of more than a million citizens during the Revolutionary and Napoleonic Wars from 1792 to 1815. Demographic growth in France, alone among the Great Powers, was almost stagnant thereafter; by 1870, its population of 36,000,000 was nearly equal to that of Austria-Hungary and already less than Germany's 41,000,000. By 1910, Germany's population had exploded to a level two-thirds greater than France's, while vast Russia's population nearly doubled from 1850 to 1910 until it was more than 70 percent greater than Germany's. While Russia's administrative and technical backwardness offset to a degree its advantage in numbers, the demographic trends clearly traced the growing danger for France vis-à-vis Germany and the danger for Germany vis-à-vis Russia. From the early 19th century perspective, should Russia ever succeed in modernizing, it would become a colossus compared to the European continent.

Population pressure was a double-edged sword dangling above the heads of European governments in the 19th century. On the one hand, fertility meant a growing labour force and potentially a larger army. On the other hand, it threatened social discord if economic growth or external safety mechanisms could not relieve the pressure. The United Kingdom adjusted to growth through urban industrialization as well as emigration to the United States and the British dominions. France felt no such pressure but was instead forced to draft a higher percentage of its manpower to fill the army ranks. Russia exported an estimated 10,000,000 people to its eastern and southern frontiers and several million more (mostly Poles and Jews) overseas. Germany, too, sent large numbers abroad, and no other nation provided more new industrial employment from 1850 to 1910. Still, Germany's landmass was small relative to Russia's and its overseas possessions unsuitable to settlement. Furthermore, its sense of beleaguerment was acute in the face of the "Slavic threat." Demographic trends thus helped to implant in the German population a feeling of both momentary strength and looming danger.

Industrialization and Trade

Industrial trends in the 19th century magnified the demographic. As with population growth, Germany was far and away the fastest-growing economic power on the Continent. This was so not only in the basic industries of coal, iron, and steel, but also in the advanced fields of electricity, chemicals, and internal combustion. Germany's swift development strained the traditional balance of power in its own society and politics. By the end of the century, Germany had become a highly urbanized and industrial society, complete with large, differentiated middle and factory-proletariat classes. However, it was still governed largely by pre-capitalist aristocrats who were becoming increasingly threatened by vocal demands for political reform.

Industrialization also made it possible to outfit and supply mass armies drawn from the growing populations. After 1815, the monarchies of Europe had shied away from arming the masses in the French revolutionary fashion, and the events of 1848 further justified their fear of an armed citizenry. But the reserve system of Prussia provided a means of making a rapid mobilization of the citizenry possible, without the risk to the regime or the elite officer corps posed by a large standing, and idle, army. (In Austria-Hungary, the crown avoided disloyalty in the army by stationing soldiers of one ethnic group on the soil of another.) After Prussia's stunning victory over France in 1871, sooner or later all the Great Powers came to adopt the German model of a mass army, supplied by a national network of railways and arms industries coordinated in turn by a general staff. The industrialization of war meant that planning and bureaucracy, technology and finance were taking the place of bold generalship and esprit in the soldier's craft.

The final contribution to the revolution in warfare innovation was planned research and development of weapons systems. Begun hesitantly in the French Navy in the 1850s and 1860s, command technology—the collaboration of state and industry in the invention of new armaments—was widely practiced by the turn of the century, adding to the insecurity that inevitably propelled the arms races. The demographic, technical, and managerial revolutions of the 19th century, in sum, made possible the mobilization of entire populations and economies for the waging of war.

The home of the Industrial Revolution was Great Britain, whose priority in the techniques of the factory system and of steam power was the foundation for a period of calm confidence known (with some exaggeration) as the Pax Britannica. The pound sterling became the preferred reserve currency of the world, making the Bank of England the hub of international finance. British textiles, machinery, and shipping dominated the markets of Asia, South America, and much of Europe. Together, the British Isles (again with some hyperbole) were "the workshop of the world," and consequently led the world in promoting free trade from 1846 on. British diplomacy, proudly eschewing alliances in favour of "splendid isolation," sought to simultaneously preserve a balance of power on the Continent and to protect the routes to India from Russian encroachment in the Middle East or Afghanistan.

However, the Pax Britannica could last for only as long as Britain's industrial hegemony. But that period of British hegemony impelled the other European nations somehow to catch up: in the short term by imposing protective tariffs to shield domestic industries and in the longer term by granting government subsidies (for railroads and other national development work) and the gradual replication of British techniques. First Belgium, France, and New England, then Germany and other states after 1850, began to challenge Britain's industrial dominance.

France (1860), Prussia (1862), and other countries reversed earlier policies and followed the British into free trade. However, a financial panic in 1873, attributed by some to overextension in Germany after receiving France's billion-franc indemnity, ended the period of rapid growth. In the depression of 1873–96

(actually years of slower, uneven growth), industrial and labour leaders formed cartels, unions, and lobbies to agitate for tariffs and other forms of state intervention to stabilize the economy. Germany's Bismarck resisted their demands until European agriculture also suffered from falling prices and lost markets after 1876, owing to the arrival of North American cereals in European ports. In 1879 the so-called alliance of rye and steel voted a German tariff on foreign manufactured goods and foodstuffs. Free trade gave way to an era of neo-mercantilism. France, Austria, Italy, and Russia followed the new (or revived) trend toward tariff protection. After 1896 the volume of world trade rose sharply again, but the sense of heightened economic competition persisted in Europe.

Social rifts between economic classes and political opponents also hardened during this period. Challenged by unrest and demands for reforms, Bismarck sponsored the first state social insurance plans. However, he also used an attempt on the Kaiser's life in 1878 as a pretext to outlaw the Social Democratic Party. While the conservative circles of society, not only farmers but the wealthier classes as well, gradually came to distrust the loyalty of the urban working class, industrialists shared few other interests with farmers. Other countries faced similar divisions between town and country, but urbanization was not advanced enough in Russia or France for socialism to acquire a mass following. On the other hand, in Britain, agriculture had long since lost out to the commercial and industrial classes, and the working class participated fully in democratic politics. The social divisions during this period of industrialization were especially acute in Germany because of the rapidity of its development and the survival of powerful pre-capitalist elites. Moreover, the German working class, while increasingly unionized, had fewer legal recourses to state policy. All this made for a series of deadlocks in German politics that would increasingly affect foreign policy after Bismarck's departure.

IMPERIALISM AND SOCIAL DARWINISM

The 1870s and 1880s, therefore, witnessed a retreat from the free market and a return to state intervention in economic affairs. The foreign counterpart to this phenomenon was the New Imperialism. The Great Powers of Europe suddenly shook off almost a century of apathy toward its overseas colonies and, in the space of 20 years, partitioned almost the entire uncolonized portion of the globe. Britain and France were the only capital-exporting countries in 1880, and in years to come their investors preferred to export capital to other European countries (especially Russia) or the Western Hemisphere rather than to their own colonies. The British remained free-trade throughout the era of the New Imperialism, a booming home economy absorbed most German capital, and Italy and Russia were large net importers of capital. Once the scramble for colonies was complete, pressure groups

did form in the various countries to argue the economic promise of imperialism, but just as often governments had to foster colonial development. In most cases, trade did not lead but followed the flag.

Why, then, was the flag planted in the first place? Sometimes, it was to protect economic interests, as when the British occupied Egypt in 1882. More often, it was for strategic reasons or in pursuit of national prestige. One necessary condition for the New Imperialism was technological prowess. Prior to the 1870s, Europeans could overpower native peoples along the coasts of Africa and Asia, but lacked the firepower, mobility, and communications that they would have needed to pacify the interior. (India was the exception, where the British East India Company had exploited an anarchic situation and allied itself with selected native rulers against others.) The tsetse fly and the *Anopheles* mosquito, indigenous insects that carried sleeping sickness and malaria, were the ultimate defenders of African and Asian jungles. However, several inventions, including shallow-draft riverboats, the steamship and telegraph, the repeater rifle and Maxim gun, and the discovery (in India) that quinine is an effective prophylactic against malaria, eventually put European colonizing forces at the advantage. By 1880, small groups of European regulars, armed with modern weapons and exercising fire discipline, could overwhelm many times their number of native troops.

The scramble for Africa should be dated, not from 1882, when the British occupied Egypt, but from the opening of the Suez Canal in 1869. The strategic importance of that waterway cannot be overstated. It was the gateway to India and East Asia, and hence, a vital interest nonpareil for the British Empire. When the Khedive of Egypt defaulted on loans owed to France and Britain, and a nationalist uprising ensued—the first such Arab rebellion against the Western presence—the French backed away from military occupation. Instead, they occupied Tunis in 1881 with Bismarck's encouragement and moral support, thus expanding their North African presence from Algeria. Prime Minister William Ewart Gladstone, otherwise an adamant anticolonialist, then established a British protectorate in Egypt. When the French reacted bitterly to the sudden presence of Britain in Egypt, Bismarck further encouraged French colonial expansion in hopes of distracting them from European power dynamics, and he then took his own country into the fray by claiming four large segments of Africa for Germany in 1884. In that year, the king of the Belgians cast his eye on the entire Congo Basin. The Berlin West Africa Conference of 1884–85 was called to settle a variety of disputes involved in European colonial occupation, and over the next 10 years all the Great Powers of Europe, except for Austria and Russia, staked out colonies and protectorates on the African continent. But whatever the ambitions and rivalries of military adventurers, explorers, and private empire-builders on the scene were, the cabinets of Europe came to agreements on colonial boundaries with

surprising neighbourliness. Colonial wars did ensue after 1894, but never between any two European colonial powers.

It has been suggested that imperial rivalries were a long-range cause of World War I. It has also been said that they were a safety valve, drawing off European energies that might otherwise have erupted in war much sooner. But the links between imperialism and the war are more subtle. The heyday of the New Imperialism, especially after 1894, created a tacit understanding among the European elites and the broad literate classes that the days of the old European balance of power were over. A new world order was dawning, and any nation left behind in the pursuit of world power would sink into obscurity. This intuition surely must have fed a growing sense of desperation among the Germans, and one of paranoia among Britons, about trends in global politics. A second point is that the New Imperialism, while it did not directly provoke World War I, did occasion a transformation of alliances that proved dangerous beyond reckoning once the Great Powers turned their attention away from their colonies and back to Europe.

The British naturalist Charles Darwin published *The Origin of Species* in 1859, and within a decade his theories of natural selection and survival of the fittest had been applied—or misapplied—to contemporary politics and economics. This pseudoscientific social Darwinism appealed to educated Europeans already demoralized by a century in which religious scripture had been criticized, and they had become conscious of the competitiveness of their own daily lives in that age of freewheeling industrial capitalism. By the 1870s, books appeared explaining the outcome of the Franco-German War, for instance, with reference to the "vitality" of the Germanic peoples by comparison to the "exhausted" Latins. Pan-Slavic literature extolled the youthful vigour of that race, of whom Russia was seen as the natural leader. A belief in the natural affinity and superiority of Nordic peoples sustained Joseph Chamberlain's conviction that an Anglo-American–German alliance should govern the world in the 20th century. Non-scholarly Anthropology during this period explained the relative merits of human races on the basis of physiognomy and brain size, a "scientific" approach to world politics occasioned by the increasing contact of Europeans with Asians and Africans. Racialist rhetoric became common currency, as when the Kaiser referred to Asia's growing population as "the yellow peril" and spoke of the next war as a "death struggle between the Teutons and Slavs." Poets and philosophers idealized combat as the process by which nature weeds out the weak and improves the human race.

By 1914, therefore, the political and moral restraints against war that had arisen after the period between 1789–1815 were significantly weakened. The old conservative notion that established governments had a heavy stake in peace, lest revolution engulf them, and the old liberal notion that national unity, democracy, and free trade would spread harmony, were all but dead. The historian cannot judge how much social Darwinism influenced specific policy decisions, but a mood of fatalism and bellicosity surely eroded the collective will to peace.

THE TRIPLE ENTENTE

In 1905, the Germans seized on Russia's temporary troubles to pressure France in Morocco. German Chancellor and Prussian Prime Minister Bernhard, prince von Bülow, believed he had much to gain. At best, he might force a breakup of the Anglo-French entente, and at worst he might provoke a French retreat and secure German rights in Morocco. But at the Algeciras Conference in 1906, when called to settle the Morocco dispute, only Austria-Hungary supported the German position. Far from breaking the Entente Cordiale, the affair prompted the British to begin secret staff talks with the French military. The United States, Russia, and even Italy, Germany's erstwhile partner in the Triple Alliance, took France's side. For some years, Italian ambitions in the Mediterranean region had been thwarted, and the attempt to conquer Abyssinia in 1896 had failed. The German alliance seemed to offer little to Italy's benefit, while Rome's other foreign objective, the Italian *irredenta* in the Tirol and Dalmatia, was aimed at Austria-Hungary. So in 1900, Italy concluded a secret agreement pledging support for France in Morocco in return for French support of Italy in Libya. The Russo-Japanese War also strengthened ties between France and Russia, while French loans again rebuilt Russia's shattered armed forces. Finally, and most critically, the defeated Russians and worried British were now willing to put to rest their old rivalry in Central Asia. The Anglo-Russian Convention of 1907 made Tibet a neutral buffer, recognized Britain's interest in Afghanistan, and partitioned Persia into spheres of influence. Foreign Secretary Sir Edward Grey also hinted at the possibility of British support for Russian policy in the Balkans, reversing a century-old tradition.

The heyday of European imperialism thus called into existence a second alliance system, the Triple Entente of France, Britain, and Russia. It was not originally conceived as a balance to German power, but that was its effect, especially in light of the escalating naval race. In 1906 the Royal Navy under the reformer Sir John Fisher launched HMS *Dreadnought*, a battleship whose size, armour, speed, and gunnery rendered all existing warships obsolete. The German government responded in kind, even enlarging the Kiel Canal at great expense to accommodate its larger ships. What were the British, dependent on imports by sea for seven-eighths of their raw materials and over half their foodstuffs, to make of German behaviour? In January 1907, a now-famous Foreign Office memo written by Senior Clerk Sir Eyre Crowe surmised that *Weltpolitik* was either a conscious bid for hegemony or a "vague, confused, and unpractical statesmanship not realizing its own drift." As Ambassador Sir Francis Bertie put it, "The Germans aim to push us into the water and steal our clothes."

For France, the Triple Entente was primarily a continental security apparatus. For Russia, it was a means of reducing points of conflict so that the antiquated tsarist system could buy time to catch up technologically with the West. For Britain the ententes, the Japanese alliance, and the "special relationship" with the United States were diplomatic props for an empire beyond Britain's capacity to defend alone. The three powers' interests by no means coincided, as disputes over Persia alone might have smashed Anglo-Russian unity if the war had not intervened. But to the Germans, the Triple Entente looked suspiciously as though it were designed to frustrate their claims to world power and prestige. German attempts to break this encirclement, however, would only alarm the entente powers and cause them to draw the loose strings into a knot. That in turn tempted German leaders, fearful that time was against them, to cut the Gordian knot with the sword. For after 1907, the focus of diplomacy shifted back to the Balkans, with European cabinets unaware, until it was too late, that alliances made with the wide world in mind had dangerously limited their freedom of action in Europe.

THE ROAD TO WAR

ANXIETY AND THE ARMS RACE

It is difficult to escape the conclusion that Europe before 1914 succumbed to hubris. The conventional images of "armed camps," "a powder-keg," or "saber rattling" almost trivialize a civilization that combined within itself immense pride in its newly expanding power and almost apocalyptic insecurity about the future. Europe bestrode the world, and yet Lord Curzon could remark, "We can hardly take up our morning newspaper without reading of the physical and moral decline of the race," and the German chief of staff, Helmuth von Moltke, could say that if Germany backed down again on Morocco, "I shall despair of the future of the German Empire." France's stagnant population and weak industry made its statesmen frantic for security, while Austrian leaders were filled with foreboding about their increasingly disaffected nationalities. Meanwhile, the tsarist regime, with the most justification, sensed doom.

Whether from ambition or insecurity, the Great Powers armed themselves as never before in peacetime, with military expenditures reaching 5 to 6 percent of their respective national incomes. Military conscription and reserve systems made available a significant percentage of the adult male population, and the impulse to create large standing armies was strengthened by the widespread belief that firepower and financial limitations would make the next war short and violent. Simple reaction also played a large role. Fear of the "Russian steam-roller" was sufficient to expand Germany's service law. Newly larger, the German army then provoked the outmanned French into an extension of national service to three years. Only Britain did without a large conscripted army, but its naval needs were proportionally more expensive.

In an age of heavy, rapid-fire artillery, infantry rifles, and railroads, but not yet including motor transport, tanks, or airplanes, a premium was placed by military staffs on mass, supply, and prior planning. European commanders assumed that in a continental war the opening frontier battles would be decisive, hence the need to mobilize the maximum number of men and move them at maximum speed to the border. The meticulous and rigid advance planning that this strategy required placed inordinate pressure on the diplomats in a crisis. Politicians might hold back their armies in hopes of saving the peace, only to risk losing the war should diplomacy fail. Furthermore, all the continental powers embraced offensive strategies. The French general staff's "cult of attack" assumed that élan could carry the day against superior German numbers. Its Plan XVII called for an immediate assault on Lorraine. The Germans' Schlieffen Plan addressed the problem of war on two fronts by throwing almost the entire German army into a

A map of Europe, 1911. Courtesy of The University of Texas Libraries, The University of Texas at Austin

sweeping offensive through neutral Belgium to capture Paris and the French army in a gigantic envelope. Troops could then be transported east to meet the slower-moving Russian army. Worked out down to the last railroad switch and passenger car, the Schlieffen Plan was an apotheosis of the industrial age: a mechanical, almost mathematical perfection that wholly ignored political factors. None of the general staffs anticipated what the war would actually be like. Had they glimpsed the horrific impending stalemate in the trenches, surely neither they nor the politicians would have run the risks they did in 1914.

Above the mass infantry armies of the early 20th century stood the officer corps, the general staffs, and, at the pinnacle, the supreme war lords: kaiser, emperor, tsar, and king. All of these men adopted military uniforms as their standard dress in these years. The army was a natural refuge for the central and eastern European aristocracies, the chivalric code of arms sustaining almost the only public service to which they could still reasonably lay claim. Even in republican France a nationalist revival after 1912 excited public morale, inspired the military buildup, and both fueled and cloaked a revanche aimed at recovery of the provinces lost 40 years before. Popular European literature poured forth bestsellers depicting the next war, and mass-circulation newspapers incited even the working classes with news of imperial adventures or the latest slight by the adversary.

PEACE MOVEMENTS

Various peace movements sprang up to counter the spirit of militarism before 1914. However, movements planned by the Socialists were the most numerous, and also the most disturbing to those responsible for national defense. The Second International took the Marxist view of imperialism and militarism as creatures of capitalist competition, and loudly warned that if the bosses provoked a war, the working classes would refuse to take part. Jean Jaurès defined the proletariat as "masses of men who collectively love peace and hate war." The 1912 Basel Conference declared the proletariat

"the herald of world peace" and proclaimed "war on war." Sober observers like George Bernard Shaw and Max Weber doubted that any putative sense of solidarity among workers would outweigh their nationalism, but the French government kept a blacklist of agitators who might try to subvert mobilization in any case. Some of Germany's leaders imagined that war might provide the opportunity to crush socialism by appeals to patriotism or martial law.

A liberal peace movement with a middle-class constituency flourished around the turn of the century. As many as 425 peace organizations are estimated to have existed in 1900, half of them in Scandinavia and most others in Germany,

A portrait of George Bernard Shaw, c. 1905. Library of Congress Prints and Photographs Division

Britain, and the United States. Among their greatest achievements were the Hague conferences of 1899 and 1907, at which the powers agreed to ban certain inhumane weapons but made no progress toward general disarmament. However, the liberal peace movement also foundered on internal contradictions. To outlaw war was to endorse the international status quo, yet liberals always stood ready to excuse wars that could claim progressive ends. They had tolerated the wars of Italian and German unification, and they would soon tolerate the Balkan Wars against the Ottoman Empire in 1912–13 and the Great War in 1914. Another solution for many peace advocates was to transcend the nation-state. Norman Angell's *The Great Illusion* (1910) argued that it already had been transcended. Angell's opinion was that interdependence among nations made war illogical and counterproductive. To Marxists, this image of capitalism was ludicrous; to Weber or Joseph Schumpeter, it was correct, but beside the point. Blood was thicker than class, or money. Politics now dominated economics, and irrationality dominated reason.

The one European statesman most sympathetic to the peace movements was, not surprisingly, Britain's Liberal foreign secretary, Sir Edward Grey. Citing the waste, social discord, and international tension caused by the naval arms race, he made several overtures to Germany in hopes of ending it. When these overhauls failed, Britain had little choice but to race more quickly than the Germans toward preparing for war. Even radical Liberals like David Lloyd George had to admit that however much they might deplore arms races in the abstract, all that was liberal and good in the world depended on the security of Britain and its control of its seas.

CRISIS IN THE BALKANS

GROWING TENSIONS AND GERMAN ISOLATION

In the end, war was not declared over the naval race, commercial competition, or imperialism. It was not sparked by the institutional violence of the armed states, either. War among nations was provoked by underground terrorism in the name of an oppressed people. It did not come over the ambitions of Great Powers to become greater, but over the fear of one Great Power that unless it took vigorous action it might cease to exist altogether. The first "world war" began in the Balkans.

In 1897, Austria-Hungary and Russia had agreed to put their dispute over the Balkans aside. When the agreement ran out in 1907, the Ottoman Empire still ruled Macedonia, ringed by Greece, Montenegro, Serbia, and Bulgaria. However, everything else had changed. For now, Austria-Hungary's only reliable ally was Germany, whose *Weltpolitik* had led it to join the competition for influence at Constantinople. Russia was looking again at the Balkans for foreign policy advantage and enjoying, for the first time, a measure of British tolerance. In Serbia, the state most threatening to Vienna because of its ethnic tie to the Serbs and Croats inside the Dual Monarchy, a fundamental political shift had occurred. Although in previous years, Vienna had neutralized Serbia by bribing the ruling Obrenović dynasty, in 1903 the rival Karageorgević clan seized control in Belgrade in a bloody coup d'état and shifted to a violently anti-Austrian policy. Finally, in 1908, a cabal of officers known as the Young Turks staged the first modernizing revolution in the Muslim world and tried to force the Sultan to adopt liberal reforms. In particular the Young Turks called for parliamentary elections, thereby placing in doubt the status of Bosnia and Hercegovina, provinces still under Ottoman sovereignty but administered by Austria-Hungary since 1878. The Austro-Hungarian foreign minister, Aloys Aehrenthal, proposed to settle the Bosnian issue and to crush Serbian ambitions finally by annexing the provinces. To this purpose he teased the Russian foreign minister, Aleksandr Petrovich Izvolsky, with talk of a quid pro quo. If Russia acquiescenced in annexation, in return Austria-Hungary would open the Dardanelles to Russian warships. When instead Aehrenthal acted unilaterally, and Izvolsky's straits proposal was rejected, the Russians felt betrayed. Their response was to increase aid and comfort to their client Serbia, and to determine never again to back down in the Balkans.

In Germany, politics were also approaching a breaking point. Chancellor von Bülow had governed both the moderate and conservative parties in the Reichstag, as well as the Kaiser, with the support of Tirpitz, on the basis of a grand compromise of which the navy was the linchpin. Agrarian interests continued to demand protection against foreign foodstuffs, but the tariffs imposed to that end harmed German industrial exports. A large armaments program, especially naval, compensated heavy industry for lost foreign markets. Furthermore, consumers suffered especially from the tariffs-plus-navy legislation arrangement; after they paid higher prices for bread, they were taxed again for the defense program. Popular resentment tended to increase the Socialist vote, and the other parties could command a majority only by banding together.

Soon, however, the expensive race to develop warships provoked a fiscal crisis that cracked the Bülow bloc and, in 1909, elevated Theobald von Bethmann Hollweg to the chancellorship. He faced the choice of ending the naval race and moderating Germany's *Weltpolitik*, or making democratic concessions to the left, or somehow rebuilding the coalition of conservative agrarians and industrialists in the teeth of Socialist opposition. Bethmann showed signs of preferring the first course of action. However, he was undercut by the pressure of industry, Tirpitz' naval propaganda, and the Kaiser's bravado, as illustrated by a damaging *Daily Telegraph* interview (1908) in which the Kaiser made inflammatory remarks about the British. When in 1912 Lord Haldane was dispatched to

Berlin to discuss a suspension of the naval arms race, the Kaiser spoiled chances for an accord by introducing a new naval bill two days before his arrival. The British then accelerated their own dreadnought construction. By now, the failure of German policy was apparent. Clearly the British would not permit Germany to challenge their sea power, while the German army agreed in 1912 to tolerate further naval expansion only if the army were granted a sharp increase in funding as well. In the 1912 elections, the Social Democrats won 110 seats and became the largest party in the Reichstag.

Germany's military and political leadership were obsessed with domestic and foreign stalemate. Reform at home meant an end to the privileged positions of the various elites; retreat abroad meant the end of Germany's dreams of world power. A bold stroke, even at the risk of war, seemed the only way out of the double impasse. In 1911, Foreign Minister Alfred von Kiderlen-Wächter tried to force the issue in Morocco, where the French clearly aimed at a formal protectorate in defiance of the Algeciras accords. Germany sent the gunboat Panther to the Moroccan port of Agadir in defense of "German interests" there. Britain again stood with France, however, and Kiderlen-Wächter acquiesced in a French Morocco in exchange for portions of French colonies in Central Africa. In France this accommodation of Germany brought down the government of Premier Joseph Caillaux, who was succeeded by Raymond Poincaré. Poincaré, a determined nationalist and advocate of military preparedness, quickly secured passage of an expansion of the standing army. In Britain, Winston Churchill, then first lord of the Admiralty, withdrew his fleet from the Mediterranean to home waters, making mandatory even closer military coordination with France.

This Second Moroccan Crisis confirmed Germany's isolation among the European powers, while the British, French, and Russian military buildups meant that time was on the side of the entente. Moltke had already raised the notion of preventive war, and in the Kaiser's war council of December 1912, he blustered, "War, the sooner the better." To be sure, jingoism of this sort could be found in every Great Power on the eve of the war, but only the leaders in Berlin—and soon Vienna—were seriously coming to view war not as simply a possibility, but as a necessity.

The final pre-war assault on the Ottoman Empire also began in 1911. Italy cashed in its bargain with France over Libya by declaring war on Turkey and sending a naval squadron as far as the Dardanelles. Simultaneously, Russian ministers in the Balkans brought about an alliance between the bitter rivals Serbia and Bulgaria in preparation for a final strike against Ottoman-controlled Europe. The First Balkan War erupted in October 1912, when Montenegro declared war on Turkey, followed quickly by Serbia, Bulgaria, and Greece. The Young Turks ended the conflict with Italy, ceding

Libya, but failed to contain the Balkan armies. In May 1913, the Great Powers imposed a settlement in which Macedonia was partitioned among the Balkan states, Crete was granted to Greece, and Albania was given its independence. Landlocked Serbia, however, bid for additional territory in Macedonia, and Bulgaria replied with an attack on Serbia and Greece, thus beginning the Second Balkan War in June 1913. In the peace that followed in August, Bulgaria lost most of its stake in the former Turkish lands plus much of the southern Dobruja region to Romania. Serbia, however, doubled its territory and, flushed with victory, turned its sights on the Austro-Hungarian provinces of Bosnia and Hercegovina.

Assassination of Archduke Ferdinand

How might the Habsburg Empire survive the rise of particularist nationalism in eastern Europe? Austrian statesmen had debated the question for 50 years, and the best answer seemed to be some form of federalism permitting political autonomy to the nationalities. Reforms of this nature had always been vetoed by the Hungarians, who stood to lose their own position vis-à-vis the German-Austrians and the minorities in their half of the empire. Conrad Franz, Graf von Hötzendorf, chief of the general staff, favoured a preventive war against Serbia to stifle nationalist agitation for good and reinforce the old order. Archduke Francis Ferdinand wrote, however, "I live and shall die for federalism; it is the sole salvation for the monarchy, if anything can save it." Out of favour with the court for his morganatic marriage and furthermore resented by conservatives and the Hungarians alike, the heir apparent was also feared by Slavic radicals as the one man who might really pacify the nationalities and so frustrate their dreams of a Greater Serbia. Hence, the archduke was a marked man among the secret societies that sprang up to liberate Bosnia.

The National Defense (Serb-Cyrillic: *Narodna Odbrana*) was formed in Serbia in 1908 to carry on pro-Serbian and anti-Austrian agitation across the border. Its nonviolent methods were deemed insufficient by others, who in 1911 formed the secret society Union or Death (*Ujedinjenje ili Smrt*), also known as the Black Hand. This society was led by the head of Serbian military intelligence, Colonel Dragutin Dimitrijević, who had been involved in the 1903 assassinations of the Obrenović family and favoured terrorist action over intellectual propaganda. With his support, if not on his direct orders, a band of youthful romantics conspired to assassinate Francis Ferdinand during his state visit to Sarajevo. On June 28, 1914, which happened to be the Serbian national holiday, the archduke and his wife rode in an open car through the streets of the Bosnian capital. A bomb was thrown at them, but missed. The archduke completed his official duties, whereupon the governor of Bosnia suggested they deviate from the planned route on the return trip for safety's sake.

Archduke Francis Ferdinand (right) and his wife, Duchess Sophie (centre), arriving in Sarajevo, Bosnia, before being assassinated by Serbian nationalist Gavrilo Princip, June 28, 1914. Time & Life Pictures/Getty Images

However, when the lead driver in the procession took a wrong turn, the cars stopped momentarily. At that moment, the 19-year-old Gavrilo Princip fired his revolver, killing both royal passengers.

Reaction in Vienna, and Europe generally, was surprisingly restrained. No one imagined that the outrage had more than local importance, much less that Bismarck's prophecy about "some damned fool thing in the Balkans" starting the next war, was about to be fulfilled. Conrad von Hötzendorf saw the deed as pretext for his preventive war against Serbia,

but the aged emperor Francis Joseph preferred to await an inquiry to determine the extent of Serbian complicity. Germany, on the other hand, pressed for a firm riposte and in the Kaiser's famous "blank check" memo promised to support whatever action Austria might take against Serbia. The Germans expected Russia to back down, since its military reforms would not be complete for several years, but even if Russia came to Serbia's aid, the German high command was confident of victory. Bethmann was less so. A move against Serbia could lead to a world war,

Gavrilo Princip waits in his jail cell to stand trial for the assassination of Archduke Francis Ferdinand, 1914. Time & Life Pictures/Getty Images

he warned on July 7. Yet Bethmann went along in the vain hope of localizing the conflict.

Austrian Foreign Minister Leopold, Graf von Berchtold, now advocated a firm policy toward Serbia, lest Austria's prestige deteriorate further and the Balkan states unite behind Russia. Gróf Tisza, the prime minister of Hungary, insisted, however, that diplomatic and legal justifications precede such a clash of arms: Austria must first present a list of demands for redress. Should Serbia accept, the empire would win a "brilliant diplomatic success"; should Serbia refuse, war could be waged with Austria-Hungary posing as the aggrieved party. In no case was Austria to annex any Serbian territory.

The Russian response to any Austrian initiative would be critical, and by chance the president and prime minister of France, Poincaré and René Viviani, were paying a state visit to St. Petersburg in July. Strangely, there is no record of the Franco-Russian conversations, but it is known that Poincaré assured the Russians that France would stand by its alliance commitments. On July 23, just after the French leaders left for home, Vienna presented its ultimatum to Belgrade. They demanded the dissolution of the secret societies, cessation of anti-Austrian propaganda, and Austrian participation in the investigation of the Sarajevo crime. Serbia was given just 48 hours to respond.

The reaction of the Russian foreign minister, Sergey Dmitriyevich Sazonov, to the news of the ultimatum was to insist on military measures. The French ambassador, Maurice-Georges Paléologue, with or without instructions from his departed chiefs, encouraged Sazonov. If Austria's prestige—and very future—were at stake in the Balkans, so too were tsarist Russia's, as the Balkans was the only region left in which Russia could demonstrate its vitality. But now, Germany was competing for influence over the Young Turks, courting Bulgaria, and plotting to smash Serbia.

PRIMARY SOURCE: WOODROW WILSON'S APPEAL FOR NEUTRALITY

"It would be the irony of fate," Woodrow Wilson remarked before his 1913 inauguration to the office of U.S. President, "if my administration had to deal chiefly with foreign affairs." His worst fears were realized when the general European war began in August 1914 and soon became the most significant crisis he had to confront. Americans reacted to the outbreak of war with a mixture of disbelief and disgust, and with a strong determination not to become involved. Wilson's message to the Senate on August 19, which is reprinted here, echoed the sentiments of most of the nation. "We must be impartial," he declared, "in thought as well as in action." The remark became famous and was quoted often in the ensuing months of the war. Source: 63 Congress, 2 Session, Senate Document No. 566.

I suppose that every thoughtful man in America has asked himself, during these last troubled weeks, what influence the European war may exert upon the United States; and I take the liberty of addressing a few words to you in order to point out that it is entirely within our own choice what its effects upon us will be, and to urge very earnestly upon you the sort of speech and conduct which will best safeguard the nation against distress and disaster.

The effect of the war upon the United States will depend upon what American citizens say and do. Every man who really loves America will act and speak in the true spirit of neutrality, which is the spirit of impartiality and fairness and friendliness to all concerned. The spirit of the nation in this critical matter will be determined largely by what individuals and society and those gathered in public meetings do and say, upon what newspapers and magazines contain, upon what ministers utter in their pulpits and men proclaim as their opinions on the street.

The people of the United States are drawn from many nations, and chiefly from the nations now at war. It is natural and inevitable that there should be the utmost variety of sympathy and desire among them with regard to the issues and circumstances of the conflict. Some will wish one nation, others another, to succeed in the momentous struggle. It will be easy to excite passion and difficult to allay it. Those responsible for exciting it will assume a heavy responsibility, responsibility for no less a thing than that the people of the United States, whose love of their country and whose loyalty to its government should unite them as Americans all, bound in honor and affection to think first of her and her interests, may be divided in camps of hostile opinion, hot against each other, involved in the war itself in impulse and opinion if not in action.

Such divisions among us would be fatal to our peace of mind and might seriously stand in the way of the proper performance of our duty as the one great nation at peace, the one people holding itself ready to play a part of impartial mediation and speak the counsels of peace and accommodation, not as a partisan but as a friend.

I venture, therefore, my fellow countrymen, to speak a solemn word of warning to you against that deepest, most subtle, most essential breach of neutrality which may spring out of partisanship, out of passionately taking sides. The United States must be neutral in fact as well as in name during these days that are to try men's souls. We must be impartial in thought as well as in action, must put a curb upon our sentiments as well as upon every transaction that might be construed as a preference of one party to the struggle before another.

My thought is of America. I am speaking, I feel sure, the earnest wish and purpose of every thoughtful American that this great country of ours, which is, of course, the first in our thoughts and in our hearts, should show herself in this time of peculiar trial a nation fit beyond others to exhibit the fine poise of undisturbed judgment, the dignity of self-control, the efficiency of dispassionate action; a nation that neither sits in judgment upon others nor is disturbed in her own counsels and which keeps herself fit and free to do what is honest and disinterested and truly serviceable for the peace of the world.

Shall we not resolve to put upon ourselves the restraints which will bring to our people the happiness and the great and lasting influence for peace we covet for them?

The German slogan "From Berlin to Baghdad," referring originally only to railroads, took on ominous new political meaning. On July 25, the Russian Council of Ministers decided that if Austrian forces entered Serbia, Russia would mobilize its army. This precipitous decision reflected Russia's size and the inadequacy of its rail network. Sazonov seems to have considered mobilization a political threat. However, given the mechanistic timetables that were integral to the planning of all the European general staffs, it could only provoke countermobilizations and an inexorable drift into war.

On July 25, Serbia accepted all the Austro-Hungarian conditions, except for those two that directly compromised its sovereignty. Two days later, Berchtold persuaded Francis Joseph to initiate war. At the same moment, the Kaiser, returning from a yachting expedition, tried belatedly to restrain Vienna. On July 28 Austria declared war and bombarded Belgrade; on the same day the tsar approved the mobilization of the Russian army against Austria, and alarms went off all over Europe. Sir Edward Grey, Kaiser William, and the Italian government all proposed negotiations, with the Austrians to occupy Belgrade as a pledge of Serbian compliance. The German ambassador in St. Petersburg assured the Russians that Austria meant to annex no Serbian territory. Unfortunately, these negotiations came as too little, and far too late. In St. Petersburg, the generals protested that partial mobilization would disrupt their contingency plans: How could Russia prepare to fight Austria-Hungary while leaving naked its border with Austria's ally Germany? The weak and vacillating Tsar Nicholas II was persuaded that partial mobilization would be adequate, and on the afternoon of July 30 he authorized general mobilization of the Russian army.

The previous day, Poincaré and Viviani had finally arrived back in Paris, where they were met with patriotic crowds and generals anxious for military precautions. In Berlin, anti-Russian demonstrations and equally anxious generals called for immediate action. On July 31, when all the other powers had begun preparations of some sort, and even the British had put the fleet to sea (thanks to Winston Churchill's foresight), Germany delivered ultimatums to Russia, demanding an end to mobilization, and to France, demanding neutrality in case of war in the east. But Russia and France could scarcely accede without abandoning the Balkans, each other, and their own security. When the ultimatums expired, the Schlieffen Plan was put into effect. Germany declared war against Russia on August 1 and against France on August 3. They also demanded safe passage for its troops through Belgium. Refused again, Germany invaded Belgium in full force.

On August 3, Italy took refuge in the fact that this was not a defensive war on Austria-Hungary's part and declared its neutrality. That left only Britain to decide between joining its entente partners in war or standing aloof and risking German domination of the Continent. Britain had little interest in the Serbian affair, and the kingdom was torn by the Irish question. The Cabinet was in doubt as late as August 2, but the prospect of the German fleet in the English Channel and German armies on the Belgian littoral finally settled the issue. On August 3, Britain demanded that Germany evacuate Belgium, Grey winning over Parliament with appeals to British interests and international law. On August 4, Britain declared war on Germany.

Thus, a great string of war declarations began. Austria-Hungary declared war against Russia on August 5; Serbia against Germany on August 6; Montenegro against Austria-Hungary on August 7 and against Germany on August 12; France and Great Britain against Austria-Hungary on August 10 and on August 12, respectively; Japan against Germany on August 23; Austria-Hungary against Japan on August 25 and against Belgium on August 28.

Romania had renewed its secret anti-Russian alliance of 1883 with the Central Powers on Feb. 26, 1914, but now chose to remain neutral. On Sept. 5, 1914, Russia, France, and Great Britain concluded the Treaty of London, each promising not to make a separate peace with the Central Powers. Thenceforth, they could be called the Allied, or Entente, Powers, or simply the Allies.

The outbreak of war in August 1914 was generally greeted with confidence and jubilation by the peoples of Europe, among whom it inspired a wave of patriotic feeling and celebration. Few people imagined how long or how disastrous a war between the great nations of Europe could be, and most believed that their country's side would be victorious within a matter of months. The war was welcomed in one of two ways: either patriotically, as a defensive one imposed by national necessity, or idealistically, as one for upholding right against might, the sanctity of treaties, and international morality.

CHAPTER 2

THE OUTBREAK OF WAR

INITIAL MILITARY FORCES AND RESOURCES

When war broke out the Allied Powers possessed greater overall demographic, industrial, and military resources than the Central Powers. They also enjoyed easier access to the oceans for trade with neutral countries, particularly with the United States. The table at the top of page 39 shows the population, steel production, and armed strengths of the two rival coalitions in 1914.

All the initial belligerents in World War I were self-sufficient in food except Great Britain and Germany. Great Britain's industrial establishment was slightly superior to Germany's (17 percent of world trade in 1913 as compared with 12 percent for Germany). However, Germany's diversified chemical industry facilitated the production of ersatz, or substitute, materials, which compensated for the worst shortages ensuing from the British wartime blockade. The German chemist Fritz Haber was already developing a process for the fixation of nitrogen from air; this process made Germany self-sufficient in explosives and thus no longer dependent on imports of nitrates from Chile.

Of all the initial belligerent nations, only Great Britain had a volunteer army, and this was quite small at the start of the war. The other nations had much larger conscript armies that required three to four years of service from able-bodied males of military age, to be followed by several years in

STRENGTH OF THE BELLIGERENTS, AUG. 4, 1941		
RESOURCES	CENTRAL POWERS	ALLIED POWERS
POPULATION (IN MILLIONS)	115.2	265.5
STEEL PRODUCTION (IN MILLIONS OF METRIC TONS)	17.0	15.3
ARMY DIVISIONS AVAILABLE FOR MOBILIZATION IN AUGUST 1914	146	212
MODERN BATTLESHIPS	20	39

LAND FORCES OF THE BELLIGERENTS, AUG. 4, 1914			
COUNTRY	REGULAR DIVISIONS (WITH NUMBER OF FIELD ARMIES)	OTHER LAND FORCES	TOTAL MANPOWER
Central Powers			
Germany	98 (8)	27 Landwehr brigades	1,900,000
Austria-Hungary	48 (6)	—	450,000
Allied Powers			
Russia	102 (6)	—	1,400,000
France	72 (5)	—	1,290,000
Serbia	11 (3)	—	190,000
Belgium	7 (1)	69,000 fortress troops	186,000
Great Britain	6 (1)	14 territorial divisions*	120,000

*Restricted in 1914 to service at home.

reserve formations. Military strength on land was counted in terms of divisions composed of 12,000–20,000 officers and men. Two or more divisions made up an army corps, and two or more corps made up an army. An army could thus comprise anywhere from 50,000 to 250,000 men.

The land forces of the belligerent nations at the outbreak of war in August 1914 are shown in the second table on page 39.

The higher state of discipline, training, leadership, and armament of the German Army reduced the importance of the initial numerical inferiority of the armies of the Central Powers. Because of the comparative slowness of mobilization, poor higher leadership, and lower scale of armament of the Russian armies, there was an approximate balance of forces between the Central Powers and the Allies in August 1914 that prevented either side from gaining a quick victory.

Germany and Austria also enjoyed the advantage of "interior lines of communication," which enabled them to send their forces to critical points on the battlefronts by the shortest route. According to one estimate, Germany's railway network made it possible to move eight divisions simultaneously from the Western Front to the Eastern Front in just four and a half days.

Even greater in importance was the advantage that Germany derived from its strong military traditions and its cadre of highly efficient and disciplined regular officers. Skilled in directing a war of movement and quick to exploit the advantages of flank attacks, German senior officers were to prove generally more capable than their Allied counterparts at directing the operations of large troop formations—a critical ability in wartime.

NAVAL FORCES

Sea power was largely determined by the number of capital ships, or dreadnought battleships and battle cruisers having extremely large guns, a navy had. Despite intensive competition from the Germans, the British had maintained their superiority in numbers, with the result that, in capital ships, the Allies had an almost two-to-one advantage over the Central Powers. The table at the top of page 41 compares the strength of the two principal rivals at sea, Great Britain and Germany.

The numerical superiority of the British Navy, however, was offset by the technological lead of the German Navy. In many categories, such as range-finding equipment, magazine protection, searchlights, torpedoes, and mines, the Germans had the technological advantage. Great Britain relied on its Royal Navy not only to ensure necessary imports of food and other supplies in wartime, but also to sever the Central Powers' access to the markets of the world. With superior numbers of warships, Great Britain could impose a blockade that gradually weakened Germany by preventing imports from overseas.

BRITISH AND GERMAN NAVAL STRENGTH, AUGUST 1914		
TYPE	BRITISH	GERMAN
dreadnought battleships	20	14
battle cruisers	9	4
pre-dreadnought battleships	39	22
armoured cruisers	34	9
cruisers	64	41
destroyers	301*	144
submarines	65	28

*Restricted in 1914 to service at home.

NAVAL ARMAMENTS

GUNS

By 1900 a major change had occurred in the handling of the very heavy main guns, those of 11- to 13.5-inch (279 to 243 mm) calibre that fired shells weighing up to 1,300 pounds (589.7 kg). In the 1890s such weapons often fired no faster than once every 5 minutes, compared to the 5 to 10 rounds per minute fired by a 6-inch (152.4 mm) gun. As power control became easier and more precise, the big guns became more effective. By 1900 it was possible for a 12-inch (305 mm) gun to fire one or two aimed shots per minute.

Meanwhile, the standard of heavy-gun marksmanship began to improve. Although rifled guns had grown bigger and muzzle velocity had increased throughout the late 19th century, there had been no corresponding improvement in fire control. For this reason, effective battle ranges had not extended much beyond 3,000 to 4,000 yards (2.7 km to 3.7 km). Finally, it was discovered that a ship's roll and pitch could be systematically compensated for, so that each shot could be fired at the same angle to the sea and reach almost exactly the same range. Greater accuracy could be achieved by firing groups of artillery shells, or salvos, bunched around the estimated range. The pattern of splashes raised by a salvo would then make corrections possible. By the end of World War I, fire control had improved enough that guns firing 15,000 to 20,000 yards (13.7 km to 18.3 km) could attain a hit rate of 5 percent. This meant that a ship firing 10 heavy guns at the rate of once or twice per minute could expect a hit after two or three minutes.

Increased range was valuable for two reasons. First, a ship that could hit at

American factory workers produce torpedoes for the U.S. Navy, c. 1914. Boyer/Roger Viollet/ Getty Images

ranges beyond the capabilities of its enemies could stand off and destroy them at leisure. Second, improved gun range increased protection against the new, longer-range torpedoes.

TORPEDOES

Modifications and adaptations of the original design quickly made the torpedo a formidable weapon. Directional control was greatly improved in the 1890s by the use of a gyroscope to control the steering rudders. Another significant improvement was the use of heat engines for propulsion. British firms, introducing both heat engines and contrarotating propellers, advanced to the high-performance, steam-driven Mark IV torpedo of 1917. Concurrently with this development, an American firm, E.W. Bliss Company, successfully used a turbine to drive a modified design. (This Bliss-Leavitt torpedo remained in extensive use until World War II.) By 1914, torpedoes were usually 18 or 21 inches (457.2 to 533.4 mm in diameter and could reach almost 4,000 yards (3.7 km) at 45 knots or 10,000 yards (9 km) at close to 30 knots.

SHIP ARMOUR

The torpedo threat forced ship designers to provide battleships with underwater protection. Schemes to place coal bunkers near the outside of the ship proved impractical. However, research during World War I showed that the basic idea of keeping the underwater explosion at a distance from the interior of the ship was correct. In the Royal Navy, existing ships were fitted with external bulges, or "blisters," to keep the explosion farther outboard. New ships were built with specially designed layers of

An aircraft is mounted on a launching catapult atop one of the main gun turrets of HMS Queen Elizabeth, moored with the British Royal Navy fleet outside of Southend, Essex, July 1919. Topical Press Agency/Hulton Archive/Getty Images

compartments designed to absorb the shock of explosion.

During the war it also became apparent that the longer firing ranges meant that more shells would fall onto a ship's deck than on its side armour. Because these ranges were experienced at the Battle of Jutland, ships designed afterward with stronger deck armour were called post-Jutland.

Ship Propulsion

While weapons were the main driving force in warship development, changes in propulsion were also important. In 1890, propulsion was exclusively by reciprocating (i.e., piston) steam engines, which were limited in power and tended to vibrate. To escape these limitations, warship designers adopted steam turbines, which ran more smoothly and had no inherent limits. Turbines were applied to destroyers from about 1900 and to battleships from 1906.

The main drawback of turbine propulsion was that really efficient turbines ran too fast to drive efficient propellers. The solution was to reduce turbine speeds to acceptable propeller speeds through gearing. By 1918, single-reduction gearing was commonplace.

Improvements in ship propulsion required more efficient methods of fueling ships. Coal was relatively inexpensive and easily available; however, it did not burn cleanly and was difficult to transfer from ship to ship at sea. On the other hand, oil burned cleanly, and it could be transferred easily at sea. Also, it had a higher thermal content than coal, so that the same weight or volume of oil could drive a ship much farther. The United States shifted to oil fuel in new ships in about 1910 and converted its remaining coal-burning warships after World War I. Beginning with the *Queen Elizabeth* class of battleships in 1915–16, Britain also switched to oil. However, the other navies followed suit only after the war.

In contrast to the steam engine, a gasoline or diesel engine often needed no tending at all, could be very compact, and could start and stop quite easily. Such engines made it possible to build small, fast coastal minesweepers, subchasers, and motor torpedo boats. Internal combustion was thought to be especially suitable to subchasers, which would have to stop their engines while listening for a submarine and then start them up suddenly when something was heard.

Capital Ships

Battleships

A battleship entering service in 1900 typically mounted a mixed battery of several different guns of various sizes: four heavy (11- to 13.5-inch [279 to 343 mm]) guns in two twin turrets, about a dozen secondary guns of 6 to 9 inches (152.4 to 228.6 mm), and small, fast-firing guns of 3 inches (76.2 mm) or less for beating off torpedo-boat attacks. These ships usually displaced 12,000 to 18,000 tons.

By 1904, however, studies reinforced by battle experience in the Spanish-

American and Russo-Japanese wars indicated that fire from large guns at longer ranges was more effective than mixed-battery fire closer in. Only bigger shells could do serious damage to well-armoured ships. Moreover, the shells fired from guns of many different calibres produced a confusing pattern of splashes in the water that made the correcting of aim and range quite difficult. Effectively increasing range, then, depended upon abandoning the multiple-calibre pattern of previous battleship armament in favour of a single-calibre armament. Several navies reached this conclusion simultaneously, but the British were the first to produce such a ship, HMS *Dreadnought*, completed in 1906. Displacing about 18,000 tons, it carried 10 12-inch (304.8 mm) guns; its only other armament consisted of 3-inch (76.2 mm) weapons intended to fight off destroyers.

The *Dreadnought* gave its name to an entirely new class of battleships of the most advanced design. By 1914 the Royal Navy had 22 dreadnoughts (another 13 were completed during World War I), Germany built a total of 19 (5 completed after 1914), and the United States completed 22 (14 of them after 1914). Japan and Italy built 6 each, while Russia and France each built 7. Although they all shared the same name, not all of these ships were strictly equivalent. Unlike its immediate German and American contemporaries, the *Dreadnought* had steam turbines in place of reciprocating engines. These enabled it to attain a speed of 21 knots, which was hitherto achieved only

by cruisers. (Contemporary battleships were generally limited to about 18 knots.) Thus, in mobility as well as in size, the *Dreadnought* began a new era.

HMS *Dreadnought* also marked a beginning of rapid development in big-gun firepower. In 1909 the Royal Navy laid down HMS *Orion*, the first "super dreadnought," which displaced 22,500 tons and was armed with 13.5-inch (3.43 mm) guns. The U.S. Navy followed with ships armed with 14-inch (355.6 mm) guns. Then, on the eve of World War I, the Royal Navy went a step further with HMS *Queen Elizabeth*, armed with 15-inch (381 mm) guns and capable, in theory, of 25 knots. Although World War I stopped the growth of British and German battleships, the United States and Japan continued to build ships exceeding 30,000 tons displacement. In 1916 both countries adopted the 16-inch (406.4 mm) gun, which fired a shell of approximately 2,100 pounds (952.5 kg). Such guns could be aimed to hit at ranges as great as 20,000 yards (18.3 kg).

The battleship saw little actual combat in World War I. However, despite submarines, aircraft, and destroyers, the outcome of the war still hinged upon control of the sea by the battleship. Had superiority in battleships passed to Germany, Britain would have been lost, and the Allies would have lost the war. The one moment when this might have happened was the only large-scale clash of battleships, the Battle of Jutland. Fought in May 1916 in mist, fog, and darkness, Jutland revealed the strengths and weaknesses of battleships and battle cruisers. Three British battle cruisers were lost. Several German battleships, thanks to watertight subdivision and efficient damage-control systems, survived despite more hits. However, Germany saw that the British advantage in battleship numbers was decisive, and instead turned to the submarine to counter the Allied blockade.

CRUISERS

HMS *Dreadnought* made earlier large cruisers obsolete, since it was nearly as fast as any of these ships. Consequently, the Royal Navy built a series of ships it called battle cruisers. These were as large as the newest battleships and were armed with battleship guns, but they were much faster (initially a top speed of 25 knots, compared with the 21 knots of battleships). The first one built was the HMS *Invincible*, completed in 1907. Many of these ships were built: 10 for the Royal Navy before 1914, 7 for Germany, and 4 for Japan.

Battle cruisers gained their superior speed by sacrificing heavy armour. As a consequence, they could not stand up to battleships. This was proved at the Battle of Jutland, where the *Invincible* was blown into two pieces by a single salvo and sunk along with two other battle cruisers. These losses led many to argue that the battle cruiser was a mistake, but during the war Britain started to build six more, three of which were eventually completed. The last of them, HMS *Hood*, launched in 1918, could be described as

a new stage in warship development. It was so large, at 41,200 tons, that it could combine contemporary battleship armour and armament (equivalent to that of HMS *Queen Elizabeth*) with the very high speed of 31 knots. Although classed as a battle cruiser, it was actually the first of a new generation of very fast battleships.

At the other end of the cruiser spectrum were small, fast "scout" cruisers used for reconnaissance and escort duties. These ships displaced from 3,000 to 7,000 tons and, by 1915, attained speeds as high as 30 knots. They were armed with guns of smaller calibre, usually 6 or 7.5 inches (152.4 to 190.5 mm). The British built many of this type of cruiser, as well as larger types that were nevertheless smaller than their battle cruisers.

DESTROYERS

The greatest impact of the self-propelled torpedo was on the design of small surface ships. Beginning in the 1880s, many nations built hundreds of small steam torpedo boats on the theory that they could bar any enemy from coastal waters. Because their hulls could be crammed with machinery, torpedo boats were quite fast. By the early 1890s, speeds as high as 25 knots were being reported. As a defense against this new fast threat, Britain deployed oversized torpedo boats, calling them torpedo boat destroyers. These craft were successful in hunting down torpedo boats. Eventually they were renamed "destroyers."

German infantrymen operating a Maxim machine gun during World War I. Imperial War Museum

The first destroyers were essentially coastal craft, displacing only about 200 tons. Their larger successors, however, could accompany battle fleets to sea. There it soon became apparent that a destroyer was, in effect, a superior sort of torpedo boat because it was capable of delivering its weapon against capital ships during or immediately after a fleet engagement. By 1914, 800- or even 1,000-ton destroyers were quite common.

During World War I British destroyer design changed radically, creating what became the postwar formula of the V and W destroyer classes. These ships had four 4-inch (101.6 mm) guns superimposed fore and aft, a high forecastle forward for greater sea-keeping ability, and two sets of twin (later triple) torpedo tubes amidships. These vessels, displacing about 1,200 tons and capable of 34 knots, made all earlier British destroyers obsolete.

In Focus: Submachine Gun

Submachine guns are lightweight, automatic small-arms weapons chambered for relatively low-energy pistol cartridges, meant to be fired from the hip or shoulder. Most types utilize relatively simple blowback actions. Using cartridges of such calibres as .45 inch or 9 millimetre, they usually have box-type magazines that hold from 10 to 50 cartridges, or occasionally drums holding more rounds. A short-range weapon, the submachine gun is rarely effective at more than 200 yards (182.9 m). However, it fires at rates as high as 650 or more rounds per minute and weighs 6 to 10 pounds (2.7 to 4.5 kg).

Developed during World War I, the submachine gun came into great demand during World War II because of the need to increase the individual soldier's firepower at close quarters. The Germans developed the first such weapons, modeling them to some extent after the Italian double-barreled Villar Perosa, or VP, a 1915 innovation that fired so fast it emptied its magazine in two seconds. The Germans identified their weapon, the first true submachine gun, as the MP18, or the Bergmann Muskete. This weapon was first issued in 1918, the last year of World War I. In Britain submachine guns came to be called machine carbines; in Germany, machine pistols; in the United States, submachine guns. An American type, the Thompson submachine gun, or tommy gun, was patented in 1920.

When Germany adopted unrestricted submarine warfare in February 1917, significant shipping losses soon forced the diversion of destroyers from fleet duty to convoy protection and antisubmarine warfare. Destroyers were not ideally suited to the escort role, as they had limited steaming range and their high-speed design made them less seaworthy than the merchant ships they were required to escort. While the Royal Navy therefore built several types of specialized convoy escort, the U.S. Navy found it easier to mass-produce its current destroyer design. These vessels, equipped with hydrophones and depth charges, as well as guns and torpedoes, overcame the submarine threat and had a large share in the safe convoy of 2 million U.S. troops to Europe without loss of a single soldier.

MACHINE GUNS AND MODERN ARTILLERY

The planning and conduct of war in 1914 were crucially influenced by both the invention of new weapons and the improvement of existing types since the Franco-German War of 1870–71. The chief developments of the intervening period had been the machine gun and the rapid-fire field artillery gun. The modern machine gun had been designed in the 1880s and '90s, was a reliable belt-fed gun capable of sustained rates of extremely rapid fire; it could fire 600 bullets per minute with a range of more than 1,000 yards (914.4 m).

The introduction of smokeless powder in the 1880s made it possible to convert the hand-cranked machine gun into a truly automatic weapon, primarily because smokeless powder's even combustion made it possible to harness the recoil so as to work the bolt, expel the spent cartridge, and reload. Hiram Stevens Maxim of the United States was the first inventor to incorporate this effect in a weapon design. The Maxim machine gun (*c.* 1884) was quickly followed by others—the Hotchkiss, Lewis, Browning, Madsen, Mauser, and other guns. Some of these guns utilized another property of the even burning of smokeless powder: small amounts of the combustion gas were diverted through a port to drive a piston or lever to open the breech as each round was fired, admitting the next round. As a result, during World War I the battlefield was from the outset dominated by the new machine gun, generally belt-fed, water-cooled, and of a calibre matching that of the rifle. Except for synchronizing with aircraft propellers, the machine gun remained little changed throughout World War I and into World War II. Since then, innovations such as sheet-metal bodies and air-cooled, quick-changing barrels have made machine guns lighter and more reliable and quick-firing. However, they still operate under the same principles as in the days of Hiram Maxim.

Most machine guns employ gas generated by the explosion of the cartridge to drive the mechanism that introduces the new round in the chamber. The machine gun thus requires no outside source of power, but instead uses the energy released by the burning propellant in a cartridge to feed, load, lock, and fire each round and to extract and eject the empty cartridge case. This automatic operation may be accomplished by any of three ways: blowback, recoil, and gas operation.

In simple blowback operation, the empty cartridge case is hurled backward by the explosion of the cartridge. Thereby the cartridge case pushes back the bolt, or breechblock, which in turn compresses a spring and is returned to the firing position upon that spring's recoil. The basic problem involved in blowback is to control the rearward motion of the bolt so that the gun's cycle of operation (i.e., loading, firing, and ejection) takes place correctly. In recoil operation, the bolt is locked to the barrel immediately after a round is fired. Both the bolt and barrel recoil, but the barrel is then returned forward by its own spring while the bolt is held to the rear by the locking mechanism until a fresh round has fallen into place in the opened breech.

More common than either of these two methods is gas operation. In this method, the energy required to operate the gun is obtained from the pressure of gas tapped off from the barrel after each cartridge explodes. In a typical gas-operated machine gun, an opening or port is provided in the side of the barrel at a point somewhere between the breech and the muzzle. When the bullet has passed this opening, some of the high-pressure gases behind it are tapped off through the hole and operate a piston or some similar device for converting the pressure of the powder gases to a thrust. This thrust is then used through a suitable mechanism to provide the energy necessary for performing the automatic functions required for sustained fire: loading, firing, and ejection.

In the realm of field artillery, the period leading up to the war saw the introduction of improved breech-loading mechanisms and brakes. Without a brake or recoil mechanism, a gun lurched out of position during firing and had to be re-aimed after each round, costing a soldier valuable time. The new improvements were epitomized in the French 75-millimetre (2.9 in) field gun; it remained motionless during firing, and it was not necessary to readjust the aim in order to bring sustained fire on a target. When used in combination with trenches and barbed-wire emplacements, machine guns and rapid-firing artillery gave a decided advantage to the defense. These weapons' rapid and sustained firepower could

British Mark I tank with antibomb roof and "tail," 1916. Courtesy of the Imperial War Museum, London; photographs, Camera Press

decimate a frontal assault by either infantry or cavalry.

There was a considerable disparity in 1914 between the deadly effectiveness of modern armaments and the doctrinal teachings of some armies regarding the rules of warfare. The South African War and the Russo-Japanese War had revealed the futility of frontal infantry or cavalry attacks on prepared positions when unaccompanied by surprise, but few military leaders foresaw that the machine gun and the rapid-firing field gun would force armies into trenches in order to survive. Instead, war was looked upon by many leaders in 1914 as a contest of national wills, spirit, and courage. A prime example of this attitude was the French Army, which was dominated by the doctrine of the offensive. French military doctrine called for headlong bayonet charges of French infantrymen against the German rifles, machine guns, and artillery. German military thinking, under the influence of Alfred, Graf von Schlieffen, sought, unlike the French, to avoid frontal assaults but rather to achieve an early decision by deep flanking attacks. At the same time, the Germans sought to make use of reserve divisions alongside regular formations from the outset of war. The Germans paid greater attention to training their officers in defensive tactics using machine guns, barbed wire, and fortifications.

TANKS

Although the concept of the armoured vehicle dates back to ancient warfare, it was only at the beginning of the 20th century that armoured fighting vehicles began to take practical form. By then the basis for them had become available with the appearance of the traction engine and the automobile. Thus, the first self-propelled armoured vehicle was built in 1900 in England when John Fowler & Company armoured one of their steam traction engines for hauling supplies in the South African War (1899–1902). The first motor vehicle used as a weapon carrier was a powered quadricycle on which F. R. Simms mounted a machine gun in 1899 in England. The inevitable next step was a vehicle that was both armed and armoured. Such a vehicle was constructed to the order of Vickers, Son and Maxim Ltd. and was exhibited in London in 1902. Two years later a fully armoured car with a turret was built in France by the Société Charron, Girardot et Voigt, and another was built concurrently in Austria by the Austro-Daimler Company.

To complete the evolution of the basic elements of the modern armoured fighting vehicle, it remained only to adopt tracks as an alternative to wheels. This became inevitable with the appearance of the tracked agricultural tractor, but there was no incentive to use tracks on the armoured vehicle for this until after the outbreak of World War I. Tracked armoured vehicles were rejected by many European powers before the war began. One was proposed in France as early as 1903 but failed to arouse the interest of military authorities, as did a similar proposal made in England in 1908. Three years later a design for a tracked armoured vehicle was rejected by the Austro-Hungarian and then by the German general staffs, and in 1912 the British War Office turned down yet another design.

The outbreak of World War I in 1914 radically changed the situation. Its opening stage of mobile warfare accelerated the development of armoured cars, numbers of which were quickly improvised in Belgium, France, and Britain. The ensuing trench warfare, which ended the usefulness of armoured cars, brought forth new proposals for tracked armoured vehicles. Most of these resulted from attempts to make armoured cars capable of moving off roads, over broken ground, and through barbed wire. The first tracked armoured vehicle was improvised in July 1915, in Britain, by mounting an armoured car body on a Killen-Strait tractor. The vehicle was constructed by the Armoured Car Division of the Royal Naval Air Service, whose ideas, backed by the first lord of the Admiralty, Winston S. Churchill, resulted in the formation of an Admiralty Landships Committee. A series of experiments by this committee led in September 1915 to the construction of the first tank, called "Little Willie." A second model, called "Big Willie," quickly followed. Designed to cross wide trenches, it was accepted by the British Army, which ordered 100 tanks of this type (called Mark I) in February 1916.

Simultaneously but independently, tanks were also developed in France. Like the very first British tank, the first French tank (the Schneider) amounted to an armoured box on a tractor chassis; 400 were ordered in February 1916. But French tanks were not used until April 1917, whereas British tanks were first sent into action on Sept. 15, 1916. Only 49 were available, and their success was limited, but on Nov. 20, 1917, 474 British tanks were concentrated at the Battle of Cambrai and achieved a spectacular breakthrough. These tanks, however, were too slow and had too short an operating range to exploit the breakthrough. In consequence, demand grew for a lighter, faster type of tank, and in 1918 the 14-ton (12.7 metric tons) Medium A appeared with a speed of 8 miles (12.9 km) per hour and a range of 80 miles (128.7 km). After 1918, however, the most widely used tank was the French Renault F.T., a light 6-ton vehicle designed for close infantry support.

When World War I ended in 1918, France had produced 3,870 tanks, and Britain 2,636. Most French tanks survived into the postwar period; these were the Renault F.T., much more serviceable than their heavier British counterparts. Moreover, the Renault F.T. fitted well with traditional ideas about the primacy of the infantry, and the French army adopted the doctrine that tanks were a mere auxiliary to infantry. France's lead was followed in most other countries; the United States and Italy both assigned tanks to infantry support and copied the design of Renault F.T. The U.S. copy was the M1917 light tank, and the Italian the Fiat 3000. The only other country to produce tanks by the end of the war was Germany, which built only about 20.

CHEMICAL WEAPONS

Although the use of chemical warfare, in the form of poisons and toxins—alone or with conventional weapons—dates back many millenia, chemical weapons did not become true weapons of mass destruction until they were introduced in their modern form in World War I. The German army initiated modern chemical warfare by launching a chlorine attack at Ypres, Belg., on April 22, 1915, killing 5,000 French and Algerian troops and momentarily breaching their lines of defense. Germany's use of gas and mustard was soon countered by similar tactics from the Allies. By war's end, both sides had used massive quantities of chemical weapons, causing an estimated 1,300,000 casualties, including 91,000 fatalities. The Russian army suffered about 500,000 of these casualties, and the British had 180,000 wounded or killed by chemical arms. One-third of all U.S. casualties in World War I were from mustard and other chemical gases, roughly the ratio for all participants combined. By the war's end, all the great powers involved had developed not only offensive chemical arms but also crude gas masks and protective overgarments to defend themselves against chemical weapon attacks. Altogether, the warring states employed more than two dozen different chemical agents during World War I, including mustard gas, which caused perhaps as many as 90 percent of all chemical casualties (though very few of these casualties were fatal) from that conflict.

Aside from chlorine gas, other choking gas agents used included phosgene, diphosgene, and chloropicrin. The blood agents included hydrogen cyanide, cyanogen, chlorine, and cyanogen bromide. Arsenic-laced sneeze agents were also used, as were tear gases like ethyl bromoacetate, bromoacetone, and bromobenzyl cyanide.

Choking agents are delivered as gas clouds to the target area, where individuals become casualties through inhalation of the vapour. The toxic agent triggers the immune system, causing fluids to build up in the lungs, which can cause death quickly through asphyxiation or oxygen deficiency if the lungs are badly damaged. The effect of the chemical agent, once an individual is exposed to the vapour, may be immediate or can take up to three hours. A good protective gas mask is the best defense against choking agents.

Blister agents were also developed and deployed in World War I. The primary form of blister agent used in that conflict was sulfur mustard, popularly known as mustard gas. Casualties were inflicted when personnel were attacked and exposed to blister agents like sulfur mustard or lewisite. Delivered in liquid or vapour form, such weapons brutally burned the skin, eyes, windpipe, and lungs. The physical results, depending on level of exposure, might be immediate or might appear after several hours. Although lethal in high concentrations, blister agents seldom kill. Modern blister agents include sulfur mustard, nitrogen mustard, phosgene oxime, phenyldichlorarsine, and lewisite. Protection against blister agents requires an effective gas mask and protective overgarments.

Blood agents, such as hydrogen cyanide or cyanogen chloride, are designed to be delivered to the targeted area in the form of a vapour. When inhaled, these agents prevent the transfer of oxygen to the cells, causing the body to asphyxiate. Such chemicals block the enzyme that is necessary for aerobic metabolism, thereby depriving red blood cells of oxygen, which has an immediate effect similar to that of carbon monoxide. Cyanogen inhibits the proper utilization of oxygen within the blood cells, thereby "starving" and damaging the heart. The best defense against blood agents is an effective gas mask.

AIR POWER

France and Germany were both aware of the military potential of aircraft, and thus began relatively large-scale manufacturing around 1909. By the outbreak of World War I in 1914, France had built a total of 2,000 airplanes, of which 1,500 were military; Germany ranked second with about 1,000 military aircraft; and Britain a distant third with 176. The United States lost its lead in aeronautics as the combined civil and military market for American airplanes was insufficient to permit the industry to grow significantly; only 49 aircraft were produced in 1914. In addition, patent rights on airplanes remained a major difficulty for the industry.

Recognizing a national need to advance aircraft technology independently, the U.S. Congress created the National Advisory Committee for Aeronautics in March 1915.

French industry, assisted by rapidly expanding facilities in its ally Great Britain, carried the production load of the Allies during the war. When the United States entered the war in 1917, however, the French government requested that it furnish more than 4,000 planes for active service by early 1918. To meet the demands of the French and the U.S. Army, the U.S. government and American aircraft manufacturers entered into a patent-licensing agreement on July 24, 1917. Thus the Manufacturers Aircraft Association was formed, which allowed its members the use of others' patents for a fixed royalty fee.

Because American aircraft manufacturers and suppliers had no experience in large-scale production, the U.S. government enlisted automobile manufacturers to mass-produce engines and airplanes. For its own use, the U.S. Army ordered the production of the two-seat British De Havilland DH-4 bomber and the American-designed Curtiss JN-4 Jennie trainer. By the end of the war 4,500 DH-4s had been built in the United States, 1,213 of which were shipped to Europe. Although U.S. production was too late to matter militarily, by the 1918 Armistice American factories were capable of producing 21,000 planes per year. Worldwide 210,000 aircraft were produced from 1914 to 1918. In the United States, the greatest success of wartime production was the very advanced 12- cylinder, water-cooled, 400-horsepower Liberty engine, developed for the DH-4.

ZEPPELINS AND AIRSHIPS

At the start of the war, the German armed forces had 10 zeppelins and three smaller airships. However, this impressive offensive capability was largely offset by the highly explosive nature of the hydrogen gas that gave the zeppelins their lifting power. After losing three zeppelins in daylight raids over heavily defended areas in the first month of the war, the army abandoned airship operations. The navy, on the other hand, with its battle fleet blockaded in port by the Royal Navy, mounted a night bombing offensive—the first

A zeppelin flying over the harbour at Kiel, Ger., on maneuvers during World War I. Encyclopædia Britannica, Inc.

aerial strategic bombardment campaign in history.

The finest of the zeppelins was the LZ-70; this craft was 740 feet (225.5 m) long, was able to fly above 16,000 feet (4.9 km), and had a range of 7,500 miles (12,070 km). The LZ-70 was shot down late in the war, however, and large rigid (metal-framed) airships were never again employed as combat aircraft. Smaller, nonrigid airships were used throughout World War I by the British for antisubmarine patrol, convoy escort, and coastal reconnaissance, achieving a remarkable record of protecting coastal convoys from German submarines. Unpowered, captive balloons also were used extensively for observation and artillery spotting in World War I.

RECONNAISSANCE AIRCRAFT

At the outbreak of World War I, heavier-than-air craft were used only for visual reconnaissance. Their feeble engines could carry little more than a pilot and, in some cases, an observer aloft. They soon proved their worth in this mission, however. RFC aviators provided reconnaissance that enabled the British and French armies to counterattack in the decisive Battle of the Marne on Sept. 6–12, 1914, turning back the invading Germans just short of Paris.

More powerful engines and better aircraft designs soon made possible specialized reconnaissance aircraft that could fly at high altitudes to avoid interception. The Germans, for example, had Rumpler two-seaters in service by 1917 that could operate as high as 24,000 feet (7.3 km). Radios were carried aloft to permit aerial observers to spot and adjust artillery fire. At first, radios were equipped with transmitters only and then, as they became lighter, with receivers for two-way communication.

FIGHTERS

The importance of aerial reconnaissance and artillery spotting (particularly the latter) made it clear that the belligerent parties able to deny the enemy use of airspaces above the battlefield would enjoy enormous advantages. This realization led to the emergence of fighters as a distinct category of aircraft. In the early days of the war, pilots and observers blazed away at enemy aircraft with pistols, rifles, and even shotguns, but to little effect. Machine guns were the obvious artillery solution. In 1913 the Vickers company in Britain had exhibited a two-seat biplane of pusher configuration, with the propeller behind the engine. It was armed with a machine gun fired by an observer who sat ahead of the pilot in a tublike crew compartment. A development of this machine, the Vickers F.B.5 Gunbus, entered service in early 1915 as the first production aircraft designed from the outset with air-to-air armament. The French armed similarly configured Voisin pushers with machine guns (one had shot down a German aircraft as early as Oct. 5, 1914), but, burdened with the extra weight of observer and gun, such aircraft were slow and unmaneuverable. In fact, their successes were mostly the result

Italian Caproni bomber of World War I. Courtesy of John W.R. Taylor

and Benz water-cooled, in-line engines, such as those that powered the streamlined Albatros D.I, D.II, and D.III series of fighters. These were faster than their Allied opponents and, most important, could carry two machine guns without sacrificing performance. The Albatros D.I pioneered a fighter configuration that was to prevail into the 1930s. This configuration featured a compact, single-seat, externally braced tractor biplane armed with two synchronized machine guns mounted ahead of the pilot on the upper fuselage decking and aimed with a simple ring-and-bead sight. Albatros fighters gave British airmen a terrible drubbing above the Arras battlefield during the "Bloody April" of 1917, but a new generation of French and British fighters with more powerful engines soon tilted the balance toward the Allies. Prominent among these were the French Spad fighters and the British S.E.5, both powered by the Spanish-designed and French-built Hispano-Suiza watercooled V-8. The British Sopwith Camel and new versions of the French Nieuport, powered by improved rotary radial engines, were also in major use.

Although Germany fell decisively behind France and Britain in aircraft production in 1917, and thus lost the war in the air, perhaps the definitive single-seat fighter of World War I was the Fokker

of accidental encounters. Light, single-seat aircraft of tractor configuration, with the propeller at the nose, had much better performance. However, efforts to arm them with machine guns firing at an angle to avoid hitting the propeller produced little success.

Most Allied fighters at that time were powered by rotary radial engines, with the cylinders arranged radially about the crankcase like the spokes of a wheel, rotating around a stationary crankshaft. These engines were relatively powerful in relation to their weight. However, their large frontal areas produced a great deal of drag, and the gyroscopic forces induced by their whirling mass posed serious aircraft control problems. In mid-1916 Germany took the lead in fighter design on the basis of its superb Daimler

D.VII of 1918. Typically powered by a 160-horsepower Mercedes engine, the D.VII was a fabric-covered biplane that differed from others in that it had a sturdy fuselage structure of welded steel tubing. Armed with two machine guns, it had a top speed of 117 miles (188.3 km) per hour. Even more powerful engines made two-seat fighters possible. The best of these was the British Bristol F.2b, powered by the 220-horsepower, water-cooled Rolls-Royce Falcon, a V-12 engine that gave the Bristol a top speed of almost 120 miles per hour (193 km). The F.2b was armed with a synchronized machine gun for the pilot and two flexible machine guns for the observer.

BOMBERS

Since they had to carry heavy disposable loads over long distances in order to be effective, specialized bombers were not developed quickly. The first bombing raids to achieve significant success (and the first to cross national boundaries) were mounted against the Zeppelin works at Friedrichshafen from Belgian bases by airmen of Britain's Royal Naval Air Service (RNAS) on Oct. 8 and Nov. 21, 1914. However, their spectacular success owed more to the highly flammable nature of the zeppelins themselves than to the destructive power of the 20-pound (9 kg) bombs used.

These raids prompted the British Admiralty to commission the development of the first specialized heavy night bomber, the Handley Page H.P. O/100, which flew for the first time in December 1915. Meanwhile, other air forces began building and putting into service strategic daytime bombers. Among the first were French Voisins. The type L was used in early 1915 to carry about 130 pounds (59 kg) of small bombs that simply lay in the bottom of the cockpit until the time came for the observer to drop them overboard manually. Later models had more powerful engines and were equipped alternatively as attack aircraft, either carrying up to 660 pounds (299.4 kg) of bombs or having a 37-millimetre (2.9 in)

Curtiss Model E flying boat. American aeronautic pioneer Glenn Hammond Curtiss piloted his Model E flying boat over Keuka Lake, near Hammondsport, N.Y., in 1912. Library of Congress, Washington, D.C. (neg. no. LC-DIG-ggbain-11555)

gun mounted in the nose. None flew faster than 84 miles (135.2 km) per hour, so the Voisins had to operate mainly under cover of darkness in the last year of the war.

Italy, too, was quick to appreciate the value of bombing attacks on enemy targets. Its big three-engined, twin-tailboom Capronis were among the finest bombers of World War I. Even larger were the Russian Ilya Muromets bombers of the tsar's Squadron of Flying Ships. Designed by Igor Sikorsky, now remembered mainly as a helicopter pioneer, these biplanes spanned about 100 feet (30. 5 m) and were descended from his "Russky Vityaz" of May 1913, the world's first successful four-engined airplane. About 80 were built, and they made 400 raids on German targets with the loss of only one plane. The best-known German strategic bombers of World War I were twin-engined Gotha "pusher" biplanes, which made several daylight raids on London in formation in the summer of 1917 before reverting to night operations. The German air force also operated a family of giant four-engined metal bombers known as Riesenflugzeug, or R-planes. Typical of these was the Staaken R.VI number R.25, which was powered by four 260-horsepower Mercedes engines. This had a takeoff weight of 25,269 pounds (11,462 kg), which included a crew of seven and a bomb load of up to 4,000 pounds (1,814 kg).

NAVAL AVIATION

Significant progress was made in naval flying in World War I. Three distinct categories of combat naval aircraft emerged during the war: long-range over-water reconnaissance and antisubmarine aircraft operating from shore bases, shorter-range floatplane reconnaissance and fighter aircraft, and ship-borne aircraft. Also in extensive British use were the long-range flying boats (so-called because their fuselages were shaped like the hull of a boat). These pioneered the technique of searching for submarines with methodical, mathematically developed search patterns. The German navy made extensive use of reconnaissance and fighter floatplanes from Belgian coastal bases to counter Allied air patrols and coastal naval operations. Some of these, notably Hansa-Brandenburg machines designed by Ernst Heinkel, rivaled their land-based equivalents in performance.

The most efficient of the long-range coastal-based airplanes were large, twin-engined flying boats designed by Glenn Curtiss and others. Despite their bulk, these aircraft were sufficiently fast and maneuverable to engage enemy zeppelins and aircraft in combat. Curtiss' flying boats were the only aircraft of U.S. design to see frontline combat service in World War I.

Carrier-based air power also advanced rapidly. In early 1916 the first landplanes (British Sopwith Pups) were flown off the 200-foot (61 m) decks of primitive carriers that had been converted from merchant ships. On Aug. 2, 1917, a pilot landed a Pup on the takeoff deck of HMS *Furious* while the ship was under way. Thus, the concept of the true aircraft carrier had been born.

Britain went on to develop more formidable naval aircraft. In October 1918, a squadron of Sopwith Cuckoos, each able to carry an 18-inch (457 mm) torpedo, was embarked on HMS *Argus*. The war ended before the squadron could go into action, but the RNAS had already used torpedoes dropped from Short seaplanes to sink enemy ships in the Mediterranean. The Cuckoo, with its modest top speed of 103 miles (165.8 km) per hour and endurance of four hours, heralded the eventual demise of the battleship in the face of air-power dominance at sea.

AIR TRANSPORT AND TRAINING

Over the four-year course of the war, techniques in military air transport showed little development. Aircraft were used on occasion to drop supplies to cut-off or besieged forces, but the methods were extremely primitive by today's standards: bags of food, medical supplies, or munitions were dropped from bomb racks or simply heaved over the side.

Conversely, flight training made enormous strides during the war. At the RFC School of Special Flying at Gosport, Eng., Major Robert Smith-Barry introduced a curriculum based on a balanced combination of academic classroom training and dual flight instruction. Philosophically, Smith-Barry's system was based not on avoiding potentially dangerous maneuvers, as had been the case theretofore. Rather, Smith-Barry's curriculum exposed the student to them in a controlled manner so that he could learn to recover from them, thereby gaining confidence and skill. Technologically, it was based on the Avro 504J, a specialized training aircraft with dual controls, good handling characteristics, and adequate power. The training aircraft also featured in-flight communication between instructor and student by means of an acoustic system of soft rubber tubing—the so-called Gosport tube. For the first time, new military pilots flew into action as masters of their airplanes. The Gosport system of training was eventually adopted at training schools throughout the world, remaining the dominant method of civil and military flight instruction into the jet age.

CHAPTER 3

THE INITIAL STAGES OF THE WAR

INITIAL STRATEGIES

THE SCHLIEFFEN PLAN

Years before 1914, successive chiefs of the German general staff foresaw that Germany might have to fight a war on two fronts at the same time. Russia, in the east, and France, in the west, whose combined strength was numerically superior to the Central Powers', indeed could potentially pose simultaneous threats to Germany. The elder Helmuth von Moltke, chief of the German general staff from 1858 to 1888, decided that Germany should stay at first on the defensive in the west and deal a crippling blow to Russia's advanced forces before turning to counterattack the French advance. His immediate successor, Alfred von Waldersee, also believed in staying on the defensive in the west. Alfred, Graf von Schlieffen, who served as chief of the German general staff from 1891 to 1905, took a contrary view, and the plan he developed was to guide Germany's initial wartime strategy. Schlieffen realized that on the outbreak of war, Russia would need six full weeks to mobilize and assemble its vast armies. Russia's immense countryside and population, sparse rail network, and inefficient government bureaucracy would make immediate mobilization impossible. Taking advantage of this fact, Schlieffen planned to initially adopt a purely defensive posture on the Eastern Front with a minimal number of troops

A portrait of Gen. Joseph Joffre, who served as commander-in-chief of the French Army from 1914 to 1916. Hulton Archive/Getty Images

facing Russia's slowly gathering armies. Germany would instead concentrate almost all of its troops in the west against France and would seek to bypass France's frontier fortifications by an offensive through neutral Belgium to the north. This offensive would sweep westward and then southward through the heart of northern France, capturing the capital and knocking that country out of the war within a few weeks. Having gained security in the west, Germany would then shift its troops to the east and destroy the Russian menace with a similar concentration of forces.

By the time of his retirement in 1905, Schlieffen had elaborated a plan for a great wheeling movement of the right (northern) wing of the German armies not only through central Belgium but also, in order to bypass the Belgian fortresses of Liège and Namur in the Meuse Valley, through the southernmost part of The Netherlands. With their right wing entering France near Lille, the Germans would continue to wheel westward until they were near the English Channel. Then, they would turn southward so as to sever the French armies' line of retreat from France's eastern frontier to the south. Finally, the outermost arc of the wheel would sweep southward west of Paris, in order to avoid exposing the German right flank to a counterstroke launched from the city's outskirts. If the Schlieffen Plan succeeded, Germany's armies would simultaneously encircle the French Army from the north, overrun all of northeastern France, and capture Paris, thus forcing

France into a humiliating surrender. The large wheeling movement that the plan envisaged required correspondingly large forces for its execution, as it also required sustaining the numerical strength of the long-stretched marching line and needed to leave adequate detachments on guard over the Belgian fortresses that had been bypassed. Accordingly, Schlieffen allocated nearly seven-eighths of Germany's available troop strength to the execution of the wheeling movement by the right and centre wings, leaving only one-eighth to face a possible French offensive on Germany's western frontier. Thus, the maximum of strength was allocated to the wheel's edge to the right. Schlieffen's plan was observed by the younger Helmuth von Moltke, who became chief of the general staff in 1906. Moltke was still in office when war broke out in 1914.

EASTERN FRONT STRATEGY

The strategy of the Central Powers' Eastern Front, on the other hand, was to occupy Russia with a small number of troops immediately, at the start of the war. Russian Poland, the westernmost part of the Russian Empire, was a thick tongue of land enclosed to the north by East Prussia, to the west by German Poland (Poznania) and by Silesia, and to the south by Austrian Poland (Galicia). It was thus obviously exposed to a two-pronged invasion by the Central Powers. However, the Germans, apart from their grand strategy of crushing France before attempting anything against Russia, took note of the poverty of Russian Poland's transportation network, and so were disinclined to overrun that vulnerable area prematurely. Austria-Hungary, however, whose frontier with Russia lay much farther east than Germany's and who was moreover afraid of disaffection among the Slav minorities, urged some immediate action to forestall a Russian offensive. Moltke therefore agreed to the Austrian general staff's suggestion for a northeastward thrust by the Austrian Army into Russian Poland—the more readily because it would occupy the Russians during the crisis in France.

The Russians, for their part, would have preferred to concentrate their immediately available forces against Austria, and to leave Germany undisturbed until their mobilization should have been completed. The French were anxious to relieve the German pressure against themselves, however. Thus, they persuaded the Russians to undertake an offensive involving two armies against the Germans in East Prussia simultaneously with one involving four armies against the Austrians in Galicia. The Russian Army, whose proverbial slowness and unwieldy organization dictated a cautious strategy, undertook an extra offensive against East Prussia that only an army of high mobility and tight organization could have hoped to execute successfully.

THE STRATEGY OF THE WESTERN ALLIES

For some 30 years after 1870, considering the likelihood of another German war, the French high command had subscribed to the strategy of an initial defensive against German attack. The defensive, however, would be followed by a counterstroke against the expected invasion: a great system of fortresses was created on the frontier, but gaps were left in order to "canalize" the German attack. France's alliance with Russia and its entente with Great Britain, however, encouraged a reversal of plan. After the turn of the century, a new school of military thinkers began to argue for an offensive strategy. The advocates of the offensive *à l'outrance* ("to the utmost") gained control of the French military machine, and in 1911 a spokesman of this school, General J.-J.-C. Joffre, was designated chief of the general staff. He sponsored the notorious Plan XVII, with which France went to war in 1914.

However, Plan XVII gravely underestimated the strength that the Germans would deploy against France. Accepting the possibility that the Germans might employ their reserve troops along with regular troops at the outset, Plan XVII estimated the strength of the German Army in the west at a possible maximum of 68 infantry divisions. The Germans actually deployed the equivalent of 83 half divisions, counting *Landwehr* (reserve troops) and *Ersatz* (low-grade substitute troops) divisions. But French military opinion crucially ignored or doubted this possibility. During the war's critical opening days, when the rival armies were concentrating and moving forward, the French Intelligence counted only Germany's regular divisions in its estimates of the enemy strength. This was a serious miscalculation. Plan XVII also miscalculated the direction and scope of the coming onslaught. Although it foresaw an invasion through Belgium, it assumed that the Germans would take the route through the Ardennes, thereby exposing their communications to attack. Basing itself on the idea of an immediate and general offensive, instead of concentrating on maintaining a strong defense, Plan XVII called for a French thrust toward the Saar into Lorraine by the 1st and 2nd armies. At the same time, on the French left (to the north), the 3rd and 5th armies, facing Metz and the Ardennes, respectively, stood ready either to launch an offensive between Metz and Thionville or to strike from the north at the flank of any German drive through the Ardennes. When war broke out, it was taken for granted that the small British Expeditionary Force (BEF) under Sir John French should be used as an adjunct to France's forces, more or less as the French might see fit. The failure of the plan was that the French remained oblivious to the gigantic German offensive that was being aimed at their left (northern) wing.

THE WAR IN THE WEST BEGINS

The German Invasion

As the war began, the Germans first had to reduce the ring fortress of Liège, which commanded the route prescribed for their 1st and 2nd armies and which was the foremost stronghold of the Belgian defenses, for the smooth working of their plan for the invasion of France. German troops crossed the frontier into Belgium on the morning of August 4, 1914. Thanks to the resolution of a middle-aged staff officer, Erich Ludendorff, a German brigade occupied the town of Liège itself in the night of August 5–6 and the citadel on August 7. However, the surrounding forts held out stubbornly until the Germans brought their heavy howitzers into action against them on August 12. These 420-millimetre (16.5 in) siege guns proved too formidable for the forts, which one by one succumbed. The vanguard of the German invasion was already pressing the Belgian field army between the Gete River and Brussels, when the last of the Liège forts fell on August 16. The Belgians then withdrew northward to the entrenched camp of Antwerp. On August 20 the German 1st Army entered Brussels while the 2nd Army appeared before Namur, the one remaining fortress barring the Meuse route into France.

The initial clashes between the French and German armies along the Franco-German and Franco-Belgian frontiers are collectively known as the Battle of the Frontiers. This group of engagements, which lasted from August 14 until the beginning of the First Battle of the Marne on September 6, was to be the largest battle of the war and was perhaps the largest battle in human history up to that time, given the fact that a total of more than 2,000,000 troops were involved.

The planned French thrust into Lorraine, totaling 19 divisions, started on

A crowd watches in the rain as German troops march into Brussels, the Belgian capital, 1914.
Henry Guttmann/Hulton Archive/Getty Images

August 14 but was shattered by the German 6th and 7th armies in the Battle of Morhange-Sarrebourg on August 20–22. Yet, this abortive French offensive had an indirect effect on the German plan; when the French attack in Lorraine developed, Moltke was tempted momentarily to postpone the right-wing sweep and instead to seek a victory in Lorraine. This fleeting impulse led him to divert to Lorraine the six newly formed *Ersatz* divisions that had been intended to increase the weight of his right wing. This was the first of several impromptu decisions by Moltke that were to fatally impair the execution of the Schlieffen Plan.

Meanwhile, the German imperial princes who commanded armies on the Germans' left, or southern wing, in Lorraine were proving unwilling to forfeit their opportunity for personal glory. Crown Prince Rupert of Bavaria ordered his 6th Army to counterattack on August 20 instead of continuing to fall back before the French advance as planned, and Crown Prince William of Germany ordered his 5th Army to do the same. The strategic result of these unplanned German offensives was merely to throw the French back onto a fortified barrier that both restored and augmented their power of resistance. Thus, the French were soon afterward enabled to dispatch troops to reinforce their left flank—a redistribution of strength that was to have far-reaching results in the decisive Battle of the Marne.

While this seesaw campaign in Lorraine was taking place, more decisive events were occurring to the northwest. The German attack on Liège had awakened Joffre to the reality of a German advance through Belgium, but not to its strength or to the wideness of its sweep. In preparing a counterattack against the German advance through Belgium, Joffre envisaged a pincer movement, with the French 3rd and 4th armies on the right and the 5th, supported by the BEF, on the left, to trap the Germans in the Meuse–Ardennes area south of Liège. The fundamental flaw in this new French plan was that the Germans had deployed about 50 percent more troops than the French had estimated, and for a vaster enveloping movement. Consequently, while the right-hand claw of the French pincer (23 divisions) collided with the German 5th and 4th armies (20 divisions) in the Ardennes and was thrown back, the left-hand claw (13 French and 4 British divisions) found itself nearly trapped between the German 1st and 2nd armies, with a total of 30 divisions, on the one hand, and the 3rd, on the other. As the French 5th Army, under General Charles Lanrezac, was checked in its offensive south of the Sambre River by a German attack on August 21, the British, who reached Mons on August 22, at first agreed to stand there to cover Lanrezac's left. However, on August 23 news of the fall of Namur and of the German 3rd Army's presence near Dinant induced Lanrezac to wisely order a general retreat.

Adolf Hitler (front left) *poses for a picture with a group of fellow German soldiers during World War I, 1914.* Time & Life Pictures/Getty Images

In Focus: Big Bertha

Several 420-millimetre (16.5 in) howitzers, known as Big Berthas, were used by advancing German forces to batter the Belgian forts at Liège and Namur in August 1914, at the start of World War I.

The guns were designed and built by Krupp, Germany's largest armaments manufacturing firm, in the years before the war for the express purpose of overcoming modern forts built of reinforced concrete. The Big Berthas were the largest and most powerful artillery produced to that time. Each gun propelled a shell weighing 2,100 pounds (952.5 kg) for a distance of almost 9 miles (14.5 km). The shells were equipped with delayed-action fuses to explode after having penetrated a fortified target. The gun and its carriage, when fully assembled, weighed about 75 tons and was operated and serviced by a crew of about 280 men. For transport to the battlefield, the howitzer was disassembled into four sections—gun barrel, mounting, carriage, and ground platform—and loaded onto railway cars, which carried them to Belgium. After they were offloaded from the train, the sections were hauled by tractor-driven wagons to the firing sites and reassembled. Big Berthas and Austrian Skoda 305-millimetre (12 in) howitzers were brought into action against the complex of Belgian forts around Liège on Aug. 12, 1914. They destroyed most of the forts in the next four days, thereby enabling the German army to sweep westward through southern Belgium on its way to invade northern France. Farther to the west, the forts around the city of Namur were similarly battered into surrender by Big Berthas and Skoda guns on August 21–25.

According to some sources, the nickname for the guns was bestowed by the Krupps in honour of Frau Bertha von Bohlen, head of the family. In popular usage, the name Big Bertha was also applied to the extreme long-range cannons with which the Germans shelled Paris in 1918. However, these guns are more properly known as Paris Guns.

Finally, on August 24, the British began their retreat from Mons, just in time to escape envelopment by the German 1st Army's westward march around their unprotected left flank.

At last Joffre realized the truth and the utter collapse of the inadequate Plan XVII. However, resolution was Joffre's greatest asset, and with imperturbable coolness he formed a new plan out of the wreckage. Joffre decided to swing the Allied centre and left back southwestward from the Belgian frontier to a line pivoted on the French fortress of Verdun, and at the same time to withdraw some strength from the right wing so as to be able to station a newly created 6th Army on the extreme left, north of Paris. This plan might, in turn, have collapsed if the Germans had not themselves departed from Schlieffen's original plan. Due to a combination of Moltke's indecisiveness, poor communications between his headquarters and the field army commanders of the German right wing, and Moltke's resulting confusion about the developing tactical situation, the Schieffen Plan in its orthodox form was all but discarded. In the first place, the German right wing was weakened by the subtraction of 11 divisions; 4 were detached to watch Antwerp and to invest French fortresses near the Belgian frontier, instead of using reserve and *Ersatz* troops for this as earlier intended, and 7 more regular divisions were transferred to check the Russian advance into East Prussia. In the second place, Alexander von Kluck, in command of the 1st Army, did, in fact, wheel inward north of Paris rather than southwest of the city.

Kluck's change of direction meant that the original wide sweep around the far (western) side of Paris would inevitably be abandoned. Now the flank of this wheeling German line would pass the near side of Paris and across the face of the Paris defenses into the valley of the Marne River. The premature inward wheel of Kluck's 1st Army before Paris had been reached thus exposed the German extreme right wing to a flank attack and a possible counter-envelopment. On September 4, Moltke decided to abandon the original Schlieffen Plan and substituted a new one. The German 4th and 5th armies should drive southeastward from the Ardennes into French Lorraine west of Verdun and then converge with the southwestward advance of the 6th and 7th armies from Alsace against the Toul–Épinal line of fortifications, so as to envelop the whole French right wing. Meanwhile, the 1st and 2nd armies, in the Marne Valley, should stand guard against any French countermove from the vicinity of Paris. But such an Allied countermove had already begun before the new German plan could be put into effect, to German misfortune.

THE FIRST BATTLE OF THE MARNE

Already on September 3, 1914, General J.-S. Gallieni, the military governor of Paris, had guessed the significance of the German 1st Army's swing inward to the Marne east of Paris. On September 4, Joffre, who had been convinced by Gallieni's arguments, decisively ordered his whole left wing to turn about from their retreat and to begin a general offensive against the Germans' exposed right flank on September 6. The French 6th Army, under M.-J. Maunoury, had been forewarned by Gallieni and actually begun attacking on September 5. The pressure of these attacks caused Kluck finally to engage the whole 1st Army in support of his right flank when he was still no farther up the Marne Valley than Meaux, with nothing but a cavalry screen stretched across the 30 miles (48.3 km) between him and Karl von Bülow's 2nd Army (at Montmirail). While the French 5th Army was turning to attack Bülow, the BEF (between the 5th and the 6th armies) was still continuing its retreat for another day. However, on September 9 Bülow learned that the British too had turned and were advancing into the gap between him and Kluck. He therefore ordered the 2nd Army to retreat, thus obliging Kluck to do likewise with the 1st.

Two German soldiers stand guard in the snow as fellow soldiers sleep in their trench near the Aisne River valley on the Western Front, 1914. Hulton Archive/Getty Images

The counterattack of the French 5th and 6th armies and the BEF developed into a general counterattack by the entire left and centre of the French Army. This counterattack is known as the First Battle of the Marne. By September 11 the German retreat extended to all the German armies.

There were several reasons for this extraordinary turn of events. Chief among them was the utter exhaustion of the German soldiery of the right wing, some of whom had marched more than 150 miles (241.4 km) under conditions of frequent battle. Their fatigue was ultimately a by-product of the Schlieffen Plan itself, for while the retreating French had been able to move troops by rail to various points within the circle formed by the front, the German troops had found their advance hampered by demolished bridges and destroyed rail lines. Their food and ammunition supplies were consequently restricted, and the troops also had to make their advance by foot. Moreover, the Germans had underestimated the resilient spirit of the French troops, who had maintained courage, morale, and confidence in their commanders. This fact was strikingly illustrated by the comparatively small number of prisoners taken by the Germans in the course of what was undeniably a precipitous French retreat.

Meanwhile, the assault by the German 6th and 7th armies on the defenses of the

In Focus: Trench Warfare

With the development of long-range artillery, trench warfare was crucial for the survival of troops meeting at relatively close range on World War I's Western Front. In trench warfare opposing armed forces attack, counterattack, and defend from relatively permanent systems of trenches dug into the ground. The opposing systems of trenches are usually close to one another. Trench warfare is resorted to when the superior firepower of the defense compels the opposing forces to "dig in" so extensively as to sacrifice their mobility in order to gain protection.

A trench system may begin simply as a collection of foxholes hastily dug by troops using their entrenching tools. These holes may subsequently be deepened so that a soldier can safely stand up in one of them, and individual foxholes may be connected to each other by shallow crawl trenches. From this beginning, a system of more permanent trenches may be constructed. In making a trench, soil from the excavation is used to create raised parapets running both in front of and behind the trench. Within the trench are firing positions along a raised forward step called a fire step, and duckboards are placed on the often muddy bottom of the trench to provide secure footing.

The tactical ancestor of modern trench warfare was the system of progressively extended trenches developed by the French military engineer Sébastien Le Prestre de Vauban for the attack of fortresses in the 17th century. Trenches remained merely a part of siegecraft until the increasing firepower of small arms and cannon compelled both sides to make use of trenches in the American Civil War (1861–65). The trench lines of the Petersburg–Richmond theatre of operations in the final months of that war were the foremost example of trench warfare in the 19th century.

Trench warfare reached its highest development on the Western Front during World War I, when armies of millions of men faced each other in a line of trenches extending from the Belgian coast through northeastern France to Switzerland. These trenches arose within the first few months of the war's outbreak, after the great offensives launched by Germany and France had shattered against the deadly, withering fire of the machine gun and the rapid-firing artillery piece. The sheer quantity of bullets and shells flying through the air in the battle conditions of that war compelled soldiers to burrow into the soil to obtain shelter and survive.

The typical trench system in World War I consisted of a series of two, three, four, or more trench lines running parallel to each other and being at least 1 mile (1.6 km) in depth. Each trench was dug in a type of zigzag so that no enemy, standing at one end, could fire for more than a few yards down its length. Each of the main lines of trenches was connected to each other and to the rear by a series of communications trenches that were dug roughly perpendicular to them. Food, ammunition, fresh troops, mail, and orders from commanding officers were delivered through these trenches. The intricate network of trenches contained command posts, forward supply dumps, first-aid stations, kitchens, and latrines. Most important, trench networks had machine-gun emplacements to defend against an assault, and dugouts deep enough to shelter large numbers of defending troops during an enemy bombardment.

The first, or front, line of trenches was known as the outpost line and was thinly held by scattered machine gunners distributed behind dense entanglements of barbed wire. The main line of resistance was a parallel series of two, three, or four lines of trenches containing the bulk of the defending troops. The defenders' artillery was posted to the rear of the main line of trenches. Each main line of trenches was fronted by fields of barbed wire intended to slow down and entangle attacking infantry. As World War I progressed, both sides, but particularly the Germans, developed trench systems of progressively greater depth and strength in order to ensure that the enemy could not achieve a breakthrough at any particular point. The Germans evolved an extremely elaborate defense system using pillboxes, or concrete shelters, for machine guns. Behind the pillboxes were more lines of barbed wire and more trenches and dugouts reinforced with concrete to withstand artillery bombardment. Behind these defenses were still more lines of trenches that were effectively out of range of the enemy's artillery fire. By 1918, the Germans had constructed some trench systems that had a depth of 14 miles (22.5 km).

Throughout most of World War I, the opposing armies on the Western Front tried to break through the enemy's trench system by mounting infantry assaults preceded by intense artillery bombardments of the defending trenches. These attacks usually failed for several reasons: partly because the preliminary bombardment alerted the defenders to the imminence of an attack, thus allowing them time to bring up reserves for a counterattack, and because the bombardments themselves turned the "no-man's-land" between the opposing sides into rough, shell-pocked terrain that slowed down the attacking infantry. The crucial elements in attacking a trench system, surprise and overwhelming numbers of infantry, were thus almost impossible to attain. The Allies' increased use of the tank in 1918 marked the beginning of the end of trench warfare, however, since the tank was invulnerable to the machine gun and rifle fire that were the trenches' ultimate defense.

French eastern frontier had already proved a predictably expensive failure, and the German attempt at a partial envelopment pivoted on Verdun was abandoned. The German right wing withdrew northward from the Marne and made a firm stand along the Lower Aisne River and the Chemin des Dames ridge. Along the Aisne, the preponderant power of the defense over the offense was reemphasized as the Germans repelled successive Allied attacks from the shelter of trenches. The First Battle of the Aisne marked the real beginning of trench warfare on the Western Front. Both sides were in the process of discovering that, in lieu of frontal assaults for which neither had the manpower readily available, the only alternative was to try to overlap and envelop the other's flank, in this case the one on the side pointing toward the North Sea and the English Channel. Thus began the "Race to the Sea," in which the developing trench networks of both sides were quickly extended northwestward until they reached the Atlantic at a point just inside coastal Belgium, west of Ostend.

The First Battle of the Marne succeeded in pushing the Germans back for a distance of 40 to 50 miles (64.4 to 80.5 km), and thus saved the capital city of Paris from capture. In this respect, it was a great strategic victory, since it enabled the French to renew their confidence and to continue the war. But the great German offensive, though unsuccessful in its object of knocking France out of the war, had enabled the Germans to capture a large portion of northeastern France. The loss of this heavily industrialized region, which contained much of the country's coal, iron, and steel production, crucial to wartime manufacturing, was a serious blow to the continuation of the French war effort.

The Belgian Army, meanwhile, had fallen back to the fortress city of Antwerp, which ended up behind the German lines. The Germans began a heavy bombardment of Antwerp on September 28, and Antwerp surrendered to the Germans on October 10.

After the failure of his first two attempts to turn the Germans' western flank (one on the Somme, the other near Arras), Joffre obstinately decided to try again yet farther north with the BEF—which in any case was being moved northward from the Aisne. The BEF, accordingly, was deployed between La Bassée and Ypres, while on the left the Belgians—who had wisely declined to participate in the projected attack—continued the front along the Yser down to the Channel. Erich von Falkenhayn, however, who on September 14 had succeeded Moltke as chief of the German general staff, had foreseen what was coming and had prepared a counterplan. One of his armies, transferred from Lorraine, was to check the expected offensive, while another was to sweep down the coast and crush the attackers' left flank. The British attack was launched

from Ypres on October 19, the German thrust began the next day. Though the Belgians of the Yser had been under increasing pressure for two days already, both Sir John French and Ferdinand Foch, Joffre's deputy in the north, were slow to appreciate what was happening to their "offensive." In the night of October 29–30, the Belgians had to open the sluices on the Yser River to save themselves by flooding the Germans' path down the coast. The Battle of Ypres had its worst crises on October 31 and November 11 and did not die down into trench warfare until November 22.

By the end of 1914, the casualties the French had so far sustained in the war totaled about 380,000 killed and 600,000 wounded. The Germans had lost only a slightly smaller number. With the repulse of the German attempt to break through at the Battle of Ypres, the strained and exhausted armies of both sides settled down into trench warfare. The trench barrier was consolidated from the Swiss frontier to the Atlantic; the power of modern defense had triumphed over the attack, and stalemate ensued. The military history of the Western Front during the next three years was to be a story of the Allies' attempts to break this deadlock.

OTHER FRONTS

THE EASTERN FRONT AND THE BATTLE OF TANNENBERG

On the Eastern Front, greater distances and quite considerable differences between

IN FOCUS: BATTLE OF VERDUN

The Battle of Verdun, fought Feb. 21–July, 1916, was one of the most devastating engagements of World War I, in which the French repulsed a major German offensive.

German General Erich von Falkenhayn believed in a strategy of attrition, and argued that Germany should bleed France to death by choosing a point of attack "for the retention of which the French would be compelled to throw in every man they have." The fortress of Verdun and its surrounding fortifications along the Meuse River was the point selected. The Germans amassed huge amounts of artillery and troops for the attack, which the French knew was impending but believed would occur elsewhere. Thus, Verdun was unprepared when one of the heaviest bombardments of the war rained down on the area. From the offensive's start on February 21, the Germans advanced with little opposition for four days until they reached Fort Douaumont, which they took. French reinforcements arrived just in time and with them General Henri Pétain, who took command and managed to slow the German advance by several French counterattacks. In March and April the hills and ridges west of the Meuse and north of Verdun were bombarded, attacked, counterattacked, taken, and retaken. In June, the Germans again assaulted the heights along the Meuse but were unable to maintain an advantage. By July they realized that their plan to seize Verdun and undermine France's will to resist had failed with a terrible loss of men—about 400,000 French casualties and nearly as many German—and material for both sides. From October until the end of the year, the French took the offensive and regained the forts and territory they had lost earlier.

the equipment and quality of the opposing armies ensured a fluidity of the front that was lacking in the west. Trench lines might form, but to break them was not difficult, particularly for the German army. Then, mobile operations of the old style could be undertaken.

Urged by the French to take offensive action against the Germans, the Russian commander in chief, Grand Duke Nicholas, took it loyally but prematurely, before the cumbrous Russian war machine was ready, by launching a pincer movement against East Prussia. Under the higher control of General Ya. G. Zhilinsky, two armies (the 1st, or Vilna, Army under P. K. Rennenkampf and the 2nd, or Warsaw, Army under A. V. Samsonov) were to converge on the German 8th Army in East Prussia from the east and the south, respectively. Rennenkampf's left flank would be separated by 50 miles (80.5 km) from Samsonov's right flank. The Russian force had a two-to-one superiority in numbers over the Germans.

Max von Prittwitz und Gaffron, commander of the 8th Army, with his headquarters at Neidenburg (Nidzica), had seven divisions and one cavalry division on his eastern front but only the three divisions of Friedrich von Scholtz's XX Corps on his southern. He was therefore dismayed to learn, on August 20, when the bulk of his forces had been

Russian prisoners, having been captured by German forces at the Battle of Tannenburg, ride the German strategic railway across a bridge, 1914. Popperfoto/Getty Images

repulsed at Gumbinnen (August 19–20) by Rennenkampf's attack from the east, that Samsonov's 13 divisions had crossed the southern frontier of East Prussia and were thus threatening his rear. He initially considered a general retreat. However, his staff objected to this, and thus he approved their counterproposal of an attack on Samsonov's left flank. For this purpose, three divisions were to be switched in haste by rail from the Gumbinnen front to reinforce Scholtz (the rest of the Gumbinnen troops could make their retreat by road). The principal exponent of this counterproposal was Lieutenant Colonel Max Hoffmann. Prittwitz, having moved his headquarters

northward to Mühlhausen (Młynary), was surprised on August 22 by a telegram announcing that General Paul von Hindenburg, with Ludendorff as his chief of staff, was coming to supersede him in command. Arriving the next day, Ludendorff readily confirmed Hoffmann's dispositions for the blow at Samsonov's left.

Meanwhile, Zhilinsky was not only giving Rennenkampf time to reorganize after Gumbinnen but even instructing him to invest Königsberg instead of pressing on to the west. When the Germans on August 25 learned from an intercepted uncoded Russian wireless message (the Russians habitually transmitted combat directives "in clear," not in code) that Rennenkampf was in no hurry to advance, Ludendorff saw a new opportunity. Developing the plan put forward by Hoffmann, Ludendorff concentrated about six divisions against Samsonov's left wing. This force, inferior in strength, could not have been decisive. Ludendorff then took the calculated risk of withdrawing the rest of the German troops, except for a cavalry screen, from their confrontation with Rennenkampf and rushing them southwestward against Samsonov's right wing. Thus, August von Mackensen's XVII Corps was taken from near Gumbinnen and moved southward to duplicate the planned German attack on Samsonov's left with an attack on his right, thus completely enveloping the Russian 2nd Army. This daring move was made possible by the notable absence of communication between the two Russian field commanders, whom Hoffmann knew to personally dislike each other. Under the Germans' converging blows, Samsonov's flanks were crushed and his centre surrounded during August 26–31. The outcome of this military masterpiece, called the Battle of Tannenberg, was the destruction or capture of almost the whole of Samsonov's army. Imperial Russia's unfortunate participation in World War I is epitomized in the ignominious outcome of the Battle of Tannenberg.

The progress of the battle was as follows. Samsonov, his forces spread out along a front 60 miles (96.6 km) long, was gradually pushing Scholtz back toward the Allenstein–Osterode (Olsztyn–Ostróda) line. On August 26, Ludendorff ordered General Hermann von François, with the I Corps on Scholtz's right, to attack Samsonov's left wing near Usdau (Uzdowo). There, on August 27, German artillery bombardments threw the hungry and weary Russians into precipitate flight. François started to pursue them toward Neidenburg, in the rear of the Russian centre, and then made a momentary diversion southward, to check a Russian counterattack from Soldau (Działdowo). Two of the Russian 2nd Army's six army corps managed to escape southeastward at this point, and François then resumed his pursuit to the east. By nightfall on August 29, his troops were in control of the road leading from Neidenburg eastward to Willenberg (Wielbark). The Russian centre, amounting to three army corps, was now caught in the maze of forest between Allenstein and the frontier of Russian Poland. It had no line of retreat, was surrounded by the Germans, and soon dissolved into mobs of hungry and exhausted men who beat feebly against the encircling German ring. They then allowed themselves to be taken prisoner by the thousands. Samsonov shot himself in despair on August 29. By the end of August, the Germans had taken 92,000 prisoners and annihilated half of the Russian 2nd Army. Ludendorff's bold recall of the last German forces facing Rennenkampf's army was wholly justified in the event, since Rennenkampf remained utterly passive while Samsonov's army was surrounded.

Having received two fresh army corps (seven divisions) from the Western Front, the Germans now turned on the slowly advancing 1st Army under Rennenkampf. The latter was attacked on a line extending from east of Königsberg to the southern end of the chain of the Masurian Lakes during September 1–15, and was driven from East Prussia. As a result of these East Prussian battles, Russia had lost about 250,000 men and, what could be afforded still less, much war matériel. But the invasion of East Prussia had at least helped to make possible the French comeback on the Marne by causing the dispatch of two German army corps from the Western Front.

Having ended the Russian threat to East Prussia, the Germans could afford to switch the bulk of their forces from that area to the Czestochowa–Kraków front in southwestern Poland, where the Austrian offensive, launched on August 20, had been rolled back by Russian counterattacks. A new plan for simultaneous thrusts by the Germans toward Warsaw and by the Austrians toward Przemyśl was brought to nothing by the end of October. The Russians could now mount counterattacks in overwhelming strength, their mobilization being at last nearly completed. The Russians then mounted a powerful effort to invade Prussian Silesia with a huge phalanx of seven armies. Allied hopes rose high as the much-heralded "Russian steamroller," as the huge Russian Army was called, began its ponderous advance. The Russian armies were advancing toward Silesia when Hindenburg and Ludendorff exploited the superiority of the German railway

network in November. When the retreating German forces had crossed the frontier back into Prussian Silesia, they were promptly moved northward by rail into Prussian Poland, and thence sent southeastward to drive a wedge between the two armies of the Russian right flank. The massive Russian operation against Silesia was disorganized, and within a week four new German army corps had arrived from the Western Front. Ludendorff was able to use them to press the Russians back by mid-December to the Bzura–Rawka line in front of Warsaw. The depletion of their munition supplies compelled the Russians to also fall back in Galicia to trench lines along the Nida and Dunajec rivers.

Austria's Serbian Campaign and the Battle of the Kolubara

The first Austrian invasion of Serbia was launched with numerical inferiority due to the diversion by part of one army originally destined for the Balkan front to the Eastern Front on August 18, 1914, and the able Serbian commander, Radomir Putnik, brought the invasion to an early end by his victories on the Cer Mountain (August 15–20) and at Šabac (August 21–24). In early September, however, Putnik's subsequent northward offensive on the Sava River had to be broken off. The Austrians had begun a second offensive, against the Serbs' western front on the Drina River. After some weeks of deadlock, the Austrians began a third offensive, which had some success in the Battle of the Kolubara, and forced the Serbs to evacuate Belgrade on November 30. However, by December 15, a Serbian counterattack had retaken Belgrade and forced the Austrians to retreat. Copious mud and exhaustion kept the Serbs from turning the Austrian retreat into a rout, but the victory sufficed to allow Serbia a long spell of freedom from further Austrian advances.

TURKEY JOINS THE CENTRAL POWERS

The entry of present-day Turkey, or the Ottoman Empire, as it was then called, into the war as a German ally was the one great success of German wartime diplomacy. Since 1909, Turkey had been under the control of the Young Turks, over whom Germany had skillfully gained a dominating influence. German military instructors permeated the Turkish Army, and Enver Paşa, the leader of the Young Turks, saw alliance with Germany as the best way of serving Turkey's interests. Germany, in particular, could provide protection against the Russian threat to the Straits. He therefore persuaded the grand vizier, Said Halim Paşa, to make a secret treaty (negotiated in late July and signed on August 2) pledging Turkey to the German side if Germany should have to take Austria-Hungary's side against Russia. The unforeseen entry of Great Britain into the war against Germany alarmed the Turks, but the timely arrival

of two German warships, the *Goeben* and the *Breslau*, in the Dardanelles on August 10 turned the scales in favour of Enver's policy. The ships were sold to Turkey in name, but they retained their German crews. The Turks began detaining British ships, and more anti-British provocations followed, both in the Straits and on the Egyptian frontier. Finally the *Goeben* led the Turkish fleet across the Black Sea to bombard Odessa and other Russian ports between October 29–30. Russia declared war against Turkey on November 1. The western Allies, after an ineffective bombardment of the outer forts of the Dardanelles on November 3, declared war likewise on November 5. Then, a British force from India occupied Basra, on the Persian Gulf, on November 21. In the winter of 1914–15 Turkish offensives in the Caucasus and in the Sinai Desert, albeit abortive, served German strategy well by tying Russian and British forces down in those peripheral areas.

DESTRUCTION OF GERMANY'S SURFACE SHIPS AND SUBMARINE WARFARE

In August 1914, Great Britain and Germany were the two great rival sea powers. Great Britain had 29 capital ships completed and 13 under construction, while Germany had built 18 capital ships and was working on 9 more. However, neither of them at first wanted a direct confrontation: the British were chiefly concerned with the protection of their trade routes, while the Germans hoped that mines and submarine attacks would gradually destroy Great Britain's numerical superiority, so that confrontation could eventually take place on equal terms.

The first significant encounter between the two navies was that of the Helgoland Bight, on Aug. 28, 1914. During this encounter, a British force under Admiral Sir David Beatty, having entered German home waters, sank or damaged several German light cruisers and killed or captured 1,000 men at a cost of one British ship damaged and 35 deaths. For the following months the Germans, in both European or British waters, confined themselves to submarine warfare. They had some notable successes: on September 22 a single German submarine, or U-boat, sank three British cruisers within an hour; on October 7 a U-boat made its way into the anchorage of Loch Ewe, on the west coast of Scotland; on October 15 the British cruiser *Hawke* was torpedoed; and on October 27 the British battleship *Audacious* was sunk by a mine.

On December 15, 1914, battle cruisers of the German High Seas Fleet set off on a sortie across the North Sea, under the command of Admiral Franz von Hipper. They bombarded several British towns and then made their way home safely. Hipper's next sortie, however, was intercepted on its way out. On Jan. 24, 1915, in the Battle of the Dogger Bank, the German cruiser *Blücher* was sunk and two other cruisers damaged before the Germans could make their escape.

Abroad on the high seas, the Germans' most powerful surface force was the East Asiatic squadron of fast cruisers, including the *Scharnhorst*, the *Gneisenau*, and the *Nürnberg*, under Admiral Graf Maximilian von Spee. For four months this fleet ranged almost unhindered over the Pacific Ocean, while the *Emden*, having joined the squadron in August 1914, was detached for service in the Indian Ocean. The Germans could thus threaten not only merchant shipping on the British trade routes but also troopships on their way to Europe or the Middle East from India, New Zealand, or Australia. The *Emden* sank merchant ships in the Bay of Bengal, bombarded Madras (September 22), haunted the approaches to Ceylon, and had destroyed 15 Allied ships in all before it was caught and sunk off the Cocos Islands on November 9, by the Australian cruiser *Sydney*.

Meanwhile, Admiral von Spee's main squadron had been threading a devious course in the Pacific from the Caroline Islands toward the Chilean coast since August and had been joined by two more cruisers, the *Leipzig* and the *Dresden*. On November 1, in the Battle of Coronel, the squadron inflicted a sensational defeat on a British force, under Sir Christopher Cradock, which had sailed from the Atlantic to hunt it down. Without losing a single ship, von Spee's squadron sank Cradock's two major cruisers and Cradock himself was killed. But the fortunes of the war on the high seas were reversed when, on December 8, the German squadron attacked the Falkland Islands in the South Atlantic. They were probably unaware of the naval strength that the British, since

Coronel, had been concentrating there under Admiral Sir Doveton Sturdee, including a force of two battle cruisers (the *Invincible* and *Inflexible*, each equipped with eight 12-inch (305 mm) guns) and six other cruisers. The German ships were suffering from wear-and-tear after their long cruise in the Pacific and were no match for the newer, faster British ships, which soon overtook them. The *Scharnhorst*, with Admiral von Spee aboard, was the first ship to be sunk, then the *Gneisenau*, followed by the *Nürnberg* and the *Leipzig*. The British ships, which had fought at long range so as to render useless the smaller guns of the Germans, sustained only 25 casualties during this engagement. When the German light cruiser *Dresden* was caught and sunk off the Juan Fernández Islands on March 14, 1915, commerce raiding by German surface ships on the high seas was at an end. Raiding was just beginning by German submarines, however.

The belligerent navies were employed as much in interfering with each other's commerce as in fighting each other. Immediately after the outbreak of war, the British had instituted an economic blockade of Germany, with the aim of preventing all supplies reaching that country from the outside world. The two routes by which supplies could reach German ports were either through the

A World War I–era German U-Boat used to attack merchant ships in British waters, c. 1916. Topical Press Agency/Hulton Archive/Getty Images

English Channel and the Dover Straits, or around the north of Scotland. A minefield laid in the Dover Straits with a narrow free lane made it fairly easy to intercept and search ships using the Channel. To the north of Scotland, however, there was an area of more than 200,000 square miles to be patrolled, and the task was assigned to a squadron of armed merchant cruisers. During the early months of the war, only absolute contraband such as guns and ammunition was restricted, but the list was gradually extended to include almost all material that might be of use to the enemy.

The prevention of the free passage of trading ships led to considerable difficulties among the neutral nations, particularly with the United States, whose trading interests were hampered by British policy. Nevertheless, the British blockade was extremely effective. During 1915, the British patrols stopped and inspected more than 3,000 vessels, of which 743 were sent into port for examination. Outward-bound trade from Germany was brought to a complete standstill.

The Germans similarly sought to attack Great Britain's economy with a campaign against its supply lines of merchant shipping. In 1915, however, their surface commerce raiders were eliminated from the conflict, they were forced to rely entirely on the submarine.

The Germans began their submarine campaign against commerce by sinking a British merchant steamship the *Glitra*, after evacuating the crew, on Oct. 20, 1914.

A number of other sinkings followed, and the Germans soon became convinced that the submarine would be able to bring the British to an early peace where their commerce raiders on the high seas had failed. On Jan. 30, 1915, Germany carried the campaign a stage further by torpedoing two Japanese liners (*Tokomaru* and *Ikaria*) without warning. They next announced, on February 4, that from February 18 they would treat the waters around the British Isles as a war zone in which all Allied merchant ships were to be destroyed. No ship, whether enemy or not, would be immune.

Yet, whereas the Allied blockade was preventing almost all trade for Germany from reaching that nation's ports, the German submarine campaign yielded less satisfactory results. During the first week of the campaign, seven Allied or Allied-bound ships were sunk out of 11 attacked, but 1,370 others sailed without being harassed by the German submarines. In the whole of March 1915, during which 6,000 sailings were recorded, only 21 ships were sunk. In April, only 23 ships were sunk from a similar number. Apart from its lack of positive success, the U-boat arm was continuously harried by Great Britain's extensive antisubmarine measures, which included nets, specially armed merchant ships, hydrophones for locating the noise of a submarine's engines, and depth bombs for destroying it underwater.

For the Germans, a worse result than any of the British countermeasures

In Focus: Sinking of the *Lusitania* and Unrestricted Submarine Warfare

The inability of the German command to perceive that a minor tactical success could constitute a strategic blunder of the most extreme magnitude was confirmed on May 7, 1915, when a German submarine sank the British liner Lusitania. *The Lusitania was on its way from New York to Liverpool, and though the ship was, in fact, carrying 173 tons of ammunition, it also had nearly 2,000 civilian passengers. When the ship sank, 1,198 people were drowned, including 128 U.S. citizens. The loss of the liner and so many of its passengers, including the Americans, aroused a wave of indignation in the United States, and it was fully expected that a declaration of war might follow. But the U.S. government clung to its policy of neutrality and contented itself with sending several notes of protest to Germany. Despite this, the Germans persisted in their policy and, on August 17, sank the* Arabic, *which also had U.S. and other neutral passengers. Following a new U.S. protest, the Germans undertook to ensure the safety of passengers before sinking liners henceforth. However, only after the torpedoing of yet another liner, the* Hesperia, *did Germany, on September 18, decide to suspend its submarine campaign in the English Channel and west of the British Isles, for fear of provoking the United States further. Thus, the German civilian statesmen had temporarily prevailed over the naval high command, which still advocated "unrestricted" submarine warfare.*

imposed on them was the long-term growth of hostility on the part of the neutral countries. Certainly the neutrals were far from happy with the British blockade, but the German declaration of the war zone and subsequent events turned them progressively away from their attitude of sympathy for Germany. The hardening of their outlook began in February 1915, when the Norwegian steamship Belridge, carrying oil from New Orleans to Amsterdam, was torpedoed and sunk in the English Channel. The Germans continued to sink neutral ships occasionally, and undecided countries soon began to adopt a hostile outlook toward this activity when the safety of their own shipping was threatened.

The Loss of the German Colonies

Germany's overseas colonies, virtually without hope of military reinforcement from Europe, defended themselves with varying degrees of success against Allied attack.

Togoland was conquered by British forces from the Gold Coast (now Ghana) and by French forces from Dahomey (now Benin) in the first month of the war. In the Cameroons (German: Kamerun), the Germans put up a more effective resistance to Allied invasions from the south, the east, the northwest, and from the sea in the west, in August 1914. The last German stronghold there, Mora, held out until Feb. 18, 1916.

Operations by South African forces in huge numerical superiority were launched against German South West Africa (Namibia) in September 1914. However, they were held up by the pro-German rebellion of certain South African officers who had fought against the British in the South African War of 1899–1902. The rebellion died out in February 1915, but the Germans in South West Africa nevertheless did not capitulate until July 9.

In Jiaozhou (Kiaochow), a small German enclave on the Chinese coast, the port of Qingdao (Tsingtao) was the object of Japanese attack from September 1914. With some help from British troops and from Allied warships, the Japanese captured it on November 7. In October, meanwhile, the Japanese had occupied the Marianas, the Caroline Islands, and the Marshalls in the North Pacific, these islands being defenseless since the departure of Admiral von Spee's naval squadron.

In the South Pacific, Western Samoa (now Samoa) fell without blood at the end of August 1914 to a New Zealand force supported by Australian, British, and French warships. In September an Australian invasion of Neu-Pommern (New Britain) won the surrender of the whole colony of German New Guinea within a few weeks.

The story of German East Africa (comprising present-day Rwanda, Burundi, and continental Tanzania) was very different, thanks to the quality of the local askaris (European-trained African troops) and to the military genius of the German commander Paul von Lettow-Vorbeck. A landing of troops from India was repelled with ignominy by the Germans in November 1914. A massive invasion from the north, comprising British and colonial troops under the South African J. C. Smuts, was launched in February 1916. This invasion was to be coordinated with a Belgian invasion from the west and with an independent British one from Nyasaland in the south. However, though Dar es Salaam fell to Smuts and Tabora to the Belgians in September, Lettow-Vorbeck maintained his small force. In November 1917 he began to move southward across Portuguese East Africa (Germany had declared war on Portugal in March 1916) and, after crossing back into German East Africa in September 1918, he turned southwestward to invade Northern Rhodesia in October. Having taken Kasama on November 9 (two days before the German armistice in Europe), he finally surrendered to Allied forces on November 25. With just some 12,000 men at the outset, he eventually tied down 130,000 or more Allied troops.

CHAPTER 4

THE STALEMATE YEARS BEGIN

By late 1914 the state of deadlock on the Western Front of the first World War had become clear to the governments of the opposing countries and even to many members of their general staffs. As each side sought a solution to this deadlock, the solutions varied in form and manner.

MAJOR DEVELOPMENTS IN 1915

DARDANELLES CAMPAIGN

Erich von Falkenhayn had succeeded the dispirited Moltke as chief of the German general staff in September 1914. By the end of 1914 Falkenhayn seems to have concluded that although the final decision would be reached in the West, Germany had no immediate prospect of success there. Therefore, the only practicable theatre of operations in the near future was the Eastern Front, however inconclusive those operations might be. Falkenhayn was convinced of the strength of the Allied trench barrier in France, so he took the momentous decision to stand on the defensive in the West.

Falkenhayn saw that a long war was now inevitable and set to work to develop Germany's resources for such a warfare of attrition. Thus, the technique of field entrenchment was carried to a higher pitch by the Germans than by any other country. Germany's military railways were expanded for the lateral movement of reserves. Furthermore, the problem of the supply of munitions and of the raw materials for their manufacture was tackled so energetically and comprehensively that an ample flow was ensured from the spring of 1915 onward—a time when the British were only awakening to the problem. Here were laid the foundations of that economic organization and utilization of resources that was to be the secret of Germany's power to resist the pressure of the British blockade.

The western Allies were divided into two camps about strategy during its stalemate with the Central Powers. General Joseph Joffre and most of the French general staff, backed by the British field marshal Sir John French, argued for continuing assaults on the Germans' entrenched line in France, despite the continued attrition of French forces that this strategy entailed. Apart from this, the French high command was singularly lacking in ideas to break the deadlock of trench warfare. While desire to hold on to territorial gains governed the German strategy, the desire to recover lost territory dominated the French.

While the French concentrated on recovering territory, British-inspired solutions to the deadlock crystallized into two main groups: one tactical, the other strategical. The first was to unlock the trench barrier by inventing a machine that would be invulnerable to machine guns and capable of crossing trenches and would thus restore the tactical balance upset by the new preponderance of defensive over offensive power. The idea of such a machine was conceived by Colonel Ernest Swinton in October 1914 and was nourished and tended in infancy by Winston Churchill, then first lord of the Admiralty. Ultimately, after months of experiment hampered by official opposition, this machine, the weapon known as the tank, came to maturity in 1916. Some of the British strategists, on the other hand, argued that instead of seeking a breakthrough on the Germans' impregnable Western Front, the Allies should turn the whole position of the Central Powers either by an offensive through the Balkans or even by a landing on Germany's Baltic coast. Joffre and his supporters won the argument, and the Balkan projects were relinquished in favour of a concentration of effort on the Western Front. But the misgivings of Joffre's opponents were not silenced, and a situation arose that revived the Middle Eastern scheme in a new, if attenuated, form.

Early in January 1915 the Russians, threatened by the Turks in the Caucasus, appealed to the British for some relieving action against Turkey. The British, after acrimonious argument among themselves, decided in favour of "a naval expedition in February to bombard and take the Gallipoli Peninsula (the western shore of the Dardanelles), with Constantinople as its objective." Though subsequently it was agreed that army troops might be provided to hold the shores if the fleet forced the Straits, the naval attack began on February 19 without army support. When at last Sir Ian Hamilton's troops from Egypt began to land on the Turkish shores on April 25, the Turks and their German commander, Otto Liman von Sanders, had had ample time to prepare adequate fortifications. The defending armies were now six times as large as when the campaign opened.

Against resolute opposition from the local Turkish commander (Mustafa Kemal, the future Atatürk), Australian and New Zealand troops won a bridgehead at Anzac Cove, north of Kaba Tepe, on the Aegean side of the peninsula, with some 20,000 men landing in the first two days. The British, meanwhile, tried to land at five points around Cape Helles. However, they only established footholds at three of them and then asked for reinforcements. Thereafter little progress was made, and the Turks took advantage of the British halt to bring into the peninsula as many troops as possible. The standstill of the enterprise led to a political crisis in London between Churchill, who, after earlier doubts, had made himself the foremost spokesman of the Dardanelles operation, and John, Lord Fisher, the first sea lord, who had always expressed doubts about it. Fisher demanded on May 14 that the operation be discontinued, and when he was overruled, resigned the next day. The Liberal government was replaced by a coalition. However, though relieved of his former post, Churchill remained in the War Council of the Cabinet.

In July the British began sending five more divisions to the peninsula, and a new plan was hatched. In the hope of cutting the Turks' north–south

IN FOCUS: ANZAC

The Australian and New Zealand Army Corps (ANZAC) was a combined corps that served with distinction in World War I during the ill-fated 1915 Gallipoli Campaign, an attempt to capture the Dardanelles from Turkey.

In 1916 Australian and New Zealand infantry divisions were sent to France. They took part in some of the bloodiest actions of the war and established reputations as elite shock troops, at the price of heavy casualties. The New Zealand Division, eventually sustained by conscription, was second to none in combat, planning, and administration. The Australians, on the other hand, eventually reaching a strength of five divisions, faced difficulty replacing losses as Australia twice rejected conscription. Grouped into a single corps commanded by Sir John Monash, who complemented the panache and the tactical skill of his soldiers with comprehensive, careful planning, the Australians nevertheless were central to defeating the German offensive of March 1918 and to the "hundred days" from August 8 to November 11 that ended the Great War. The ANZAC cavalry units remained in the Middle East, playing a major role in the 1917–18 Palestine campaign. A unique mentality based on concepts of manhood, mateship, and meritocracy is frequently cited as the key to Australian and New Zealand soldiers' valour and effectiveness. In Australia and New Zealand, ANZAC Day—April 25 (the date of the Gallipoli landing)—has been a major occasion for expressing national sentiment.

communications down the peninsula by seizing the Sari Bair heights, which commanded the Straits from the west, the British reinforced the bridgehead at Anzac Cove. In the night of August 6–7, they landed more troops at Suvla Bay (Anafarta Limanı), farther to the north. Within a few days, both the offensive from Anzac Cove and the new landing had proved ineffectual to the success of their strategy. More argument ensued in the War Council, and only late in the year was it acknowledged that the initially promising but ill-conducted enterprise should be given up. The evacuation of the troops was carried out from Suvla Bay and from Anzac Cove under cover of darkness in December 1915, and from the Cape Helles beaches in January 1916. The Dardanelles campaign thus came to a frustrating end. Had it succeeded, the campaign might well have ended Turkey's participation in the war. In failing, however, it had cost about 214,000 casualties and achieved nothing.

THE WESTERN AND EASTERN FRONTS, 1915

THE WESTERN FRONT

Repeated attacks in February–March 1915 on the Germans' Western trench barrier in Champagne won the French only 500 yards (460 metres) of ground at a cost of 50,000 men. Britain's Sir Douglas Haig and his 1st Army, between Armentières and Lens, tried a new experiment at Neuve-Chapelle on March 10, when its artillery opened an intense bombardment on a 2,000-yard (1.8 km) front. Then, after 35 minutes, they lengthened its range so that the attacking British infantry, behind the second screen of shells, could overrun the trenches ravaged by the first. The experiment's immediate result was merely the loss of life, rather than any ground gained, both because shortage of munitions made the second barrage inadequate and because there was a five-hour delay in launching the infantry assault, against which the Germans, having overcome their initial surprise, had time to rally their resistance. It was clear to the Allies that this small-scale tactical experiment had missed success by only a narrow margin and that there was scope for its development. But the Allied commands seemingly missed the true lesson, which was that a surprise attack could be successfully made immediately following a short bombardment that compensated for its brevity by its intensity. Instead, they drew the superficial deduction that mere volume of shellfire was the key to reducing a trench line prior to an assault. Not until 1917 did they revert to the Neuve-Chapelle method. It was left to the Germans to profit from the experiment. In the meantime, a French offensive in April against the Germans' Saint-Mihiel salient, southeast of Verdun, sacrificed 64,000 men to no effect.

The Germans, in accordance with Falkenhayn's strategy, remained generally on the defensive in the West. They did, however, launch an attack on the Allies' Ypres salient (where the French

Both the horses and rider of this German resupply team have been equipped with gas masks, c. 1918. Hulton Archive/Getty Images

IN FOCUS: PARIS GUN

Several long-range cannons produced by the German arms manufacturer Krupp during World War I were called Paris Guns. The guns were so called because they were specially built to shell Paris at a range, never before attained, of approximately 75 miles (121 km).

The guns were fabricated by adding a tube to the barrel of a 380-millimetre (15 in) naval gun. The barrel was thus elongated to about 112 feet (34.2 m), weighed 138 tons, and needed supports to hold it straight. A charge of 550 pounds (249.5 kg) of gunpowder was used to propel a shell out of the barrel at a velocity of 5,260 feet (1.6 km) per second. The extremely long range of the guns was achieved by sending the shells on a trajectory 24 miles (38.6 km) up into the stratosphere, where atmospheric drag was almost nonexistent. After modifications, the Paris Guns were initially 210 millimetres (8.3 in) in calibre, but successive firings eroded the inner linings of the gun barrels and their calibre was increased to about 240 millimetres (9.5 in). The Paris Guns were moved to their emplacements near the German front lines on railway tracks and successively carried out an intermittent bombardment of Paris over a period of about 140 days, beginning in March 1918.

The Paris Guns killed about 250 Parisians and wrecked a number of buildings during 1918, but they did not appreciably affect French civilian morale or the larger course of the war. The name Big Bertha, which was derisively applied to the guns by Parisians under bombardment from them, is more properly applied to the 420-millimetre (16.5 in) howitzers used by the German army to batter Belgian forts in August 1914, at the start of the war.

had in November 1914 taken the place of the British). There, on April 22, 1915, they used chlorine gas, a choking agent, for the first time on the Western Front. However, they made the mistake of discharging it from cylinders (which were dependent on a favourable wind) rather than lobbing it onto the enemy trenches in artillery shells. The gas did throw the agonized defenders into chaotic flight; but the German high command, having been disappointed by the new weapon's performance under adverse conditions in Poland earlier in the year, had failed to provide adequate reserves to exploit its unforeseen success. By the end of a month-long battle, the Allies' front was only slightly retracted.

On May 9, meanwhile, the Allies had launched yet another premature offensive. They combined a major French onslaught between Lens and Arras with two thrusts by Haig's 1st Army, from Festubert and from Fromelles, against the Aubers Ridge north of Lens. The French prolonged their effort until June 18, losing 102,000 men without securing any gain; the British, still short of shells against the Germans' mass of machine guns, already had suspended their attacks three weeks earlier.

An even worse military failure was the joint offensive launched by the Allies on Sept. 25, 1915. While 27 French divisions with 850 heavy guns attacked on a front 18 miles long in Champagne, north and east of Reims, simultaneous blows were delivered in distant Artois by 14 French divisions with 420 heavy guns on a 12-mile front south of Lens and by six British divisions with only 117 guns at Loos north of Lens. All of these attacks were disappointing failures, partly because they were preceded by prolonged bombardments that gave away any chance of surprise and allowed time for German reserves to be sent forward to close up the gaps that had been opened in the trench defenders' ranks by the artillery bombardment. At Loos the British use of chlorine gas was less effective than Haig had hoped, and his engagement of all his available forces for his first assault came to nothing when his commander in chief, Sir John French, was too slow in sending up reserves. The French on both their fronts likewise lost, through lack of timely support, most of what they had won by their first attacks. In all, for a little ground, the Allies paid 242,000 men, against the defenders' loss of half as many men.

Having subsequently complained bitterly about Sir John French's management of operations, Haig was appointed British commander in chief in his place in December.

THE EASTERN FRONT

The Russians' plans for 1915 prescribed the strengthening of their flanks in the north and in Galicia before driving westward again toward Silesia. Their preparations for a blow at East Prussia's southern frontier were forestalled. Germany's General Erich Ludendorff, striking suddenly eastward from East Prussia, enveloped four Russian divisions in the Augustów forests, east of the Masurian Lakes, in the second week of February. However, in Galicia the winter's fighting culminated in the fall of Przemyśl to the Russians on March 22.

For the Central Powers, the Austrian spokesman, Conrad, primarily required some action to relieve the pressure on his Galician front. Falkenhayn was willing to help him for that purpose without departing from his own general strategy of attrition, which was already coming into conflict with Ludendorff's desire for a sustained effort toward decisive victory over Russia. The plan they finally adopted, with the aim of smashing the Russian centre in the Dunajec River sector of Galicia by an attack on the 18-mile front from Gorlice to Tuchów (south of Tarnów), was conceived with tactical originality. In order to maintain the momentum of advance, no daily objectives were to be set for individual corps or divisions. Instead, each should make all possible progress before the Russians could bring their reserves up, on the assumption that the rapid advance of some attacking units would contagiously promote the subsequent advance of others that had at first met more resistance. In late April, 14 divisions, with 1,500 guns, were quietly concentrated for the stroke against the six Russian divisions present. Mackensen

A portrait of German field marshal August von Mackensen, c. 1914. Topical Press Agency/
Hulton Archive/Getty Images

was in command, with Hans von Seeckt, sponsor of the new tactic of infiltration, as his chief of staff.

The Gorlice attack was launched on May 2 and achieved success beyond all expectation. Routed on the Dunajec, the Russians tried to stand on the Wisłoka, then fell back again. By May 14, Mackensen's forces were on the San, 80 miles from their starting point, and at Jarosław they even forced the Russians to re-cross that river. Strengthened with more German troops from France, Mackensen then struck again, taking Przemyśl on June 3 and Lemberg (Lvov) on June 22. The Russian front was now bisected, but Falkenhayn and Conrad had foreseen no such result and had made no preparations to exploit it promptly. Their consequent delays enabled the Russian armies to retreat without breaking up entirely.

Falkenhayn then decided to pursue a new offensive. Mackensen was instructed to veer northward, so as to catch the Russian armies in the Warsaw salient between his forces and Hindenburg's, which were to drive southeastward from East Prussia. Ludendorff disliked the plan as being too much of a frontal assault: the Russians might be squeezed by the closing-in of the two wings, but their retreat to the east would not be cut off. He once more urged his spring scheme for a wide enveloping maneuver through Kovno (Kaunas) on Vilna (Vilnius) and Minsk, in the north. Falkenhayn opposed this plan, fearing that it would mean more troops and a deeper commitment, and on July 2

the German emperor decided in favour of Falkenhayn's plan, over Ludendorff's protestations.

The results of the plan justified Ludendorff's reservations. The Russians held Mackensen at Brest-Litovsk and Hindenburg on the Narew River long enough to enable the main body of their troops to escape through the unclosed gap to the east. Though by the end of August all of Poland had been occupied and 750,000 Russians had been taken prisoner in four months of fighting, the Central Powers had missed their opportunity to break Russia's ability to carry on the war.

Too late, Falkenhayn in September allowed Ludendorff to try what he had been urging much earlier, a wider enveloping movement to the north on the Kovno–Dvinsk–Vilna triangle. The German cavalry, in fact, approached the Minsk railway, far beyond Vilna. However, the Russians' power of resistance was too great for Ludendorff's slender forces, whose supplies moreover began to run out. By the end of the month his operations were suspended. The crux of this situation was that the Russian armies had been allowed to draw back almost out of the net of German forces before the long-delayed Vilna maneuver was attempted. Meanwhile, an Austrian attack eastward from Lutsk (Luck), begun later in September and continued into October, incurred heavy losses for no advantage at all. By October 1915 the Russian retreat, after a nerve-wracking series of escapes from the salients the Germans had systematically created and then sought to cut off, had come to a definite halt along a line running from the Baltic Sea just west of Riga southward to Czernowitz (Chernovtsy) on the Romanian border.

OTHER FRONTS

THE CAUCASUS

The Caucasian front between Russia and Turkey comprised two battlegrounds: Armenia in the west, Azerbaijan in the east. While the ultimate strategic objectives for the Turks were to capture the Baku oilfields in Azerbaijan and to penetrate Central Asia and Afghanistan in order to threaten British India, they needed first to capture the Armenian fortress of Kars. The fortress, together with that of Ardahan, had been a Russian possession since 1878.

A Russian advance from Sarıkamış (Sarykamysh, south of Kars) toward Erzurum in Turkish Armenia in November 1914 was countered in December when the Turkish 3rd Army, under Enver himself, launched a three-pronged offensive against the Kars–Ardahan position. This offensive was catastrophically defeated in battles at Sarıkamış and at Ardahan in January 1915. However, the Turks, ill-clad and ill-supplied in the Caucasian winter, lost many more men through exposure and exhaustion than in fighting (their 3rd Army was reduced in one month from 190,000 to 12,400 men, the battle casualties being 30,000). Turkish forces, which had meanwhile invaded neutral Persia's part of Azerbaijan and taken Tabriz on January 14, were expelled by a Russian counterinvasion in March.

During this campaign, the Armenians had created disturbances behind the Turkish lines in support of the Russians and had threatened the already arduous Turkish communications. On June 11, 1915, the Turkish government decided to deport the Armenians. In the process of deportation, the Turkish authorities committed atrocities on a vast scale: Armenian deaths have been estimated at some 600,000. Subsequently, the Armenians perpetrated similar atrocities against the Turkish population of the Armenian country, but perforce on a smaller scale.

A portrait of Grand Duke Nicholas of Russia, c. 1918. Hulton Archive/Getty Images

Grand Duke Nicholas, who had hitherto been commander in chief of all Russia's armies, was superseded by Emperor Nicholas himself in September 1915; the Grand Duke was then sent to command in the Caucasus. He and General N. N. Yudenich, the victor of Sarıkamış, started a major assault on Turkish Armenia in January 1916; Erzurum was taken on February 16, Trabzon on April 18, Erzincan on August 2; and a long-delayed Turkish counterattack was held at Oğnut. Stabilized to Russia's great advantage in the autumn, the new front in Armenia was thereafter affected less by Russo-Turkish warfare than by the consequences of impending revolution in Russia.

MESOPOTAMIA

The British occupation of Basra, Turkey's port at the head of the Persian Gulf, in November 1914 had been justifiable strategically because of the need to protect the oil wells of southern Persia and the Abadan refinery. The British advance of 46 miles (74 km) northward from Basra to al-Qurnah in December and the farther advance of 90 miles (144.8 km) up the Tigris to al-ʿAmārah in May–June 1915 ought to have been reckoned enough for all practical purposes. However, the advance was continued in the direction of the fatally magnetic Baghdad, ancient capital of the Arab caliphs of Islam. Al-Kūt was occupied in September 1915, and the advance was pushed on until the British, under Major General Charles Townshend,

were 500 miles away from their base at Basra. They fought a profitless battle at Ctesiphon, only 18 miles from Baghdad, on November 22 but then had to retreat to al-Kūt. There, from December 7, Townshend's 10,000 men were besieged by the Turks; and there, on April 29, 1916, they surrendered themselves into captivity.

THE EGYPTIAN FRONTIERS

Even after the evacuation from Gallipoli, the British maintained 250,000 troops in Egypt. A major source of worry to the British was the danger of a Turkish threat from Palestine across the Sinai Desert to the Suez Canal. That danger waned, however, when the initially unpromising rebellion of the Hāshimite amir Ḥusayn ibn ʿAlī against the Turks in the Hejaz was developed by the personal enterprise of an unprofessional soldier of genius, T. E. Lawrence, into a revolt infecting the whole Arabian hinterland of Palestine and Syria and threatening to sever the Turks' vital Hejaz Railway (Damascus–Amman–Maʿān–Medina). Sir Archibald Murray's British troops at last started a massive advance in December 1916 and captured some Turkish outposts on the northeastern edge of the Sinai Desert. However, they made a pusillanimous withdrawal from Gaza in March 1917 at the very moment when the Turks were about to surrender the place to them; the attempt the next month to retrieve the mistake was repulsed with heavy losses. In June the command was transferred from Murray to Sir Edmund

Allenby. In striking contrast to Murray's performance was Lawrence's capture of Aqaba (al-'Aqabah) on July 6, 1917, when his handful of Arabs got the better of 1,200 Turks there.

ITALY AND THE ITALIAN FRONT

On April 26, 1915, Great Britain, France, and Russia concluded the secret Treaty of London with Italy. The treaty induced the latter to discard the obligations of the Triple Alliance and to enter the war on the side of the Allies by the promise of territorial aggrandizement at Austria-Hungary's expense. Italy was offered not only the Italian-populated Trentino and Trieste but also South Tirol (to

consolidate the Alpine frontier), Gorizia, Istria, and northern Dalmatia. On May 23, 1915, Italy accordingly declared war on Austria-Hungary.

The Italian commander, General Luigi Cadorna, decided to concentrate his effort on an offensive moving eastward from the province of Venetia across the comparatively low ground between the head of the Adriatic and the foothills of the Julian Alps, or across the lower valley of the Isonzo (Soča) River. Against the risk of an Austrian descent on his rear from the Trentino (which bordered Venetia to the northwest) or on his left flank from the Carnic Alps (to the north), he thought that limited advances would be precaution enough.

Italian troops serving in World War I pose for a photograph with their weapons, c. 1915. Archive Holding Inc./The Image Bank/Getty Images

The Italians' initial advance eastward, begun late in May 1915, was soon halted, largely because of the flooding of the Isonzo, and trench warfare set in. Cadorna, however, was determined to make progress and so embarked on a series of persistent renewals of the offensive, known collectively as the Battles of the Isonzo. The first four of these (June 23–July 7; July 18–August 3; October 18–November 4; and November 10–December 2) achieved nothing worth the cost of the 280,000 men lost; and the fifth (March 1916) was equally fruitless. The Austrians had shown on this front a fierce resolution that was often lacking when they faced the Russians. In mid-May 1916 Cadorna's program was interrupted by an Austrian offensive from the Trentino into the Asiago region of western Venetia. Though the danger of an Austrian breakthrough from the mountainous borderland into the Venetian plain in the rear of the Italians' Isonzo front was averted, the Italian counteroffensive in mid-June recovered only one-third of the territory overrun by the Austrians north and southwest of Asiago. The Sixth Battle of the Isonzo (August 6–17), however, did win Gorizia for the Italians. On August 28, Italy finally declared war on Germany as well. The next three months saw three more Italian offensives on the Isonzo, none of them really profitable. In the course of 1916, the Italians had sustained 500,000 casualties, twice as many as the Austrians, and were still entrenched on the Isonzo.

SERBIA AND THE SALONIKA EXPEDITION

Serbia had brusquely repulsed Austria's three attempted invasions of Serbia in 1914 with a series of counterattacks. By the summer of 1915 the Central Powers were doubly concerned with conquering Serbia, both for reasons of prestige and for the sake of establishing secure rail communications with Turkey across the Balkans. In August, Germany sent reinforcements to Austria's southern front. The Central Powers concluded a treaty with Bulgaria, whom they drew to their side by the offer of territory to be taken from Serbia, on Sept. 6, 1915. The Austro-German forces attacked southward from the Danube on October 6; and the Bulgars, undeterred by a Russian ultimatum, struck at eastern Serbia on October 11 and at Serbian Macedonia on October 14.

The western Allies, surprised in September by the prospect of a Bulgarian attack on Serbia, hastily decided to send help through neutral Greece's Macedonian port of Salonika, relying on the collusion of Greece's pro-Entente prime minister, Eleuthérios Venizélos. Troops from Gallipoli, under the French general Maurice Sarrail, reached Salonika on October 5. However, on that day Venizélos fell from power, thus thwarting the Allies' plan. The Allies advanced northward up the Vardar into Serbian Macedonia but found themselves prevented from junction with the Serbs by the westward thrust of the Bulgars. Driven back over the Greek

IN FOCUS: BATTLES OF THE ISONZO

A series of 12 battles were fought between 1915 and 1917 along the Isonzo River on the eastern sector of the Italian Front in World War I.

Although it is now located in present-day Slovenia, the Isonzo River at the time ran roughly north-south just inside Austria along its border with Italy at the head of the Adriatic Sea. The river is flanked by rugged peaks, and the Austrians already had fortified these mountains prior to Italy's entry into the war on May 23, 1915, giving them quite a considerable advantage over the Italians. The Italian general Luigi Cadorna launched his first attack against the Austrians on June 23. For 14 days, the Italian army attempted to cross the river and scale the heights beyond, but they were beaten back. Again during July 18–August 3, October 18–November 3, and November 10–December 2, the Italians attacked, but they penetrated only a few miles into the Austrian sector at the cost of heavy losses. From March 9 to 17, 1916, Cadorna tried to cross the river again—and again failed. In the sixth battle, August 6–17, 1916, Gorizia was captured and a bridgehead was secured across the Isonzo, the first real victories. In the next three battles, September 14–17, October 10–12, and November 1–4, the Italians changed their tactics to short, intense attacks in order to limit their casualties, but they still could not penetrate the formidable natural barriers protected by Austrian artillery. In the 10th battle, May 12–June 8, 1917, Cadorna struck in two places with massed troops and a larger number of guns but gained only a few yards of ground.

During August 19–September 12 the Italians struck again, this time with a total of 51 divisions and 5,200 guns, and they slowly pushed forward, dislodging the Austrians as they advanced. The Germans feared that the Austrian front might collapse against the Italian attack and sent reinforcements. On October 24 the Austrian-German forces took the offensive, beginning with a heavy bombardment. By afternoon the Italian army was in a rout. War-weary and demoralized territorial troops threw down their arms, the Austrians poured over the Isonzo, and Caporetto fell, though many Italian units continued to fight as they retreated toward the Piave River. There, they held the line on November 7, after one of the worst defeats in Italian history.

frontier, the Allies were merely occupying the Salonika region by mid-December. The Serbian Army, meanwhile, to avoid double envelopment, had begun an arduous winter retreat westward over the Albanian mountains to refuge on the island of Corfu.

In the spring of 1916 the Allies at Salonika were reinforced by the revived Serbs from Corfu as well as by French, British, and some Russian troops, and the bridgehead was expanded westward to Vodena (Edessa) and eastward to Kilkis. However, the Bulgars, who in May obtained Fort Rupel (Klidhi, on the Struma) from the Greeks, in mid-August not only overran Greek Macedonia east of the Struma but also, from Monastir (Bitola), invaded the Florina region of Greek Macedonia, to the west of the

Allies' Vodena wing. The Allied counter-offensive took Monastir from the Bulgars in November 1916, but more ambitious operations, from March to May 1917, proved abortive. The Salonika front was tying down some 500,000 Allied troops without troubling the Central Powers in any significant way.

MAJOR DEVELOPMENTS IN 1916

THE WESTERN FRONT AND THE BATTLE OF VERDUN

Although in 1914 the centre of gravity of World War I had been on the Western Front, in 1915 it shifted to focus on the Eastern. However, by 1916, it shifted once more moved back to France. Though the western Allies had dissipated some of their strength in the Dardanelles, Salonika, and Mesopotamia, the rising tide of Britain's new armies and of its increased munition supplies promised the means for an offensive far larger in scale than any before to break the trench deadlock. Britain's armies in France had grown to 36 divisions by the end of 1915. By that time voluntary enlistments, though massive, had nevertheless proved to be inadequate to meet Britain's needs. By January 1916, the Military Service Act replaced voluntary service with conscription.

In December 1915 a conference of the leaders of the French, British, Belgian, and Italian armies, with representatives present from the Russian and Japanese armies, was held at Joffre's headquarters. They adopted the principle of coordinating a simultaneous general offensive in 1916 by France, Great Britain, Russia, and Italy. However, military action by Germany was to dislocate this scheme, and only the British offensive came fully into operation.

By the winter of 1915–16, Falkenhayn regarded Russia as paralyzed and Italy as inconsiderable. He considered the time at last ripe for positive action against France, after whose collapse Great Britain would have no effective military ally on the European continent and would be brought to terms rather by submarine warfare than by land operations. For his offensive in the West, however, Falkenhayn clung always to his method of attrition. He believed that a mass breakthrough was unnecessary and that instead the Germans should aim to bleed France of its manpower by choosing a point of attack "for the retention of which the French Command would be compelled to throw in every man they have." The town of Verdun and its surrounding complex of forts was chosen for many reasons: because it was a menace to the main German lines of communications, because it was within a French salient and thus cramped the defenders, and because of the certainty that the French would sacrifice any number of men to defend Verdun for reasons of patriotism associated with the town itself.

The keynote of Falkenhayn's tactical plan was to place a dense semicircle of German heavy and medium artillery to

French troops under shellfire huddle together during the Battle of Verdun, 1916. General Photographic Agency/Hulton Archive/Getty Images

the north and east of Verdun and its outlying fortresses and then to stage a continuous series of limited infantry advances upon the forts. These advances would draw the French infantry into defending or trying to retake the forts, in the process of which they would be pulverized by German artillery fire. In addition, each German infantry advance would have its way smoothed by a brief but extremely intense artillery bombardment that would clear the targeted ground of defenders.

Although French Intelligence had given early warnings of the Germans' offensive preparations, the French high command was so preoccupied with its own projected offensive scheme that the

warning of the impending German attack fell on deaf ears. At 7:15 AM on Feb. 21, 1916, the heaviest German artillery bombardment yet seen in the war began on a front of 8 miles (12.9 km) around Verdun, and the French trenches and barbed wire fields there were flattened out or upheaved in a chaos of tumbled earth. At 4:45 PM the German infantry advanced—although for the first day only on a front of two and a half miles. From then until February 24 the French defenders' lines east of the Meuse River crumbled away. Fort-Douaumont, one of the most important fortresses, was occupied by the Germans on February 25. By March 6, when the Germans began to attack on the west bank of the Meuse as well as on the east

IN FOCUS: ERICH MARIA REMARQUE

(b. June 22, 1898, Osnabrück, Ger.–d. Sept. 25, 1970, Locarno, Switz.), Erich Maria Remarque, who wrote under the pseudonym of Erich Paul Remark, is chiefly remembered as the author of Im Westen nichts Neues *(1929;* All Quiet on the Western Front*), which became perhaps the best-known and most representative novel dealing with World War I.*

Remarque was drafted into the German army at the age of 18 and was wounded several times. After the war he worked as a racing-car driver and as a sportswriter while working on All Quiet on the Western Front. *The novel's events are those in the daily routine of soldiers who seem to have no past or future apart from their life in the trenches. Its title, the language of routine communiqués, is typical of its cool, terse style, which records the daily horrors of war in laconic understatement. Its casual amorality was in shocking contrast to the wars' patriotic rhetoric. The book was an immediate international success, as was the American film made from it in 1930. It was followed by a sequel,* Der Weg zurück *(1931;* The Road Back*), dealing with the collapse of Germany in 1918. Remarque wrote several other novels, most of them dealing with victims of the political upheavals of Europe during World Wars I and II. Some had popular success and were filmed (e.g.,* Arc de Triomphe, *1946), but none achieved the critical prestige of his first book.*

Remarque left Germany for Switzerland in 1932, before his books were banned by the Nazis in 1933. In 1939 he went to the United States, where he was naturalized in 1947. After World War II he returned to Europe and settled in Porto Ronco, Switz., on Lake Maggiore, where he lived with his second wife, the American actress Paulette Goddard, until his death.

bank, the French had come to see that something more than a feint was intended. To relieve the pressure on France, the Russians made a sacrificial attack on the Eastern Front at Lake Naroch; the Italians began their fifth offensive on the Isonzo; and the British took over the Arras sector of the Western Front, thus becoming responsible for the whole line from the Yser southward to the Somme. Meanwhile, General Philippe Pétain was entrusted with commanding the defense of Verdun. He organized repeated counterattacks that slowed the German advance, and, more importantly, he worked to keep open the one road leading into Verdun that had not been closed by German shelling. This was the Bar-le-Duc road, which became known as La Voie Sacrée (the "Sacred Way") because vital supplies and reinforcements continued to be sent to the Verdun front along it despite constant harassment from the German artillery.

Slowly but steadily, the Germans moved forward on Verdun. They took Fort-Vaux, southeast of Fort-Douaumont, on June 7 and almost reached the Belleville heights, the last stronghold before Verdun itself, on June 23. Pétain was preparing to evacuate his troops from the east bank of the Meuse when the

Allies' offensive on the Somme River was at last launched. Thereafter, the Germans assigned no more divisions to the Verdun attack.

Preceded by a week of bombardment, which gave ample warning of its advent, the Somme offensive began on July 1, 1916. The 11 British divisions of Rawlinson's new 4th Army coordinated attacks on a 15-mile (24 km) front between Serre, north of the Ancre, and Curlu, north of the Somme, while five French divisions attacked at the same time on an 8-mile (12.9 km) front mainly south of the Somme, between Curlu and Péronne. With incredibly misplaced optimism, Haig had convinced himself that the British infantry would be able to walk forward irresistibly over ground cleared of defenders by the artillery. But the unconcealed preparations for the assault and the long preliminary bombardment had given away any chance of surprise, and the German defenders were well prepared for what was to come. In the event, the 60,000 attacking British infantrymen, moving forward in symmetrical alignment at a snail's pace, enforced by each man's 66 pounds (30 kg) of cumbrous equipment were mowed down in masses by the German machine guns. The day's casualties were the heaviest ever sustained by a British army. The French participants in the attack had twice as many guns as the British and did better against a weaker system of defenses, but almost nothing could be done to exploit this comparative success.

IN FOCUS: FIRST BATTLE OF THE SOMME

The First Battle of the Somme was fought July 1–Nov. 13, 1916. It was a costly and largely unsuccessful Allied offensive on the Western Front during World War I.

The Germans were securely entrenched and strategically located when the British and French launched their frontal attack on a 21-mile (33.8 km) front north of the Somme River. A week-long artillery bombardment preceded the British infantry's "going over the top," but the latter were nevertheless mowed down as they assaulted the virtually impregnable German positions. The British sustained nearly 60,000 casualties (20,000 dead) on the first day of the attack. The Somme offensive then deteriorated into a battle of attrition. In September the British introduced their new weapon, the tank, into the war for the first time, but with little effect. In October torrential rains turned the battlefield into an impassable sea of mud, and by mid-November the Allies had advanced only 5 miles (8 km).

Although the figures have been much disputed, the casualties from the First Battle of the Somme perhaps amounted to roughly 650,000 German, 195,000 French, and 420,000 British. Because of the absolutely staggering number of casualties incurred by all involved, the Battle of the Somme became a metaphor for futile and indiscriminate slaughter. Even though their attack itself was unsuccessful, by taking the offensive in the Somme, the Allies managed to relieve the German pressure on Verdun, however, and the subsequent fighting did much to wear down the German army by destroying its prewar cadres.

Resigning himself now to limited advances, Haig concentrated his next effort on the southern sector of his Somme front. The Germans' second position there (Longueval, Bazentin, and Ovillers) fell on July 14, but again the opportunity of exploitation was missed. Thenceforward, at great cost in lives, a methodical advance was continued, gaining little ground but straining the German resistance. The first tanks to be used in the war, though in numbers far too small to be effective, were thrown into the battle by the British on September 15. In mid-November early rains halted operations. The four-month Battle of the Somme was a miserable failure except that it diverted German resources from the attack on Verdun. It cost the British 420,000 casualties, the French 195,000, and the Germans 650,000.

At Verdun, the summer slackening of German pressure enabled the French to organize counterattacks. Surprise attacks directed by General Robert Nivelle and launched by General Charles Mangin's army corps recovered Fort-Douaumont on October 24, Fort-Vaux on November 2, and places north of Douaumont in mid-December. Pétain's adroit defense of Verdun and these counterattacks had deprived Falkenhayn's offensive of its strategic fulfillment. However, France had been so much weakened in the first half of 1916 that it could scarcely satisfy the Allies' expectations in the second. Verdun was one of the longest, bloodiest, and most ferocious battles of the war. French casualties during the whole of Verdun amounted to about 400,000; German casualties reached about 350,000.

The Battle of Jutland

The summer of 1916 saw the long-deferred confrontation of Germany's High Seas Fleet and Great Britain's Grand Fleet in the Battle of Jutland—history's biggest naval battle, which both sides claimed as a victory.

Admiral Reinhard Scheer, who became commander in chief of the High Seas Fleet in January 1916, planned to contrive an encounter on the open sea between his fleet and some part of the British fleet in separation from the whole, so that the Germans could exploit their momentary superiority in numbers to achieve victory. Scheer's plan was to ensnare Admiral Beatty's squadron of battle cruisers at Rosyth, midway up Britain's eastern coast, by stratagem and destroy it before any reinforcements from the Grand Fleet's main base at Scapa Flow could reach it.

To set the trap, five battle cruisers of the German High Seas Fleet, together with four light cruisers, were to sail northward, under Hipper's command, from Wilhelmshaven, Ger., to a point off the southwestern coast of Norway. Scheer himself, with the battle squadrons of the High Seas Fleet, was to follow, 50 miles (80 km) behind, to catch Beatty's forces in the gap once they had been lured eastward across the North Sea in pursuit of Hipper. But the signal for the German operation to begin, made in the afternoon of May 30, was intercepted and partially decoded by the British. Before midnight, the whole British Grand Fleet was on its way to a rendezvous off Norway's south-western coast and roughly across the planned route of the German fleet.

At 2:20 PM on May 31, when Admiral John Jellicoe's Grand Fleet squadrons from Scapa Flow were still 65 miles (104.6 km) away to the north, Beatty's advance guard of light cruisers—5 miles (8 km) ahead of his heavier ships—and Hipper's scouting group learned quite accidentally of one another's proximity. An hour later, the two lines were drawn up for battle, and in the next 50 minutes the British suffered severely, and the *Indefatigable* was sunk. When Beatty's battle cruisers came up, however, the German cruisers, in their turn, sustained such damage that Hipper sent a protective screen of German destroyers in to launch a torpedo attack. The British had lost another battle cruiser, the *Queen Mary*, before the German High Seas Fleet was sighted by a British patrol to the south, at 4:35 PM. On this report Beatty ordered his ships north-ward, to lure the Germans toward the Grand Fleet under Jellicoe's command.

Not until 6:14 PM, after Jellicoe's squadrons and Beatty's light cruisers had been within sight of one another for nearly a quarter of an hour, was the German fleet precisely located—only just in time for Jellicoe to deploy his ships to the best advantage. Jellicoe arrayed the Grand Fleet end-to-end in a line so that their combined broadsides could be brought to bear on the approaching German ships, who could in turn reply only with the forward guns of their lead-ing ships. The British ships in effect formed the horizontal stroke and the German ships the vertical stroke of the letter "T," with the British having deployed into line at a right angle to the German ships' forward progress. This maneuver was in fact known as "crossing the ene-my's T" and was the ideal situation dreamed of by the tacticians of both navies, since by "crossing the T" one's forces temporarily gained an overwhelm-ing superiority of firepower.

For the Germans, this was a moment of unparalleled risk. Three factors helped prevent the destruction of the German ships in this trap: their own excellent con-struction, the steadiness and discipline of their crews, and the poor quality of the British shells. The *Lützow*, the *Derfflinger*, and the battleship *König* led the line and were under broadside fire from some 10 British battleships, yet their main guns remained undamaged. They fought back to such effect that one of their salvoes fell full on the *Invincible* and blew it up. This success, however, did little to relieve the intense bombardment from the other British ships, and the German fleet was still pressing forward into the steel trap of the Grand Fleet.

Relying on the magnificent seaman-ship of the German crews, Scheer extricated his fleet from the appalling danger into which it had run by a simple but, in practice, extremely difficult maneu-ver. At 6:30 PM he ordered a turn of 180°

for all his ships at once, which was executed without collision. The German battleships reversed course in unison and steamed out of the jaws of the trap, while German destroyers spread a smoke screen across their rear. The smoke and worsening visibility left Jellicoe in doubt about what had happened, and the British had lost contact with the Germans by 6:45 PM.

Yet the British Grand Fleet had maneuvered in such a way that it ended up between the German High Seas Fleet and the German ports, and this was the situation Scheer most dreaded, and so at 6:55 PM Scheer ordered another reverse turn, perhaps hoping to pass around the rear of the British fleet. But the result for him was a worse position than that from which he had just escaped: his battle line had become compressed, and his leading ships found themselves again under intense bombardment from the broadside array of the British ships. Jellicoe had succeeded in crossing the Germans' "T" again. The *Lützow* now received irreparable damage, and many other German ships were damaged at this point. At 7:15 PM, therefore, to cause a diversion and win time, Scheer ordered his battle cruisers and destroyers ahead to virtually immolate themselves in a massed charge against the British ships.

This was the crisis of the Battle of Jutland. As the German battle cruisers and destroyers steamed forward, the German battleships astern became confused and disorganized in trying to execute their reverse turn. Had Jellicoe ordered the Grand Fleet forward through the screen of charging German battle cruisers at that moment, the fate of the German High Seas Fleet would likely have been sealed. As it was, fearing and overestimating the danger of torpedo attacks from the approaching destroyers, Jellicoe ordered his fleet to turn away, and the two lines of battleships steamed apart at a speed of more than 20 knots. They did not meet again, and when darkness fell, Jellicoe could not be sure of the route of the German retreat. By 3:00 AM on June 1 the Germans had safely eluded their pursuers.

Despite their various tactical successes in the battle, the British had sustained greater losses than the Germans in both ships and men. In all, the British lost three battle cruisers, three cruisers, eight destroyers, and 6,274 officers and men in the Battle of Jutland. The Germans lost one battleship, one battle cruiser, four light cruisers, five destroyers, and 2,545 officers and men. The losses inflicted on the British, however, were not enough to affect the numerical superiority of their fleet over the Germans in the North Sea, where their domination remained practically unchallengeable during the course of the war. Henceforth, the German High Seas Fleet chose not to venture out from the safety of its home ports.

RUSSIA STUMBLES

In the hope of diverting German strength from the attack at Verdun on the Western Front, the Russians gallantly but prematurely opened an offensive north and south of Lake Naroch (Narocz, east of Vilna) on March 18, 1916. The offensive continued until March 27, though they won very little ground at great cost and only for a short time. They then reverted to preparations for a major offensive in July. The main blow, it was planned, should be delivered by A. E. Evert's central group of armies, assisted by an inward movement of A. N. Kuropatkin's army in the northern sector of the front. But at the same time, A. A. Brusilov's southwestern army group was authorized to make a supposedly diversionary attack in its own sectors. In the event, Brusilov's attack became by far the more important operation of the offensive.

Surprised by the Austrians' Asiago offensive in May, Italy promptly appealed to the Russians for action to draw the enemy's reserves away from the Italian fronts, and the Russians responded by advancing their timetable again. Brusilov undertook to start his attack on June 4, on the understanding that Evert's should be launched 10 days later.

Thus began an offensive on the Eastern Front that was to be Imperial Russia's last really effective military effort. Popularly known as Brusilov's offensive, it had such an astonishing initial success as to revive Allied dreams about the irresistible Russian "steamroller." Instead, its ultimate achievement was to sound the death knell of the Russian monarchy. Brusilov's four armies were distributed along a very wide front, with Lutsk at the northern end, Tarnopol and Buchach (Buczacz) in the central sector, and Czernowitz at the southern end. Having struck first in the Tarnopol and Czernowitz sectors on June 4, Brusilov on June 5 took the Austrians wholly by surprise when he launched A. M. Kaledin's army toward Lutsk. The Austrian defenses crumbled at once, and the attackers pushed their way between two Austrian armies. As the offensive was developed, the Russians were equally successful in the Buchach sector and in their thrust into Bukovina, which culminated in the capture of Czernowitz. By June 20, Brusilov's forces had captured 200,000 prisoners.

Evert and Kuropatkin, however, instead of striking in accordance with the agreed plan, found excuses for procrastination. The Russian chief of general staff, M. V. Alekseyev, therefore tried to transfer this inert couple's reserves to Brusilov, but the Russians' lateral communications were so poor that the Germans had time to reinforce the Austrians before Brusilov was strong enough to make the most of his victory. Although his forces in Bukovina advanced as far as the Carpathian Mountains, a counterstroke by Alexander von Linsingen's Germans in the Lutsk sector checked Russian progress at the decisive point. Further Russian drives from the centre of Brusilov's front were launched in July. However, by early September the opportunity of exploiting the summer's victory was lost. Brusilov had driven the Austrians from Bukovina and from much of eastern Galicia and had inflicted huge losses of men and equipment on them, but he had

IN FOCUS: U-BOATS

By the eve of World War I, all of the major navies included submarines in their fleets, but these craft were relatively small, were considered of questionable military value, and generally were intended for coastal operations. The most significant exception to the concept of coastal activity was the German Deutschland class of merchant U-boats, each 315 feet (96 m) long with two large cargo compartments. These submarines could carry 700 tons of cargo at 12- to 13-knot speeds on the surface and at 7 knots submerged. The Deutschland itself became the U-155 when fitted with torpedo tubes and deck guns, and, with seven similar submarines, it served in a combat role during the latter stages of the war. In comparison, the "standard" submarine of World War I measured slightly over 200 feet (61 m) in length and displaced less than 1,000 tons on the surface.

The prewar submarines generally had been armed with self-propelled torpedoes for attacking enemy ships. During the war, submarines also were fitted with deck guns. This permitted them to approach enemy merchant ships on the surface and signal them to stop for searching, as part of an early war policy, and later to sink small or unarmed ships that did not warrant expenditure of torpedoes. Most war-built submarines had one and sometimes two guns of about 3- or 4-inch (76.2 or 101.6 mm) calibre; however, several later German submarines carried 150-millimetre (5.9 in) guns (including the Deutschland class in military configuration).

A notable armament variation was the submarine modified to lay mines during covert missions off an enemy's harbours. The Germans constructed several specialized submarines with vertical mine tubes through their hulls; some U-boats carried 48 mines in cargo, in addition to their torpedoes.

Also noteworthy was the development, during the war, of the concept of an antisubmarine submarine. British submarines sank 17 German U-boats during the conflict; the early submarine-versus-submarine successes led to British development of the R-class submarine intended specifically for this role. Antisubmarine craft were relatively small, 163 feet (49.7 m) long and displacing 410 tons on the surface, with only one propeller (most contemporary submarines had two). Diesel engines could drive them at nine knots on the surface, but once submerged, large batteries permitted their electric motors to drive them underwater at the high speed of 15 knots for two hours. (Ten knots was a common speed for submerged submarines until after World War II.) Thus, they were both maneuverable and fast. Advanced underwater listening equipment (asdic, or sonar) was installed, and six forward torpedo tubes made these craft potent weapons. Although these submarines appeared too late into the war to have any actual effect on its outcome, they pioneered a new concept in the development of the submarine.

All World War I-era submarines were propelled by diesels on the surface and by electric motors submerged, except for the British Swordfish and K class. These submarines, intended to operate as scouts for surface warships, required the high speeds then available only from steam turbines. The K-boats steamed at 23.5 knots on the surface, while electric motors gave them a 10-knot submerged speed.

depleted his own armies by about 1,000,000 men in doing so. However, a large portion of this number consisted of deserters or prisoners. This loss seriously undermined both the morale and the material strength of Russia. Brusilov's offensive also had indirect results of great consequence. First, it had compelled the Germans to withdraw at least seven divisions from the Western Front, where they could be ill spared from the Verdun and Somme battles. Second, it hastened Romania's unfortunate entry into the war.

Disregarding Romania's military backwardness, the Romanian government of Ionel Brătianu declared war against Austria-Hungary on Aug. 27, 1916. In entering the war, Romania succumbed to the Allies' offers of Austro-Hungarian territory, and to the belief that the Central Powers would be too much preoccupied with other fronts to mount any serious riposte against a Romanian offensive. Some 12 of Romania's 23 divisions, in three columns, thus began on August 28 a slow westward advance across Transylvania, where at first there were only five Austro-Hungarian divisions to oppose them.

The riposte of the Central Powers was swifter than the progress of the invasion. Germany, Turkey, and Bulgaria declared war against Romania on August 28, August 30, and September 1, respectively. Falkenhayn had plans already prepared for attacking Romania. Though the miscarriage of his overall program for the year led to his being replaced by Hindenburg as chief of the German general staff on August 29, Falkenhayn's recommendation that Mackensen should direct a Bulgarian attack on southern Romania was approved. Falkenhayn himself went to command on the Transylvanian front, for which five German, as well as two more Austrian divisions were found available as reinforcements.

Mackensen's forces from Bulgaria stormed the Turtucaia (Tutrakan) bridgehead on the Danube southeast of Bucharest on September 5. His subsequent advance eastward into the Dobruja caused the Romanians to switch their reserves to that quarter instead of reinforcing their Transylvanian enterprise, which thereupon came to a halt. Falkenhayn soon attacked. First, at the southern end of the 200-mile (321.9 km) front, he threw one of the Romanian columns back into the Roter Turm (Turnu Roşu) Pass, then in the centre, he defeated another at Kronstadt (Braşov) by October 9. For a month, however, the Romanians withstood Falkenhayn's attempts to drive them out of the Vulcan and Szurduk (Surduc) passes into Walachia. But just before winter snows blocked the way, the Germans took the two passes and advanced southward to Tîrgu Jiu, where they won another victory. Then Mackensen, having turned westward from the Dobruja, crossed the Danube near Bucharest, on which his and Falkenhayn's armies converged.

Bucharest fell to the Central Powers on December 6, and the Romanian Army, a crippled force, could only fall back north-eastward into Moldavia, where it had the belated support of Russian troops. After Romania's defeat, the Central Powers had access to its wheat fields and oil wells, and the Russians had 300 more miles (482.8 km) of front to defend.

German Strategy and Submarine Warfare

Both Admiral Scheer and General Falkenhayn doubted whether the German submarines could do any decisive damage to Great Britain so long as their warfare was restricted in deference to the protests of the United States, following the sinking of so many ships carrying large numbers of neutral passengers. After a tentative reopening of the submarine campaign on Feb. 4, 1916, the German naval authorities in March gave the U-boats permission to sink without warning all ships except passenger vessels. The German civilian statesmen, however, who paid due attention to their diplomats' warnings about U.S. opinion, were soon able to prevail over the generals and the admirals. On May 4 the scope of the submarine campaign was again severely restricted.

The controversy between the statesmen and the advocates of unrestricted warfare was not dead yet. Hindenburg, chief of the general staff from August 29, had Ludendorff as his quartermaster general. Ludendorff was quickly won over

to supporting the chief of the Admiralty staff, Henning von Holtzendorff, in his arguments against the German chancellor, Theobald von Bethmann Hollweg, and the foreign minister, Gottlieb von Jagow. Whereas Bethmann and some other statesmen were hoping for a negotiated peace, Hindenburg and Ludendorff were committed to a military victory. The British naval blockade, however, threatened to starve Germany into collapse before a military victory could be achieved, and soon Hindenburg and Ludendorff got their way: it was decided that, from Feb. 1, 1917, submarine warfare should be unrestricted and overtly so.

Wilson Offers to Mediate a Peace Treaty and the Zimmermann Telegram

There were few efforts by any of the Central or Allied Powers to achieve a negotiated peace in the first two years of the war. By 1916 the most promising signs for peace seemed to exist only in the intentions of two statesmen in power—the German chancellor Bethmann and the U.S. president Woodrow Wilson. Wilson, having proclaimed the neutrality of the United States in August 1914, strove for the next two years to maintain it. Early in 1916 he sent his confidant, Colonel Edward M. House, to sound London and Paris about the possibility of U.S. mediation between the belligerents. House's conversations with the British foreign secretary, Sir Edward Grey, resulted in the House–Grey Memorandum (Feb. 22,

TELEGRAM RECEIVED.

CANCELED
...ter 1-8-58
W. .. ...erson, State Dept.

By *Mach 9 Eckhoff Archivist*

Date *Oct. 22, 1958*

FROM 2nd from London # 5747.

"We intend to begin on the first of February unrestricted submarine warfare. We shall endeavor in spite of this to keep the United States of America neutral. In the event of this not succeed- ing, we make Mexico a proposal of alliance on the following basis: make war together, make peace together, generous financial support and an under- standing on our part that Mexico is to reconquer the lost territory in Texas, New Mexico, and Arizona. The settlement in detail is left to you. You will inform the President of the above most secretly as soon as the outbreak of war with the United States of America is certain and add the suggestion that he should, on his own initiative, invite ~~write~~ Japan to immediate adherence and at the same time mediate between Japan and ourselves. Please call the President's attention to the fact that the ruthless employment of our submarines now offers the prospect of compelling England in a few months to make peace." Signed, ZIMMERMANN.

The receipt of this information has so greatly exercised the British Government that they have lost no time in communicating it to me to transmit to you, in order that our Government may be able without delay to make such disposition as

may

The Zimmermann Telegram, decrypted and translated, 1918, changed U.S. opinion on war against Germany. National Archives and Records Administration

1916), declaring that the United States might enter the war if Germany rejected Wilson's mediation but that Great Britain reserved the right to initiate U.S. mediatory action. However, by mid-1916, the imminent approach of the presidential election in the United States caused Wilson to suspend his moves for peace.

In Germany, meanwhile, Bethmann had succeeded, with difficulty, in postponing the declaration of unrestricted submarine warfare. Wilson, though he was reelected president on Nov. 7, 1916, let another month pass without working toward peace, and during that period the German victory over Romania was taking place. Thus, while Bethmann lost patience with waiting for Wilson to act, the German military leaders came momentarily to think that Germany, from a position of strength, might now propose a peace acceptable to themselves. Having been constrained to agree with the militarists that if his proposals were rejected by the Allies, unrestricted submarine warfare should be resumed, Bethmann was allowed to announce, on December 12, the terms of a German offer of peace—terms, however, that were militarily so far-reaching as to preclude the Allies' possible acceptance of them. The main stumbling block was Germany's insistence upon its annexation of Belgium and of the occupied portion of northeastern France.

On Dec. 18, 1916, Wilson invited both belligerent camps to state their "war aims." The Allies were secretly encouraged by the U.S. secretary of state to offer terms too sweeping for German acceptance.

The Germans, on the other hand, suspecting collusion between Wilson and the Allies, agreed in principle to the opening of negotiations but left their statement of December 12 practically unchanged. Privately, they decided that Wilson should not actually take part in any negotiation that he might bring about. By mid-January 1917, the December overtures had ended.

Strangely enough, Wilson's next appeal, a speech on Jan. 22, 1917 preaching international conciliation and a "peace without victory," elicited a confidential response from the British expressing readiness to accept his mediation. In the opposite camp, Austria-Hungary would likewise have listened readily to peace proposals, but Germany had already decided, on January 9, to declare unrestricted submarine warfare. Bethmann's message restating Germany's peace terms and inviting Wilson to persevere in his efforts was delivered on January 31, but was paradoxically accompanied by the announcement that unrestricted submarine warfare would begin the next day.

Wilson severed diplomatic relations between the United States and Germany on Feb. 3, 1917, and asked Congress, on February 26, for power to arm merchantmen and to take all other measures to protect U.S. commerce. But American opinion was still not ready for war, and the Germans wisely abstained from attacks on U.S. shipping. What finally changed the tenor of public feeling was the publication of the Zimmermann Telegram.

Arthur Zimmermann had succeeded Jagow as Germany's secretary of state for foreign affairs in November 1916. In that same month the Mexican president, Venustiano Carranza, whose country's relations with the United States had been critical since March, had virtually offered bases on the Mexican coast to the Germans for their submarines. Zimmermann sent a coded telegram to his ambassador in Mexico on Jan. 16, 1917, instructing him to propose to the Mexican government that if the United States should enter the war against Germany, Mexico should become Germany's ally with a view to recovering Texas, New Mexico, and Arizona from the United States. Intercepted and decoded by the British Admiralty Intelligence, this message was communicated to Wilson on February 24. It was published in the U.S. press on March 1, and it immediately set off a nationwide demand for war against Germany.

MAJOR DEVELOPMENTS IN 1917

SPRING OFFENSIVES ON THE WESTERN FRONT

The western Allies were, with good reason, profoundly dissatisfied with the poor results of their enterprises of 1916, and this dissatisfaction was signalized by two major changes made at the end of the year. In Great Britain, the government of H. H. Asquith, already turned into a coalition in May 1915, was replaced in December 1916 by a coalition under David Lloyd George. During that same month in France the post of commander in chief of the army was transferred from Joffre to General Robert Nivelle.

As for the military situation, the fighting strength of the British Army on the Western Front had grown to about 1,200,000 men and was still growing. That of the French Army had been increased by the incorporation of colonial troops to some 2,600,000, so that, including the Belgians, the Allies disposed an estimated 3,900,000 men against 2,500,000 Germans. To the Allies, these figures suggested an offensive on their part.

Nivelle, who owed his appointment to the contrast between the brilliant success of his recent counterattacks at Verdun and the meagre results of Joffre's strategy of attrition, was deeply imbued with the optimism of which experience was by now curing Joffre. He also had ideas of national glory and, accordingly, modified plans made by Joffre in such a way as to assign to the French Army the determinant role in the offensive that, it was calculated, must decide the issue on the Western Front in 1917. Nivelle's plan in its final stage was that the British should make preparatory attacks not only north of the wilderness of the old Somme battlefields but also south of them (in the sector previously held by French troops). Also, these preparatory attacks should attract the German reserves. Finally, that the French should launch the major offensive in Champagne (their forces in that sector having been strengthened both by new troops from the overseas colonies and by those transferred from the Somme). The tactics Nivelle planned to use were based on those he had employed so successfully at Verdun. But he placed an optimistic overreliance on his theory of combining "great violence with great mass," which basically consisted of intense artillery bombardments followed by massive frontal attacks.

Meanwhile, Ludendorff had foreseen a renewal of the Allied offensive on the Somme, and he used his time to frustrate Nivelle's plans and to strengthen the German front in two different ways. First, the hitherto rather shallow defenses in Champagne were by mid-February reinforced with a third line, out of range of the French artillery. Second, Ludendorff decided to anticipate the attack by falling back to a new and immensely strong line of defense. This new line, called the Siegfriedstellung, or "Hindenburg Line," was rapidly constructed across the base of the great salient formed by the German lines between Arras and Reims. From the German position east of Arras, the line ran southeastward and southward, passing west of Cambrai and Saint-Quentin to rejoin the old German line at Anizy (between Soissons and Laon). After a preliminary step backward on February 23, a massive withdrawal of all German troops from the westernmost bulges of the great salient to the new and shorter line was smoothly and quickly made on March 16. The major towns within the areas evacuated by the Germans (i.e., Bapaume, Péronne, Roye, Noyon, Chauny,

and Coucy) were abandoned to the Allies, but the area was left as a desert. The roads were mined, trees cut down, wells fouled, and houses demolished, and the ruins were strewn with explosive booby traps.

This baffling and unexpected German withdrawal dislocated Nivelle's plan, but unperturbed by warnings from all quarters about the changed situation, Nivelle insisted on carrying it out. The Battle of Arras, with which the British started the offensive on April 9, 1917, began well enough for the attackers. This successful beginning was thanks to much-improved artillery methods and to a new poison gas shell that paralyzed the hostile artillery. Vimy Ridge, at the northern end of the 15-mile battlefront, fell to the Canadian Corps. However, the exploitation of this success was frustrated by the congestion of traffic in the British rear, and though the attack was continued until May 5, stiffer German resistance prevented exploitation of the advances made in the first five days.

Nivelle's own offensive in Champagne, launched on April 16 on the Aisne front from Vailly eastward toward Craonne and Reims, proved to be a fiasco. The attacking troops were trapped in a web of machine-gun fire, and by nightfall the French had advanced about 600 yards (548.6 m) instead of the 6 miles (9.7 km) anticipated in Nivelle's program. Only on the wings was any appreciable progress achieved. The results compared favourably with Joffre's offensives, as some 28,000 German prisoners were taken at a cost to the French of just under 120,000 casualties. But the effect on French morale was worse, because Nivelle's fantastic predictions of the offensive's success were more widely known than Joffre's had ever been. With the collapse of Nivelle's plan, his fortunes were buried in the ruins, and after some face-saving delay he was superseded as commander in chief by Pétain on May 15, 1917.

This change was made too late to avert a more harmful sequel, for in late April a mutiny broke out among the French infantry and spread until 16 French army corps were affected. The authorities chose to ascribe it to seditious propaganda, but the mutinous outbreaks always occurred when exhausted troops were ordered back into the line. The aggravated troops signaled their grievances by such significant cries as: "We'll defend the trenches, but we won't attack." Pétain restored tranquillity by addressing and meeting the just grievances of the troops. His reputation for sober judgment restored the troops' confidence in their leaders, and he made it clear that he would avoid future reckless attacks on the German lines. However, following the April mutinies, the military strength of France could never be fully restored during the war.

Pétain insisted that the only rational strategy was to keep to the defensive until new factors had changed the conditions sufficiently to justify taking the offensive with a reasonable hope of success. His constant advice was: "We must wait for the Americans and the tanks." Tanks were now belatedly being built in large numbers, and this emphasis on arming armoured vehicles showed a dawning recognition that machine warfare had superseded mass infantry warfare.

AMERICA DECLARES WAR

After the rupture of diplomatic relations with Germany on Feb. 3, 1917, events pushed the United States inexorably along the road to war. On March 9, using his authority as commander in chief, Wilson ordered the arming of American merchant ships so that they could defend themselves against German U-boat attacks. Three U.S. merchant ships were

U.S. Army recruits at Camp Pike, Arkansas, in 1918, following the United States' entry into World War I in April 1917. Library of Congress, Washington, D.C.

Army recruiting poster featuring "Uncle Sam," designed by James Montgomery Flagg, 1917. The Library of Congress, Washington, D.C.

sunk by German submarines during March 16–18, with heavy loss of life. Supported by his Cabinet, by most newspapers, and by a large segment of public opinion, Wilson made the decision on March 20 for the United States to declare war on Germany. On March 21, he called Congress to meet in special session on April 2. He delivered a ringing war message to that body, and the war resolution was approved by the Senate on April 3 and by the House of Representatives on April 6. The presidential declaration of war followed immediately.

The entry of the United States was the turning point of the war, because it made the eventual defeat of Germany possible. It had been foreseen in 1916 that if the United States went to war, the Allies' military effort against Germany would be upheld by U.S. supplies and by enormous extensions of credit. These expectations were amply and decisively fulfilled. The United States' production of armaments was to meet not only its own needs but also France's and Great Britain's. In this sense, the American economic contribution alone was decisive in the influence of its entry into the war. By April 1, 1917, the Allies had exhausted their means of paying for essential supplies from the United States, and it is difficult to see how they could have maintained the war effort if the United States had remained neutral. American loans to the Allies worth $7,000,000,000 between 1917 and the end

New recruits to the U.S. Army prepare to depart from Woodhaven, Long Island, N.Y., c. 1918. The sign at the front reads, "Express, Woodhaven to Berlin, No Sleepers." FPG/Hulton Archive/Getty Images

IN FOCUS: SCHENCK V. UNITED STATES

On March 3, 1919, the U.S. Supreme Court ruled in Schenck v. United States *that the freedom of speech protection afforded in the U.S. Constitution's First Amendment could be restricted if the words spoken or printed represented to society a "clear and present danger."*

In June 1917, shortly after the United States' entry into World War I, Congress passed the Espionage Act, which made it illegal during wartime to "willfully make or convey false reports or false statements with intent to interfere with the operation or success of the military or naval forces of the United States or to promote the success of its enemies . . . [or] willfully cause or attempt to cause insubordination, disloyalty, mutiny, or refusal of duty, in the military or naval forces of the United States, or shall willfully obstruct the recruiting or enlistment service of the United States, to the injury of the service or of the United States."

Charles T. Schenck was general secretary of the U.S. Socialist Party, which opposed the implementation of a military draft in the country. The party printed and distributed some 15,000 leaflets that called for men who were drafted to resist military service. Schenck was subsequently arrested for having violated the Espionage Act; he was convicted on three counts and sentenced to 10 years in prison for each count.

Oral arguments at the Supreme Court were heard on Jan. 9, 1919, with Schenck's counsel arguing that the Espionage Act was unconstitutional and that his client was simply exercising his freedom of speech guaranteed by the First Amendment. On March 3, the court issued a unanimous ruling upholding the Espionage Act and Schenck's conviction. Writing for the court, Oliver Wendell Holmes, Jr., argued: "Words which, ordinarily and in many places, would be within the freedom of speech protected by the First Amendment may become subject to prohibition when of such a nature and used in such circumstances as to create a clear and present danger that they will bring about the substantive evils which Congress has a right to prevent." Throughout the 1920s, however, the court abandoned the clear and present danger rule and instead utilized an earlier-devised "bad [or dangerous] tendency" doctrine, which enabled speech to be limited even more broadly, as seen in, for example, Gitlow v. New York (1925).

of the war maintained the flow of U.S. arms and food across the Atlantic.

The American military contribution was as important as the economic one. A system of conscription was introduced by the Selective Service Act of May 18, 1917, but many months were required for the raising, training, and dispatch to Europe of an expeditionary force. There were still only 85,000 U.S. troops in France when the Germans launched their last great offensive in March 1918. However, there were 1,200,000 there by the following September. The U.S. commander in Europe was General John J. Pershing.

The U.S. Navy was the second largest in the world, Great Britain's Royal Navy being the largest, when America entered

PRIMARY DOCUMENT: GEORGE M. COHAN'S "OVER THERE"

"Over There" was actor and songwriter George M. Cohan's main contribution to the U.S. war effort—and no meager contribution it was. Enrico Caruso sang it on the steps of the New York Public Library and sold thousands of dollars worth of Liberty Bonds, and it was adopted by the men of the American Expeditionary Force as their favorite marching song. Congress authorized Cohan a special medal for the song in 1940, and it was sung by a new generation of American soldiers in World War II. Legion Airs: Songs of the Armed Forces, Lee O. Smith, ed., New York, 1960.

Johnnie get your gun, get your gun, get your gun,
Take it on the run, on the run, on the run;
Hear them calling you and me;
Every son of liberty.
Hurry right away, no delay, go today,
Make your daddy glad, to have had such a lad,
Tell your sweetheart not to pine,
To be proud her boy's in line.
Chorus:
Over there, over there,
Send the word, send the word over there,
That the Yanks are coming, the Yanks are coming,
The drums rum-tumming everywhere.
So prepare, say a prayer,
Send the word, send the word to beware,
We'll be over, we're coming over,
And we won't come back till it's over over there.
Johnnie get your gun, get your gun, get your gun,
Johnnie show the Hun, you're a son-of-a-gun,
Hoist the flag and let her fly,
Like true heroes do or die.
Pack your little kit, show your grit, do your bit,
Soldiers to the ranks from the towns and the tanks,
Make your mother proud of you,
And to liberty be true.

the war in 1917. The Navy soon abandoned its plans for the construction of battleships and instead concentrated on building the destroyers and submarine chasers so desperately needed to protect Allied shipping from the U-boats. By July 1917, there were already 35 U.S. destroyers stationed at Queenstown (Cobh) on the coast of Ireland—enough to supplement British destroyers for a really effective transatlantic convoy system. By the end of the war, there were more than 380 U.S. craft stationed overseas.

The U.S. declaration of war also set an example to other states in the Western Hemisphere. Cuba, Panama, Haiti, Brazil, Guatemala, Nicaragua, Costa Rica, and Honduras were all at war with Germany by the end of July 1918. The Dominican Republic, Peru, Uruguay, and Ecuador contented themselves with the severance of relations.

The Russian Revolutions

The Russian Revolution of March (February, Old Style) 1917 put an end to the autocratic monarchy of Imperial Russia and replaced it with a provisional government. But the latter's authority was at once contested by soviets, or "councils of workers' and soldiers' deputies," who claimed to represent the masses of the people and, thus, the rightful conductors of the revolution. The March Revolution was an event of tremendous magnitude. Militarily, it appeared to the western Allies as a disaster and to the Central Powers as a golden opportunity. While the Russian Army remained in the field against the Central Powers with a broken spirit, the Russian people were utterly tired of a war that the imperial regime for its own reasons had undertaken without being morally or materially prepared for it. The Russian army had been poorly armed, poorly supplied, poorly trained, and poorly commanded and had suffered a long series of defeats. The soviets' propaganda—including the notorious Order No. 1 of the Petrograd Soviet (March 14, 1917), which called for committees of soldiers and sailors to take control of their units' arms and to ignore any opposition from their officers— served to subvert the remnants of discipline in troops who were already deeply demoralized.

But the leaders of the provisional government foresaw that a German victory in the war would bode ill for Russia in the future, and they were also conscious of their nation's obligations toward the western Allies. A. F. Kerensky, minister of war from May 1917, thought that a victorious offensive would enhance the new government's authority, besides relieving pressure on the Western Front. The offensive, however, which General L. G. Kornilov launched against the Austrians in eastern Galicia on July 1, 1917, was brought to a sudden halt by German reinforcements after 10 days of spectacular advances, and it turned into a catastrophic rout in the next three weeks. By October the advancing Germans had won control of most of Latvia and of the approaches to the Gulf of Finland.

Meanwhile, anarchy was spreading throughout Russia. The numerous non-Russian peoples of the former empire were one after another claiming autonomy or independence from Russia—whether spontaneously or at the prompting of the Germans in occupation of their countries. Finns, Estonians, Latvians, Lithuanians,

Vladimir Lenin addresses a rally gathered in Moscow, 1917. Popperfoto/Getty Images

and Poles were, by the end of 1917, all in various stages of the dissidence from which the independent states of the postwar period were to emerge. At the same time, Ukrainians, Georgians, Armenians, and Azerbaijanis were no less active in their own nationalist movements.

The provisional government's authority and influence were rapidly fading away in Russia proper during the late summer and autumn of 1917. The Bolshevik Revolution of November (October, Old Style) 1917 overthrew the provisional government and brought to power the Marxist Bolsheviks under the leadership of Vladimir Lenin. The Bolshevik Revolution spelled the end of Russia's participation in the war. Lenin's decree on land, of November 8, undermined the Eastern Front by provoking a homeward rush of soldiers anxious to profit from the expropriation of their former landlords. On November 8, likewise, Lenin issued his decree on peace, which offered negotiations to all belligerents but precluded annexations and indemnities, and stipulated a right of self-determination for all peoples concerned. Finally, on November 26, the new Bolshevik government unilaterally ordered a cessation of hostilities both against the Central Powers and against the Turks.

Primary Document: The Archangel Expedition

After the overthrow of the Kerensky regime by the Bolsheviks in the October 1917 revolution, the new rulers of Russia immediately set about ending their country's involvement in the World War. Public opinion in western Europe and in America had been sympathetic to the revolution at first, but sentiment changed when the Lenin-Trotsky regime sued for a separate peace with Germany in March 1918. For a time, there was hope that the White, or anti-Bolshevik, Russians would be able to reinstate the "legitimate" government of the country. To this end, several detachments of American troops were sent to join Allied forces already in Archangel in northern Russia. The following aide-mémoire, sent by Secretary of State Robert Lansing to the Allied ambassadors on July 17, 1918, explained U.S. policy with regard to Russia. [United States Department of State] Papers Relating to Foreign Relations of the United States, 1918, Supplement on Russia, Vol. II, pp. 287–290.

The whole heart of the people of the United States is in the winning of this war. The controlling purpose of the government of the United States is to do everything that is necessary and effective to win it. It wishes to cooperate in every practicable way with the Allied governments, and to cooperate ungrudgingly; for it has no ends of its own to serve and believes that the war can be won only by common counsel and intimate concert of action.

It has sought to study every proposed policy or action in which its cooperation has been asked in this spirit, and states the following conclusions in the confidence that, if it finds itself obliged to decline participation in any undertaking or course of action, it will be understood that it does so only because it deems itself precluded from participating by imperative considerations either of policy or of fact.

In full agreement with the Allied governments and upon the unanimous advice of the Supreme War Council, the government of the United States adopted, upon its entrance into the war, a plan for taking part in the fighting on the Western front into which all its resources of men and material were to be put, and put as rapidly as possible; and it has carried out that plan with energy and success, pressing its execution more and more rapidly forward and literally putting into it the entire energy and executive force of the nation. This was its response, its very willing and hearty response, to what was the unhesitating judgment alike of its own military advisers and of the advisers of the Allied governments.

It is now considering, at the suggestion of the Supreme War Council, the possibility of making very considerable additions even to this immense program which, if they should prove feasible at all, will tax the industrial processes of the United States and the shipping facilities of the whole group of associated nations to the utmost. It has thus concentrated all its plans and all its resources upon this single absolutely necessary object.

In such circumstances it feels it to be its duty to say that it cannot, so long as the military situation on the Western front remains critical, consent to break or slacken the force of its present effort by diverting any part of its military force to other points or objectives. The United States is at a great distance from the field of action on the Western front; it is at a much greater distance from any other field of action. The instrumentalities by which it is to handle its armies and its stores have at great cost and with great difficulty been created in France. They do not exist elsewhere. It is practicable for her to do a great deal in France; it is not practicable for her to do anything of importance or on a large scale upon any other field. The American government, therefore, very respectfully requests its associates to accept its deliberate judgment that it should not dissipate its force by attempting important operations elsewhere.

It regards the Italian front as closely coordinated with the Western front, however, and is willing to divert a portion of its military forces from France to Italy if it is the judgment and wish of the Supreme Command that it should do so. It wishes to defer to the decision of the commander in chief in this matter, as it would wish to defer in all others, particularly because it considers these two fronts so closely related as to be practically but separate parts of a single line and because it would be necessary that any American troops sent to Italy should be subtracted from the number used in France and be actually transported across French territory from the ports now used by the armies of the United States.

It is the clear and fixed judgment of the government of the United States, arrived at after repeated and very searching reconsiderations of the whole situation in Russia, that military intervention there would add to the present sad confusion in Russia rather than cure it, injure her rather than help her, and that it would be of no advantage in the prosecution of our main design—to win the war against Germany. It cannot, therefore, take part in such intervention or sanction it in principle.

Military intervention would, in its judgment, even supposing it to be efficacious in its immediate avowed object of delivering an attack upon Germany from the east, be merely a method of making use of Russia, not a method of serving her. Her people could not profit by it, if they profited by it at all, in time to save them from their present distresses, and their substance would be used to maintain foreign armies, not to reconstitute their own.

Military action is admissible in Russia, as the government of the United States sees the circumstances, only to help the Czechoslovaks consolidate their forces and get into successful cooperation with their Slavic kinsmen and to steady any efforts at self-government or self-defense in which the Russians themselves may be willing to accept assistance. Whether from Vladivostok or from Murmansk and Archangel, the only legitimate object for which American or Allied troops can be employed, it submits, is to guard military stores which may subsequently be needed by Russian forces and to render such aid as may be acceptable to the Russians in the organization of their own self-defense. For helping the Czechoslovaks there is immediate necessity and sufficient justification. Recent developments have made it evident that that is in the interest of what the Russian people themselves desire, and the government of the United States is glad to contribute the small force at its disposal for that purpose.

It yields, also, to the judgment of the Supreme Command in the matter of establishing a small force at Murmansk, to guard the military stores at Kola, and to make it safe for

Russian forces to come together in organized bodies in the north. But it owes it to frank counsel to say that it can go no further than these modest and experimental plans. It is not in a position, and has no expectation of being in a position, to take part in organized intervention in adequate force from either Vladivostok or Murmansk and Archangel.

It feels that it ought to add, also, that it will feel at liberty to use the few troops it can spare only for the purposes here stated and shall feel obliged to withdraw those forces in order to add them to the forces at the Western front if the plans in whose execution it is now intended that they should cooperate should develop into others inconsistent with the policy to which the government of the United States feels constrained to restrict itself.

At the same time the government of the United States wishes to say with the utmost cordiality and goodwill that none of the conclusions here stated is meant to wear the least color of criticism of what the other governments associated against Germany may think it wise to undertake. It wishes in no way to embarrass their choices of policy. All that is intended here is a perfectly frank and definite statement of the policy which the United States feels obliged to adopt for herself and in the use of her own military forces. The government of the United States does not wish it to be understood that in so restricting its own activities it is seeking, even by implication, to set limits to the action or to define the policies of its associates.

It hopes to carry out the plans for safeguarding the rear of the Czechoslovaks operating from Vladivostok in a way that will place it and keep it in close cooperation with a small military force like its own from Japan and, if necessary, from the other Allies, and that will assure it of the cordial accord of all the Allied powers; and it proposes to ask all associated in this course of action to unite in assuring the people of Russia in the most public and solemn manner that none of the governments uniting in action either in Siberia or in northern Russia contemplates any interference of any kind with the political sovereignty of Russia, any intervention in her internal affairs, or any impairment of her territorial integrity either now or hereafter, but that each of the associated powers has the single object of affording such aid as shall be acceptable, and only such aid as shall be acceptable, to the Russian people in their endeavor to regain control of their own affairs, their own territory, and their own destiny.

It is the hope and purpose of the government of the United States to take advantage of the earliest opportunity to send to Siberia a commission of merchants, agricultural experts, labor advisers, Red Cross representatives, and agents of the Young Men's Christian Association accustomed to organizing the best methods of spreading useful information and rendering educational help of a modest sort, in order in some systematic manner to relieve the immediate economic necessities of the people there in every way for which opportunity may open. The execution of this plan will follow and will not be permitted to embarrass the military assistance rendered in the rear of the westward-moving forces of the Czechoslovaks.

An armistice between Lenin's Russia and the Central Powers was signed at Brest-Litovsk on Dec. 15, 1917. The ensuing peace negotiations were complicated. On the one hand, Germany wanted peace in the east in order to be free to transfer troops thence to the Western Front. At the same time, Germany was concerned about exploiting the principle of national self-determination in order to transfer as much territory as possible into its own safe orbit from that of revolutionary Russia. On the other hand, the Bolsheviks wanted peace in order to be free to consolidate their regime in the east with a view to being able to extend it westward as soon as the time should be ripe. The Germans, despite the armistice, invaded the Ukraine to cooperate with the Ukrainian nationalists against the Bolsheviks there, and furthermore resumed their advance in the Baltic countries and in Belorussia. Following this, Lenin rejected his colleague Leon Trotsky's stopgap policy ("neither peace nor war") and accepted Germany's terms in order to save the Bolshevik Revolution. By the Treaty of Brest-Litovsk (March 3, 1918), Soviet Russia recognized Finland and the Ukraine as independent; renounced control over Estonia, Latvia, Lithuania, Poland, and most of Belorussia; and ceded Kars, Ardahan, and Batumi to Turkey.

GREEK AFFAIRS

Greece's attitude toward the war was long uncertain: whereas King Constantine I and the general staff stood for neutrality, Eleuthérios Venizélos, leader of the Liberal Party, favoured the Allied cause. As prime minister from 1910, Venizélos wanted Greece to participate in the Allies' Dardanelles enterprise against Turkey in 1915, but his arguments were overruled by the general staff. The Allies occupied Lemnos and Lesbos regardless of Greece's neutrality. Constantine dismissed Venizélos from office twice in 1915, but Venizélos still commanded a majority in Parliament. The Bulgarians' occupation of Greek Macedonia in summer 1916 provoked another political crisis. Venizélos left Athens for Crete late in September, set up a government of his

Greek prime minister Eleutherios Venizelos, 1914. Topical Press Agency/ Hulton Archive/Getty Images

own there, and transferred it early in October to Salonika. On November 27, Venizélo's government declared war on Germany and Bulgaria. Finally, the Allies, on June 11, 1917, deposed King Constantine. Venizélos then returned to Athens to head a reunified Greek government, which on June 27 declared war on the Central Powers.

The Battle of Caporetto

On the Italian front, Cadorna's 10th Battle of the Isonzo in May–June 1917 won very little ground. However, his 11th battle strained Austrian resistance very severely, especially from August 17 to September 12, during which time General Luigi Capello's 2nd Army captured much of the Bainsizza Plateau (Banjška Planota), north of Gorizia. To avert an Austrian collapse, Ludendorff decided that the Austrians must take the offensive against Italy and that he could, with difficulty, lend them six German divisions for that purpose.

The Austrian offensive against Italy was boldly planned, very ably organized, and well executed. Two Austrian armies, under General Svetozar Borojević von Bojna, attacked the eastern end of the Italians' Venetian salient on the Bainsizza Plateau and on the low ground near the Adriatic shore. At the same time, the German 14th Army, comprising the six German divisions and nine Austrian ones under Otto von Below, with Konrad Krafft von Dellmensingen as his chief of staff, on

Oct. 24, 1917, began to force its way over the barrier of the Julian Alps at the northeastern corner of the Venetian salient, with Caporetto approximately opposite the middle point of the line. The Italians, completely surprised by this thrust, which threatened their forces both to the north and to the south, fell back in confusion. Below's van reached Udine, the former site of the Italian general headquarters, by October 28 and was on the Tagliamento River by October 31. Below's success had far exceeded the hopes of the planners of the offensive, and the Germans could not exploit their speedy advance as effectively as they wished. Cadorna, with his centre shattered, managed by precipitate retreat to save the wings of his army. By November 9, he was able to rally his remaining 300,000 troops behind the Piave River, north of Venice. The Italians had sustained about 500,000 casualties, and 250,000 more had been taken prisoner. General Armando Diaz was then appointed commander in chief in Cadorna's place. The Italians managed to hold the Piave front against direct assaults and against attempts to turn its left flank by an advance from the Trentino. The Italians' defense was helped by British and French reinforcements that had been rushed to Italy when the collapse began. A conference of the military and political leaders of the Allies was held at Rapallo in November, and out of this conference there sprang the joint Supreme War Council at Versailles was established, as was a unified military command.

BRITAIN CAPTURES MESOPOTAMIA

The British forces in Mesopotamia, neglected hitherto and discouraged by the disaster at al-Kūt, received better attention from London in the second half of 1916. Sir Frederick Stanley Maude, who became commander in chief in August, did so much to restore their morale that by December, he was ready to undertake the recapture of al-Kūt as a first step toward capturing Baghdad.

By a series of outflanking movements, the British made their way gradually and methodically up the Tigris, compelling the Turks to extend their defenses upstream. When the final blow at al-Kūt was delivered by a frontal attack on Feb. 22, 1917, British forces were already crossing the river from the west bank behind the town. However, though al-Kūt fell two days later, most of the Turkish garrison extricated itself from the threatened encirclement. Unable to hold a new line on the Diyālā River, the Turkish commander, Kâzim Karabekir, evacuated Baghdad, which the British entered on March 11. In September the British position in Baghdad was definitively secured by the capture of ar-Ramādī, on the Euphrates about 60 miles (96.6 km) to the west. In early November, the main Turkish force in Mesopotamia was driven from Tikrīt, on the Tigris midway between Baghdad and Mosul.

Within a year, Maude changed the Mesopotamian scene from one of despair to one of victory for the British. However, he died of cholera on Nov. 18, 1917. His successor in command in Mesopotamia was Sir William Marshall.

BRITAIN CAPTURES PALESTINE

After assuming command in Egypt, Allenby set his sights on advancing on Palestine. Allenby transferred his headquarters from Cairo to the Palestinian front and devoted the summer of 1917 to preparing a serious offensive against the Turks. On the Turkish side, Falkenhayn, now in command at Aleppo, was at this time himself planning a drive into the Sinai Peninsula for the autumn. However, the British were able to strike first.

The Turkish front in southern Palestine extended from Gaza, on the coast, southeastward to Abu Hureira (Tel Haror) and thence to the stronghold of Beersheba. Allenby began his operation with a heavy bombardment of Gaza from October 20 onward, in order to disguise his real intention of achieving a breakthrough at Abu Hureira, a prerequisite in reaching Beersheba. When Beersheba had been seized by converging movements on October 31, a feint attack on Gaza was launched next day to draw the Turkish reserves thither. Then, the main attack, delivered on November 6, broke through the weakened defenses at Abu Hureira and into the plain of Philistia. Falkenhayn had attempted a counterstroke at Beersheba, but the collapse of the Turkish centre necessitated a general retreat. By November 14, the Turkish forces were split in two divergent groups, the port of Jaffa was taken, and Allenby wheeled his main force to the right for an advance inland on Jerusalem. On December 9, the British successfully occupied Jerusalem.

Summer and Fall Offensives on the Western Front

After Nivelle's failure, Pétain decided to remain temporarily on the defensive, which gave Haig the opportunity to fulfill his desire for a British offensive in Flanders. Haig took the first step on June 7, 1917, with a long-prepared attack on the Messines Ridge, north of Armentières, on the southern flank of his Ypres salient. This attack by General Sir Herbert Plumer's 2nd Army proved an almost complete success; it owed much to the surprise effect of 19 huge mines simultaneously fired after having been placed at the end of long tunnels under the German front lines. The capture of the ridge inflated Haig's confidence. Despite the recommendations of General Sir Hubert Gough, in command of the 5th Army, to use a step-by-step method for the offensive, Haig committed himself to Plumer's view that they "go all out" for an early breakthrough. Haig disregarded the well-founded meteorological forecast that from the beginning of August, rain would be turning the Flanders countryside into an almost impassable swamp. The Germans, meanwhile, were well aware that an offensive was coming from the Ypres salient:

the flatness of the plain prevented any concealment of Haig's preparations, and a fortnight's intensive bombardment (4,500,000 shells from 3,000 guns) served to underline the obvious—without, however, destroying the German machine gunners' concrete pillboxes.

Thus, when the Third Battle of Ypres began on July 31, only the left wing's objectives were achieved. On the crucial right wing the attack was a failure. Four days later, the ground was already swampy. When the attack was resumed on August 16, very little more was won on the right, but Haig was still determined to persist in his offensive. Between September 20 and October 4, thanks to an improvement in the weather, the infantry was able to advance into positions cleared by bombardment, but no farther. Haig launched another futile attack on October 12, followed by three more attacks, scarcely more successful, in the last 10 days of October. At last, on November 6, when his troops advanced a very short distance and occupied the ruins of Passchendaele (Passendale), barely 5 miles (8 km) beyond the starting point of his offensive, Haig felt that enough had been done. Having prophesied a decisive success without "heavy losses," he in fact had lost 325,000 men and inflicted no comparable damage on the Germans.

Pétain, less pretentious and merely testing what might be done with his rehabilitated French Army, had at least as much to show for himself as Haig. In August the French 2nd Army under General M.-L.-A.

Guillaumat fought the last battle of Verdun, winning back all the remainder of what had been lost to the Germans in 1916. In October General P.-A.-M. Maistre's 10th Army, in the Battle of Malmaison, took the ridge of the Chemin des Dames, north of the Aisne to the east of Soissons, where the front in Champagne joined the front in Picardy south of the Somme.

The British, at least, closed the year's campaign with an operation of some significance for the future. When the offensive from Ypres died out in the Flanders mud, they looked again at their tanks, of which they now had a considerable force but which they could hardly use profitably in the swamps. A Tank Corps officer, Colonel J.F.C. Fuller, had already suggested a large-scale raid on the front southwest of Cambrai, where a swarm of tanks, unannounced by any preparatory bombardment, could be released across the rolling downland against the German trenches. This comparatively modest scheme might have been wholly successful if left unchanged, but the British command transformed it: Sir Julian Byng's 3rd Army was not only to actually try to capture Cambrai but also to push on toward Valenciennes. On November 20, therefore, the attack was launched, with 324 fighting tanks leading Byng's six divisions. The first massed assault of tanks in history took the Germans wholly by surprise, and the British achieved a far deeper penetration and at less cost than in any of their past offensives. Unfortunately, however, all of Byng's troops and tanks had been thrown into the first blow, and, as he was not reinforced

in time, the advance came to a halt several miles short of Cambrai. A German counterstroke, on November 30, broke through on the southern flank of the new British salient and threatened Byng's whole army with disaster before being checked by a further British counterattack. In the end, three-quarters of the ground that the British had won was reoccupied by the Germans and Cambrai was not captured. Even so, the Battle of Cambrai had proved that surprise and the tank in combination could unlock the trench barrier.

THE FAR EAST

China's entry into the war in 1917 on the side of the Allies was motivated not by any grievance against the Central Powers but by the Beijing government's fear lest Japan, a belligerent since 1914, should monopolize the sympathies of the Allies and of the United States when Far Eastern affairs came up for settlement after the war. Accordingly, in March 1917 the Beijing government severed its relations with Germany; and on August 14 China declared war not only on Germany but also on the western Allies' other enemy, Austria-Hungary. China's contribution to the Allied war effort was to prove negligible in practical effects, however.

NAVAL OPERATIONS

ALLIED CONVOYS

Since Germany's previous restrictions of its submarine warfare had been

In Focus: The Battle of Cambrai

The Battle of Cambrai, a British offensive from November to December 1917 on the Western Front, marked the first large-scale, effective use of tanks in warfare.

Carried out by the 3rd Army under General Sir Julian Byng in order to relieve pressure on the French front, the offensive consisted of an assault against the Germans' Hindenburg line along a 10-mile (16 km) front some 8 miles (12.9 km) west of Cambrai in northern France. The chosen terrain, rolling chalk downland, was especially suitable for tank movement. Nineteen British divisions were assembled for the offensive, supported by tanks (476 in all, of which about 324 were fighting tanks; the rest were supply and service vehicles) and five horsed cavalry divisions. For the initial attack, eight British divisions were launched against three German divisions.

Attacking by complete surprise on November 20, the British fighting tanks ripped through German defenses in depth and took some 7,500 prisoners at low cost in casualties. Bad weather intervened, however, so that the cavalry could not exploit the breakthrough, and adequate infantry reinforcements were not available. By November 29 the offensive had been halted after an advance of about 6 miles (9.7 km). On November 30 the Germans counterattacked with 20 divisions, and by December 5 the British had been driven back almost to their original positions. Casualties on both sides were nearly equal—about 45,000 each. Despite the British failure to exploit the initial success of their tanks, the battle demonstrated that armour was the key to a decision in the trenches on the Western Front.

motivated by fear of provoking the United States into war, the U.S. declaration of war in April 1917 removed any reason for the Germans to retreat again from their already declared policy of unrestricted warfare. Consequently, the U-boats, having sunk 181 ships in January, 259 in February, and 325 in March, sank 430 more ships in April. The April sinkings represented 852,000 gross tons, to be compared both with the 600,000 postulated by the German strategists as their monthly target and with the 700,000 that the British in March had pessimistically foretold for June. The Germans had calculated that if the world's merchant shipping could be sunk at the monthly rate of 600,000 tons, the Allies, being unable to build new merchant ships fast enough to replace those lost, could not carry on the war for more than five months. At the same time, the Germans, who had 111 U-boats operational when the unrestricted campaign began, had embarked on an extensive building program that, when weighed against their current losses of one or two U-boats per month, promised a substantial net increase in the U-boats' numbers. During April, one in every four of the merchant ships that sailed from British ports was destined to be sunk, and by the end of

May the quantity of shipping available to carry the vital foodstuffs and munitions to Great Britain had been reduced to only 6,000,000 tons.

The April total, however, proved to be a peak figure—primarily because the Allies at last adopted the convoy system for the protection of merchant ships. Previously, a ship bound for one of the Allies' ports had set sail by itself as soon as it was loaded. The sea was thus dotted with single and unprotected merchant ships, and a scouting U-boat could rely on several targets coming into its range in the course of a cruise. The Allies' convoy system remedied this by having groups of merchant ships sail within a protective ring of destroyers and other naval escorts. It was logistically possible and economically worthwhile to provide this kind of escort for a group of ships. Furthermore, the combination of convoy and escort would force the U-boat to risk the possibility of a counterattack in order to sink the merchant ships, thus giving the Allies a prospect of reducing the U-boats' numbers. Despite the manifest and seemingly overwhelming benefits of the convoy system, the idea was novel and, like any untried system, met with powerful opposition from within the military. It was only in the face of extreme necessity, due to excessive loss of ships and cargo, and under great pressure from Lloyd George that the system was tried, more or less as a last resort.

The first convoy sailed from Gibraltar to Great Britain on May 10, 1917; the first from the United States sailed later in May; ships using the South Atlantic sailed in convoy from July 22. During the later months of 1917, the use of convoys caused an abrupt fall in the sinkings by U-boats: 500,500 tons in May, 300,200 in September, and only about 200,600 in November. The USS *Alcedo*, a former civilian yacht commissioned for convoy duty, was the first U.S. Navy ship to be sunk by a German submarine, *UC-71*, on November 5, en route to Brest, France. Just two days later, the U.S. Navy scored its first German submarine when the USS *Fanning* and the USS *Nicholson* sank *U-58* off Milford Haven, Wales. The convoy system was so quickly vindicated that in August, it was extended to shipping outward-bound from Great Britain. The Germans themselves soon observed that the British had grasped the principles of antisubmarine warfare, and that sailing ships in convoys considerably reduced the opportunities for attack.

THE CHANNEL AND NORTH SEA MINE BARRAGES

Apart from employing a system of convoys to protect ships from submarine attacks, the Allies improved their antisubmarine technology (hydrophones, depth charges, etc.) and extended their minefields. In 1918, moreover, Admiral Sir Roger Keyes, in command at Dover, set up a system whereby the English Channel was patrolled by surface craft with searchlights, so that U-boats passing through it had to submerge themselves to depths at which they were liable to strike the mines that had been laid for them. Subsequently, most of the U-boats renounced the Channel as a way into the Atlantic and instead took the passage north of Great Britain, thus losing precious fuel and time before reaching the heavily traveled sea lanes of the western approaches to Great Britain. Thus, in the summer of 1918, U.S. minelayers laid more than 60,000 mines (13,000 of them British) in a wide belt across 180 miles of the North Sea between Scotland and Norway. This operation known as the North Sea Mine Barrage, obstructed the U-boats' only access from Germany to the Atlantic other than the closely guarded Channel.

The cumulative effect of all these measures was the gradual containment and, ultimately, the defeat of the U-boat campaign, which never again achieved the staggering success of its April 1917 numbers. While sinkings by submarines, after that month, steadily fell, the losses of U-boats showed a slow but steady rise, and more than 40 were destroyed in the first six months of 1918. At the same time, the replacement of merchant vessels in the building program improved steadily, until the size of the merchant fleet eventually far surpassed the number of ships lost to submarines. In October 1918, for example, 511,000 tons of new Allied merchant ships were launched, while only 118,559 tons were lost.

PEACE MOVES

Until the end of 1916, the pursuit of peace was confined to individuals and to small groups, rather than nations or their governments. However, in the following months it began to acquire a broad popular backing. Semi-starvation in towns, mutinies in the armies, and casualty lists that seemed to have no end made more and more people question the need and the wisdom of continuing the war.

Francis Joseph, Austria's venerable old emperor, died on Nov. 21, 1916. The new emperor, Charles I, and his foreign minister, Graf Ottokar Czernin, initiated peace moves in the spring of 1917. Unfortunately, they did not concert their diplomatic efforts, and the channels of negotiation they opened between Austria-Hungary and the Allies had dried up by that summer.

In Germany, Matthias Erzberger, a Roman Catholic member of the Reichstag, had, on July 6, 1917, proposed that territorial annexations be renounced in order to facilitate a negotiated peace. During the ensuing debates Bethmann Hollweg resigned the office of chancellor. The emperor William II appointed the next chancellor, Ludendorff's nominee Georg Michaelis, without consulting the Reichstag. The Reichstag, offended, proceeded to pass its *Friedensresolution*, or "peace resolution," of July 19 by 212 votes. The peace resolution was a string of innocuous phrases expressing Germany's desire for peace, but was without a clear

An undated portrait of Pope Benedict XV by the artist Fabres Antonio. Imagno/Hulton Archive/Getty Images

renunciation of annexations or indemnities. The Allies took almost no notice of it.

Erzberger's proposal of July 6 had been intended to pave the way for Pope Benedict XV's forthcoming note to the belligerents of both camps. Dated Aug. 1, 1917, this note advocated a German withdrawal from Belgium and from France, the Allies' withdrawal from the German colonies, and the restoration not only of Serbia, Montenegro, and Romania but also of Poland to independence. France and Great Britain declined to give an express reply pending Germany's statement of its attitude about Belgium, on which Germany avoided committing itself.

Another unofficial peace move was made in London on Nov. 29, 1917. The *Daily Telegraph* published a letter from Lord Lansdowne suggesting negotiations on the basis of the status quo antebellum. However, Lloyd George rejected Lansdowne's theses on December 14.

By 1918, the U.S. president Woodrow Wilson had made himself the chief formulator and spokesman of the war aims of the Allies and the United States. The first nine months of 1918 saw Wilson's famous series of pronouncements on his war aims: the Fourteen Points (January 8), the "Four Principles" (February 11), the "Four Ends" (July 4), and the "Five Particulars" (September 27). Most important, not least because of Germany's deluded reliance on them in its eventual suing for peace, were the Fourteen Points: (1) open covenants of peace and the renunciation of secret diplomacy, (2) freedom of navigation on the high seas in wartime as well as peace, (3) the maximum possible freedom of trade, (4) a guaranteed reduction of armaments, (5) an impartial colonial settlement accommodating not only the colonialist powers but also the peoples of the colonies, (6) the evacuation of all Russian territory and respect for Russia's right of self-determination, (7) the complete restoration of Belgium, (8) a complete German withdrawal from France and satisfaction for France about Alsace-Lorraine, (9) a readjustment of Italy's frontiers on an ethnic basis, (10) an open prospect of autonomy for the peoples of Austria-Hungary, (11) the restoration of Romania, Serbia, and Montenegro, with free access to the sea for Serbia and international guarantees of the Balkan states' independence and integrity, (12) the prospect of autonomy for non-Turkish peoples of the Ottoman Empire and the unrestricted opening of the Straits, but secure sovereignty for the Turks in their own areas, (13) an independent Poland with access to the sea and under international guarantee, and (14) "a general association of nations," to guarantee the independence and integrity of all states, great and small. The three subsequent groups of pronouncements mainly consisted of idealistic expansions of themes implicit in the Fourteen Points, with increasing emphasis on the wishes of subject populations. However, the first of the "Four Ends" was that every arbitrary power capable by itself of disturbing world peace should be rendered innocuous.

Wilson's peace campaign was a significant factor in the collapse of the German people's will to fight, or to support Germany's military actions, and also a significant factor in the decision of the German government to sue for peace in October 1918. Indeed, the Germans conducted their preliminary peace talks exclusively with Wilson. Furthermore, the Armistice, when it came on Nov. 11, 1918, was formally based upon the Fourteen Points and additional Wilsonian pronouncements, with two just reservations by the British and French relating to freedom of the seas and reparations.

CHAPTER 5

THE STALEMATE BREAKS, 1918

GERMANY REGROUPS TO ATTACK IN THE WEST

In 1917, the German strength on the Western Front was being steadily increased by the transfer of divisions from the Eastern Front, where they were no longer needed since Russia had withdrawn from the war. Facing an imminent German offensive, the Allies' main problem was how to withstand a massive attack pending the arrival of massive reinforcements from the United States. Eventually Pétain persuaded the reluctant Haig that the British with 60 divisions should extend their sector of the front from 100 to 125 miles as compared with the 325 miles (523 km) to be held by the French with approximately 100 divisions. Haig thus devoted 46 of his divisions to the front from the Channel to Gouzeaucourt (southwest of German-held Cambrai) and 14 to the remaining third of the front from Gouzeaucourt past German-held Saint-Quentin to the Oise River.

On the German side, between Nov. 1, 1917, and March 21, 1918, the German divisions on the Western Front were increased from 146 to 192, the newly arrived troops having been drawn from Russia, Galicia, and Italy. By these means, the German armies in the west were reinforced by a total of about 570,000 men. General Erich Ludendorff's interest was to strike from his temporary position of strength—before the arrival of the major U.S. contingents—and at the same time to ensure that his German offensive should not fail for the same reasons the Allies' offensives of the past three years had failed. Accordingly he formed an offensive strategy based on taking the tactical line of least resistance. The main German attacks would begin with brief, but extremely intense, artillery bombardments using a high proportion of poison gas and smoke shells. These would incapacitate the Allies' forward trenches and machine-gun emplacements and would obscure their observation posts. Then a second and lighter artillery barrage would begin to creep forward over the Allied trenches at a walking pace (in order to keep the enemy under fire), with the masses of German assault infantry advancing as closely as possible behind it. The key to the new tactics was that the assault infantry would bypass machine-gun nests and other points of strong resistance instead of waiting for reinforcements to mop up the obstructions before continuing the advance, as had been the previous practice on both sides. The Germans would instead continue to advance in the direction of the least enemy resistance. Advancing this way would ensure the mobility of the German troops, and the deep infiltration of its advance would result in large amounts of territory being taken.

Such tactics demanded exceptionally fit and disciplined troops and a high level of military training. Ludendorff accordingly drew the best troops from all the Western Front forces at his disposal and formed them into elite shock divisions.

The troops were systematically trained in the new tactics, and every effort was also made to conceal the actual areas at which the German main attacks would be made.

Ludendorff's main attack was to be on the weakest sector of the Allies' front, the 47 miles (75.6 km) between Arras and La Fère (on the Oise). Two German armies, the 17th and the 2nd, were to break through the front between Arras and Saint-Quentin, north of the Somme. Then, they were to wheel right so as to force most of the British back toward the Channel, while the 18th Army, between the Somme and the Oise, protected the left flank of the advance against counterattack from the south. Code-named "Michael," this offensive was to be supplemented by three other attacks: "St. George I" against the British on the Lys River south of Armentières; "St. George II" against the British again between Armentières and Ypres; and "Blücher" against the French in Champagne. It was finally decided to use 62 divisions in the main attack, "Michael."

OPERATION MICHAEL

Preceded by an artillery bombardment using 6,000 guns, "Michael" was launched on March 21, 1918, and was helped by an early morning fog that hid the German advance from the Allied observation posts. The attack, which is known as the Second Battle of the Somme or the Battle of Saint-Quentin, took the British altogether by surprise. However, it did not develop as Ludendorff had foreseen. While the

A portrait of Field Marshal Ferdinand Foch, who became Supreme Allied Commander in March 1918, c. 1916. Hulton Archive/Getty Images

18th Army under von Hutier achieved a complete breakthrough south of the Somme, the major attack to the north was held up, mainly by the British concentration of strength at Arras. For a whole week Ludendorff, in violation of his new tactical emphasis, vainly persisted in trying to carry out his original plan instead of exploiting the unexpected success of the 18th Army, though the latter had advanced more than 40 miles (64.4 km) westward and had reached Montdidier by March 27. At last, however, the main effort of the Germans was converted into a drive toward Amiens, which began in force on March 30. By that time the Allies had

recovered from their initial dismay, and French reserves were coming up to reinforce the British line. The German drive was halted east of Amiens and so too was a renewed attack on April 4. After these latest attacks, Ludendorff then suspended his Somme offensive. This offensive had yielded the largest territorial gains of any operation on the Western Front since the First Battle of the Marne, more than three years before, in September 1914.

The collapse of one-third of the British front at least produced one overdue benefit for the Allies. On March 26, Marshal Ferdinand Foch was appointed to coordinate the Allies' military operations at Haig's own suggestion; and on April 14 he was named commander in chief of the Allied armies. Previously, Haig had resisted the idea of a generalissimo.

Operations St. George I and II

On April 9, the Germans began their operation "St. George I," against British forces with an attack on the extreme northern front between Armentières and the canal of La Bassée, their aim being to advance across the Lys River toward Hazebrouck. Such was the initial success of this attack that "St. George II" was launched the very next day, with the capture of Kemmel Hill (Kemmelberg), southwest of Ypres, as its first objective. Armentières fell, and Ludendorff came to think for a time that this Battle of the Lys might be turned into a major effort. The British, however, after being driven back

IN FOCUS: THE SECOND BATTLE OF THE SOMME

The Second Battle of the Somme, or Battle of Saint-Quentin (March 21–April 5, 1918), was a partially successful German offensive against Allied forces on the Western Front in the last year of the war.

The German commander, General Erich Ludendorff, believed that it was essential for Germany to use the troops freed from the Eastern Front by the collapse of Imperial Russia to achieve a victory on the Western Front in the spring of 1918, before American troops arrived in sufficient numbers to effectively reinforce the war-weary Allies. His first offensive was directed against the rather weak British armies north of the Somme River, between Arras and La Fère. The British trenches were shelled and gassed before a massive morning attack in dense fog, which took the British by surprise, as they could not see the advancing German troops. Their first and second lines of British soldiers quickly fell, and by March 22 the shattered British 5th Army was in retreat and had lost contact with the French to the south. The Germans moved rapidly forward, hoping to drive a permanent wedge between the French and the British, but by March 28, the Allies had assembled new troops that checked the German advance east of Amiens. The German offensive had obtained the single largest territorial gain on the Western Front since the early months of the war in late 1914. The Germans had advanced almost 40 miles and had taken about 70,000 prisoners, but in spite of these gains the Allied lines were only bent, not broken, as Ludendorff had hoped. The German tactical virtuosity, unconnected to any broader strategic concept, only exhausted Germany's limited resources.

10 miles (16 km), halted the Germans short of Hazebrouck. By then, French reinforcements began to come up. Thus, when the Germans had taken Kemmel Hill (April 25), Ludendorff decided to suspend exploitation of the advance, for fear of a counterstroke against his front's new bulge.

DOUGHBOYS AND OPERATION BLÜCHER

Thus far, Ludendorff had fallen short of strategic results, but he could claim huge tactical successes—the British casualties incurred under his command alone amounted to more than 300,000. Ten British divisions had to be broken up

temporarily, while the German strength mounted to 208 divisions, of which 80 were still in reserve. A restoration of the balance, however, was now in sight. A dozen U.S. divisions had arrived in France, and great efforts were being made to swell the stream. Furthermore, Pershing, the U.S. commander, had placed his troops, affectionately known as "doughboys," at Foch's disposal for use wherever required. The first significant action by American troops, with French air and artillery support, occurred at the village of Cantigny, which the U.S. 1st Division captured on May 28 and held against a sustained German counterattack. Known as the Battle of Cantigny, the doughboy's determination to hold onto the village, with casualties of more than a quarter of their troops, demonstrated the fighting spirit of American troops. However, this minor battle was overshadowed by the last great German offensive, which already had begun along the Aisne River.

Ludendorff had finally launched Operation "Blücher" on May 27, on a front extending from Coucy, north of Soissons, eastward toward Reims. Fifteen German divisions suddenly attacked the seven French and British divisions opposing them swarming over the ridge of the Chemin des Dames and across the Aisne River. By May 30, the Germans were on the Marne, between Château-Thierry and Dormans. Their advance was halted at the Marne by the U.S. 3rd Division under the command of Major General Joseph Dickman, who earned the sobriquet of "Rock of the Marne" for his stubborn defense of the main bridge connecting the twin city of Château-Thierry. Once again the attack's initial success went far beyond Ludendorff's expectation or intention. However, when the Germans tried to push westward against the right flank of the Allies' Compiègne salient, which was sandwiched between the Germans' Amiens and Champagne bulges, they were checked by counter-attacks. These responses included the taking of Château-Thierry (June 3–4) by the U.S. 2nd and 3rd Divisions, with help from the French 10th Colonial Division. The 2nd Division's Marine Corps were then tasked with clearing the nearby Belleau Wood (Bois de Belleau). The Battle of Belleau Wood (June 6–26) was

the first major engagement by American forces and had the dubious distinction of the highest casualties sustained by the marines before World War II. Control of the woods changed some half dozen times, with American casualties of 9,777, including 1,811 dead.

Overtaken by the inordinate fruition of his own offensives, Ludendorff paused for a month's recuperation. The tactical success of his own blows had been his undoing; yielding to their influence, he had pressed each too far and too long, using up his own reserves and causing an undue interval between blows. He had driven three great wedges into the Allied lines, but none had penetrated far enough to sever a vital rail artery, and this strategic failure left the Germans with a front whose several bulges invited flanking counterstrokes. Moreover, Ludendorff had used up many of his shock troops in the attacks, and the remaining troops, though strong in numbers, were not as well-trained. The Germans were to end up sustaining a total of 800,000 casualties in their great 1918 offensives. Meanwhile, the Allies were now receiving U.S. troops at the rate of 300,000 men per month.

THE SECOND BATTLE OF THE MARNE

Following Operation Blücher, the next German offensive, which opened the Second Battle of the Marne, was launched in Champagne on July 15. It came to nothing: a German thrust from the front east of Reims toward Châlons-sur-Marne was frustrated by the "elastic defense" that Pétain had recently been prescribing but that the local commanders had failed to practice against the offensive of May 27. A drive from Dormans, on the left flank of the Germans' huge Soissons–Reims bulge, across the Marne toward Épernay, simply made the Germans' situation more precarious when Foch's long-prepared counterstroke was launched on July 18. In this great counterstroke one of Foch's armies assailed the Germans' Champagne bulge from the west, another from the southwest, one more from the south, and a fourth from the vicinity of Reims. Masses of light tanks—a relatively new weapon on which Ludendorff had placed little reliance, preferring gas instead in his plans for the year—played a vital part in forcing the French forcing Germans into a hasty retreat. By August 2, the French had pushed the Champagne front back to a line following the Vesle River from Reims and then along the Aisne to a point west of Soissons.

THE BATTLE OF AMIENS

Having recovered the initiative after the Second Battle of the Marne, the Allies were determined not to lose it. For their next blow, they chose again the front north and south of the Somme. The British 4th Army, including Australian and Canadian forces, with 450 tanks, struck the Germans with maximum surprise on Aug. 8, 1918. Overwhelming the German forward divisions, who had failed to entrench themselves adequately since their recent

occupation of the "Michael" bulge, the 4th Army advanced steadily for four days. Over the course of those four days, they took 21,000 prisoners and inflicted as many or more casualties at the cost of only about 20,000 casualties to themselves, and halted only when it reached the desolation of the old battlefields of 1916. Several German divisions simply collapsed in the face of the offensive, their troops either fleeing or surrendering. The Battle of Amiens was thus both a striking material and moral success for the Allies. However, Ludendorff put it differently: "August 8 was the black day of the German Army in the history of the war ... It put the decline of our fighting power beyond all doubt ... The war must be ended." After Amiens, he informed Emperor William II and Germany's political chiefs that peace negotiations should be opened before the situation became worse. The conclusions reached at a German Crown Council held at Spa were that "We can no longer hope to break the war-will of our enemies by military operations," and "the objects of our strategy must be to paralyse the enemy's war-will gradually by a strategic defensive." In other words, the German high command had abandoned hope of victory or even of holding their gains. After crushing defeat at Amiens, they hoped only to avoid outright surrender.

THE HINDENBURG LINE AND THE BATTLE OF SAINT-MIHIEL

Meanwhile, the French had retaken Montdidier and were thrusting toward

Lassigny (between Roye and Noyon). On August 17, they began a new drive from the Compiègne salient south of Noyon. Then, in the fourth week of August, two more British armies went into action on the Arras–Albert sector of the front, the one advancing directly eastward on Bapaume, the other operating farther to the north. From then on, Foch delivered a series of hammer blows along the length of the German front, launching a series of rapid attacks at different points, each broken off as soon as its initial impetus waned. All of the attacks were close enough in time to attract German reserves, which consequently were unavailable to defend against the next Allied attack along a different part of the front. By the early days of September, the Germans were back where they had been before March 1918—behind the Hindenburg Line.

The Allies' recovery was consummated by the first feat executed by Pershing's U.S. forces as an independent army (hitherto the U.S. divisions in France had fought only in support of the major French or British units): the U.S. 1st Army on September 12 erased the triangular Saint-Mihiel salient that the Germans had been occupying since 1914 (between Verdun and Nancy). Saint-Mihiel was the greatest air battle of the war. Nearly 1,500 Allied airplanes faced about 500 German aircraft during the battle (Sept. 12–16). The Allied forces, which included American, French, and British aircraft, was led by U.S. Colonel William (Billy) Mitchell.

Because of the clear evidence of the Germans' decline, Foch decided to seek victory in the coming autumn of 1918 instead of postponing the attempt until 1919. In order to ensure a victorious outcome, all the Allied armies in the west were to combine in a simultaneous offensive.

OTHER DEVELOPMENTS

NATIONALIST MOVEMENTS

The growth of the national movements toward the end of the war, which, under the eventual protection of the Allies, were to result in the foundation of new states or the resurrection of long-defunct ones at the end of the war. There were three such movements: that of the Czechs, with the more backward Slovaks in tow; that of the South Slavs, or Yugoslavs (Serbs, Croats, and Slovenes); and that of the Poles. The Czech country, namely Bohemia and Moravia, belonged in 1914 to the Austrian half of the Habsburg monarchy, the Slovak to the Hungarian half. The Yugoslavs had already been represented in 1914 by two independent kingdoms, Serbia and Montenegro, but they were also predominantly numerous in territories still under Habsburg rule: Serbs in Bosnia and Hercegovina (an Austro-Hungarian condominium) and in Dalmatia (an Austrian possession); Croats in Croatia (Hungarian), in Istria (Austrian), and in Dalmatia; Slovenes in Istria and in Illyria (Austrian likewise). Poland was divided into three parts:

Germany had the north and the west as provinces of the Kingdom of Prussia; Austria had Galicia (including an ethnically Ukrainian extension to the east); Russia controlled the rest.

The Czechs had long been restless under the Austrian regime, and one of their leading intellectual spokesmen, Tomáš Masaryk (in fact a Slovak), had already envisaged the carving of Czechoslovak and Yugoslav states out of Austria-Hungary in December 1914. In 1916 he and a fellow émigré, Edvard Beneš, based respectively in London and in Paris, organized a Czechoslovak National Council. The western Allies

A portrait of Tomas Garrigue Masaryk, president of Czechoslovakia, c. 1910. Imagno/Hulton Archive/Getty Images

committed themselves to the Czechoslovak idea from 1917 onward, when Russia's imminent defection from the war made them ready to exploit any means at hand for the disabling of Austria-Hungary. Furthermore, Wilson's sympathy for the cause was implicit in his successive peace pronouncements of 1918.

For the South Slavs of Austria-Hungary the Yugoslav Committee, with representatives in Paris and in London, was founded in April 1915. On July 20, 1917, this committee and the Serbian government in exile made the joint Corfu Declaration forecasting a South Slav state to comprise Serbs, Croats, and Slovenes.

The Polish nationalist leaders in the first years of the war were uncertain whether to rely on the Central Powers or on the Allies for a restoration of Poland's independence. So long as the western Allies hesitated to encourage Polish nationalism for fear of offending imperial Russia, the Central Powers seemed to be the most likely sponsors; and Austria at least allowed Józef Piłsudski, from 1914, to organize his volunteer Polish legions to serve with Austrian forces against the Russians. Austria's benevolence, however, was not reflected by Germany; and when the Two Emperors' Manifesto of Nov. 5, 1916, provided for the constitution of an independent Polish kingdom, it was clear that this kingdom would consist only of Polish territory conquered from Russia, not of any German or Austrian territory. When, after the March Revolution of 1917, the Russian provisional government had recognized

Poland's right to independence, Roman Dmowski's Polish National Committee, which from 1914 had been functioning in a limited way under Russian protection, could at last count seriously on the sympathy of the western Allies. While Piłsudski declined to raise a Polish army to fight against the new Russia, a Polish army was formed in France, as well as two army corps in Belorussia and in the Ukraine, to fight against the Central Powers. The Bolshevik Revolution and Wilson's Fourteen Points together consummated the alignment of the Poles on the side of the western powers.

Germany Takes Control of Eastern Europe

The Treaty of Brest-Litovsk (March 3, 1918), negotiating a separate peace between Russia and Germany, gave Germany a free hand to do what it liked with Russia's former land possessions in eastern Europe. While their plan of 1916 for a kingdom of Poland was under way, the Germans took new measures for the other countries. Lithuania, recognized as independent, was to be a kingdom under some German prince. Latvia and Estonia were to be merged into a grand duchy of the Baltikum under the hereditary rule of Prussia. An expeditionary force of 12,000 men, under General Graf Rüdiger von der Goltz, was sent to Finland to uphold the Finnish general C.G.E. Mannerheim's nationalist forces against the Red Guards, whom the Bolsheviks, despite their recognition of Finland's independence, were

now promoting there. Finally, the Ukrainian nationalist government, which had already been challenged by a Communist one before its separate peace with the Central Powers (Brest-Litovsk, February 9), was promptly displaced by a new regime after the advance of German and Austro-Hungarian troops into its territory.

The Romanian armistice of December 1917 was converted into the Treaty of Bucharest on May 7, 1918. Under this treaty's terms, southern Dobruja was ceded to Bulgaria; northern Dobruja was put under the joint administration of the Central Powers; and the latter obtained virtual control of Romania's oil fields and communications. Romania, on the other hand, had some consolation from Bessarabia, whose nationalists, after receiving Romanian assistance against the Bolsheviks, had voted in March 1918 for their country's conditional union with Romania.

Even Transcaucasia began to slide into the German camp. The short-lived federal republic was dissolved by its three members' individual declarations of independence—Georgia's on May 26, Armenia's and Azerbaijan's on May 28. Treaties of friendship were promptly signed between Georgia and Germany and between Armenia and Turkey, and Turkish troops advanced into Azerbaijan, where they occupied Baku on September 15. The western Allies, meanwhile, were hoping that some new semblance of an Eastern Front could be conjured up if they supported the various and growing forces in Russia that were opposed to the peacemaking Bolsheviks. Since the Black Sea and the Baltic were closed to them, the Allies could land troops only on Russia's distant Arctic and Pacific shores. Thus, the Allied "intervention" in Russia on the side of the anti-Bolshevik ("White") forces began with an Anglo-French landing at Murmansk, in the far north, on March 9, 1918. The subsequent reinforcement of Murmansk made possible the occupation of the Murmansk railway as far south as Soroka (now Belomorsk). A further landing at Arkhangelsk in the summer raised the total Allied strength in northern Russia to some 48,000 (including 20,000 Russian "Whites"). By this time, moreover, there were some 85,000 interventionist troops in Siberia, where a strong Japanese landing at Vladivostok in April had been followed by British, French, Italian, and U.S. contingents. A "White" provisional government of Russia was set up at Omsk, with Admiral A. V. Kolchak as its dominant personality. The "White" resistance in the south of European Russia, which had been growing since November 1917, was put under the supreme command of General A. I. Denikin in April 1918.

THE BALKAN FRONT

At Salonika the Allies' politically ambitious but militarily ineffective commander in chief, General Sarrail, was replaced at the end of 1917 by General Guillaumat. Guillaumat was in turn succeeded in July 1918 by General L.-F.-F. Franchet d'Espèrey, who launched a major offensive in September with six Serbian and two French divisions against a seven-mile front held by only one Bulgarian division.

The initial assault, preceded by heavy bombardment at night, began in the morning of Sept. 15, 1918. By nightfall on September 16, a five-mile penetration was achieved. The next day, the Serbs advanced 20 miles forward, while French and Greek forces on their flanks widened the breach to 25 miles. A British attack, launched on September 18 on the front between the Vardar and Lake Doiran, prevented the Bulgars from transferring troops westward against the right flank of the penetration. By September 19, the Serbian cavalry had reached Kavadarci, at the apex of the Crna–Vardar triangle. Two days later the whole Bulgarian front west of the Vardar had collapsed.

While Italian forces in the extreme west advanced on Prilep, the elated Serbs, with the French beside them, pressed on up the Vardar Valley. The British in the east now made such headway as to take Strumica, across the old Bulgarian frontier, on September 26. Facing sure defeat, the Bulgars then sued for an armistice. Still, a bold French cavalry thrust up the Vardar from Veles (Titov Veles) and took Skopje, the key to the whole system of communications for the Balkan front, on September 29. Bulgarian delegates signed the Armistice of Salonika, accepting the Allies' terms unreservedly the same day.

THE TURKISH FRONTS

In the summer of 1918, the British–Turkish front in Palestine ran from the Jordan

River westward north of Jericho and Lydda to the Mediterranean just north of Jaffa. North of this front there were three Turkish "armies" (in fact, barely stronger than divisions): one to the east of the Jordan, two to the west. These armies depended for their supplies on the Hejaz Railway, the main line of which ran from Damascus southward, east of the Jordan, and which was joined at Déraa (Dar'ā) by a branch line serving Palestine.

Liman von Sanders, Falkenhayn's successor as commander of the Turkish forces in Syria–Palestine, was convinced that the British would make their main effort east of the Jordan. Allenby, however, was really interested in taking a straight northerly direction. He reckoned that the Palestine branch rail line at 'Afula and Beisān, some 60 miles (96.6 km) behind the Turkish front, could be reached by a strategic "bound" of his cavalry and that their fall would isolate the two Turkish armies in the west.

Having by ruse and diversion induced the Turks to reduce their strength in the west, Allenby struck there on Sept. 19, 1918, with a numerical superiority of 10 to one. In this Battle of Megiddo, a British infantry attack swept the astonished defenders aside and opened the way for the cavalry, which rode 30 miles north up the coastal corridor before swinging inland to cut the Turks' northward lines of retreat. 'Afula, Beisān, and even Nazareth, farther north, were in British hands the next day.

When the Turks east of the Jordan River began to retreat on September 22,

the Arabs had already severed the railway line and were lying in wait for them. A British cavalry division from Beisān was also about to push eastward to intercept their withdrawal. Simultaneously, two more British divisions and another force of Arabs were racing on toward Damascus, which fell on October 1. The campaign ended with the capture of Aleppo and the junction of the Baghdad Railway. In 38 days Allenby's forces had advanced 350 miles and taken 75,000 prisoners at a cost of less than 5,000 casualties.

In Mesopotamia, meanwhile, the British had taken Kifrī, north of the Diyālā left-bank tributary of the Tigris, in January 1918. They also took Khān al-Baghdāḥī, up the Euphrates, in March. Pressing northward from Kifrī, they took Kirkūk in May but evacuated it soon afterward.

The British centre in Mesopotamia, advancing up the Tigris in October, was about to capture Mosul when the hostilities were suspended. The Ottoman government, seeing eastern Turkey defenseless, feared Allied advance against Istanbul from the west now that Bulgaria had collapsed. Thus, they decided to capitulate. On October 30, the Armistice of Mudros was signed, on a British cruiser off Lemnos. The Turks, by its terms, were to open the Straits to the Allies, demobilize their forces, allow the Allies to occupy any strategic point that they might require, and also, to use all Turkey's ports and railways. They also were ordered to surrender their remaining garrisons in Arabia, Syria, and Mesopotamia. With the signing of the Armistice of Mudro, the centuries-old Ottoman Empire finally had come to an end.

The Italian Front

After the stabilization of the Italian front on the Piave River at the end of 1917, the Austrians made no further move until the following June. They then tried not only to force the Tonale Pass and enter northeastern Lombardy but also to make two converging thrusts into central Venetia. One thrust was to move southeastward from the Trentino and the other southwestward across the lower Piave. The whole offensive came to worse than nothing, the attackers losing 100,000 men.

Armando Diaz, the Italian commander in chief, was meanwhile deliberately abstaining from positive action until Italy should be ready to strike with success assured. In the offensive he planned, three of the five armies lining the front from the Monte Grappa sector to the Adriatic end of the Piave were to drive across the river toward Vittorio Veneto. This would cut communications between the two Austrian armies opposing them.

When Germany, in October 1918, was at last asking for an armistice, Italy's time had obviously come. On October 24, the anniversary of Caporetto, the offensive opened. An attack in the Monte Grappa sector was repulsed with heavy loss, though it served to attract the Austrian reserves. Furthermore, the flooding of the Piave prevented two of the three central armies from advancing simultaneously with the third. However, the latter of the armies, comprising one Italian and one British corps, having under cover of darkness and fog occupied Papadopoli Island farther downstream, won a foothold on the left bank of the river on October 27. The Italian reserves were then brought up to exploit this bridgehead.

Mutiny was already breaking out in the Austrian forces, and on October 28 the Austrian high command ordered a general retreat. Vittorio Veneto was occupied the next day by the Italians, who were also pushing on already toward the Tagliamento. On November 3 the Austrians obtained an armistice.

The Collapse of Austria-Hungary

In the Austro-Hungarian empire, the duality of the Habsburg monarchy had been underlined from the very beginning of the war. Whereas the Austrian parliament, or Reichsrat, had been suspended in March 1914 and was not reconvened for three years, the Hungarian parliament in Budapest continued its sessions, and the Hungarian government proved itself constantly less amenable to dictation from the military than had the Austrian. The Slav minorities, however, showed little sign of anti-Habsburg feeling before Russia's March Revolution of 1917. In May 1917, however, the Reichsrat was reconvened, and just before the opening session the Czech intelligentsia sent a manifesto to its deputies calling for "a democratic Europe . . . of autonomous states." The Bolshevik Revolution of November 1917 and the Wilsonian peace pronouncements from January 1918 onward encouraged either socialism or nationalism, or alternatively, a combination of both tendencies, among all peoples of the Habsburg monarchy.

Emperor Charles I of Austria and his wife, Empress Zita, at their coronation, 1916. Charles was the last Habsburg emperor to reign over Austria-Hungary. Keystone/Hulton Archive/Getty Images

Early in September 1918, the Austro-Hungarian government proposed in a circular note to the other powers that a conference be held on neutral territory for a general peace. This proposal was quashed by the United States on the ground that the U.S. position had already been enunciated by the Wilsonian pronouncements (the Fourteen Points, etc.). However, when Austria-Hungary, after the collapse of Bulgaria, appealed on October 4 for an armistice based on those very pronouncements, the answer from the United States on October 18 was that the U.S. government was now committed to the Czechoslovaks and to the Yugoslavs, who might not be satisfied with the "autonomy" postulated heretofore. The emperor Charles had, in fact, granted autonomy to the peoples of the Austrian Empire (as distinct from the Hungarian Kingdom) on October 16. However, this concession was ignored internationally and served only to facilitate the process of disruption within the monarchy: Czechoslovaks in Prague and South Slavs in Zagreb had already set up organs ready to take power.

The last scenes of Austria-Hungary's dissolution were performed very rapidly. On October 24 (when the Italians launched their very timely offensive), a Hungarian National Council prescribing peace and severance from Austria was set up in Budapest. On October 27, they sent a note accepting the U.S. note of October 18 to Washington from Vienna, but it remained unacknowledged. On October 28 the Czechoslovak committee in Prague passed a "law" for an independent state, while a similar Polish committee was formed in Kraków for the incorporation of Galicia and Austrian Silesia into a unified Poland. On October 29, while the Austrian high command was asking the Italians for an armistice, the Croats in Zagreb declared Slavonia, Croatia, and Dalmatia to be independent, pending the formation of a national state of Slovenes, Croats, and Serbs. On October 30 the German members of the Reichsrat in Vienna proclaimed an independent state of German Austria.

The solicited armistice between the Allies and Austria-Hungary finally was signed at the Villa Giusti, near Padua, on Nov. 3, 1918, to become effective on November 4. Under its provisions, Austria-Hungary's forces were required to evacuate not only all territory occupied since August 1914 but also South Tirol, Tarvisio, the Isonzo Valley, Gorizia, Trieste, Istria, western Carniola, and Dalmatia. All German forces should be expelled from Austria-Hungary within 15 days or interned, and the Allies were free to use of Austria-Hungary's internal communications, and to take possession of most of its warships.

Count Mihály Károlyi, chairman of the Budapest National Council, had been appointed prime minister of Hungary by his king, the Austrian emperor Charles, on October 31. However, he had promptly started to dissociate his country from Austria—partly in the vain hope of obtaining a separate Hungarian armistice. Charles, the last Habsburg to rule in Austria-Hungary, renounced the right to participate in Austrian affairs of government on November 11. On November 13, he renounced his right to participate in Hungarian affairs as well.

THE ALLIES LAUNCH THE FINAL ATTACK ON THE WESTERN FRONT

In planning their final offensive of the war, the Allied commanders eventually agreed that Pershing's U.S. troops should advance across the difficult terrain of the Argonne Forest, so that the combined Allied offensive would consist of converging attacks against the whole German position west of a line drawn from Ypres to Verdun. Thus, the Americans from the front northwest of Verdun and the French from eastern Champagne were to launch attacks on September 26, the former on the west bank of the Meuse, the latter west of the Argonne Forest, with Mézières as their ultimate objective. This would threaten not only the Germans' supply line along the Mézières–Sedan–Montmédy railway and the natural line of retreat across Lorraine but also the hinge of the Antwerp–Meuse defensive line that the Germans were now preparing. The British were to attack the Hindenburg Line between

Cambrai and Saint-Quentin on September 27 and to try to reach the key rail junction of Maubeuge, so as to threaten the Germans' line of retreat through the Liège gap. The Belgians, with Allied support, were to begin a drive from Ypres toward Ghent on September 28.

The Americans took Vauquois and Montfaucon in the first two days of their offensive but were soon slowed down. On October 14, when their attack was suspended, they had only reached Grandpré, less than halfway to Mézières. The French advance meanwhile was halted on the Aisne. The British, though they had broken through the German defenses by October 5 and thenceforward had open country in front of them, could not pursue the Germans fast enough to endanger their withdrawal. Nevertheless, the piercing of the Hindenburg Line unnerved the German supreme command as Belgians were in possession of all the heights around Ypres.

GERMAN COLLAPSE

Georg von Hertling had taken the place of Georg Michaelis as Germany's chancellor in November 1917, but had proved no more capable than Michaelis of restraining Ludendorff and Hindenburg; thus, he tendered his resignation on Sept. 29, 1918, the day of the Bulgarian armistice and of the major development of the British attack on the Western Front. Pending the appointment of a new chancellor, Ludendorff and Hindenburg obtained the Emperor's consent to an immediate peace move with the Western powers. On October 1, they even disclosed their despondency to a meeting of the leaders of all the national political parties, thus undermining the German home front by a sudden revelation of facts long hidden from the public and its civilian leaders. This new and bleak honesty about Germany's deteriorating military situation gave an immense impetus to the native German forces of pacifism and internal discord. On October 3 the new chancellor Prince Maximilian of Baden was appointed. He was internationally known for his moderation and honorability. However, Max demanded a few days' interval lest Germany's overture for peace should appear too obviously an admission of imminent collapse, the military leaders insisted on an immediate move. A German note to Wilson, requesting an armistice and negotiations on the basis of Wilson's own pronouncements, was sent off in the night of October 3–4.

The United States answered on October 8 requiring that Germany preliminarily assent to negotiations on the sole question of the means of putting Wilson's principles into practice, and also, to the withdrawal of German forces from Allied soil. The German government's note of October 12 accepted these requirements and suggested a mixed commission to arrange the postulated evacuation. On October 14, however, the U.S. government sent a second note, which coupled allusions to Germany's "illegal and inhuman" methods of warfare with demands that the conditions of the

IN FOCUS: SERGEANT YORK

(b. Dec. 13, 1887, Pall Mall, Tenn., U.S.—d. Sept. 2, 1964, Nashville, Tenn.), Sergeant Alvin York, a celebrated American hero of World War I, was immortalized by the film version of his life story, Sergeant York (1941).

A blacksmith from Cumberland Hill, Tenn., York was denied status as a conscientious objector and was drafted into the army during World War I. While serving in the 82nd Infantry Division at the Meuse-Argonne Offensive (October 1918), he was among a patrol of 17 men ordered to take out a German machine-gun emplacement that was checking his regiment's advance. Behind enemy lines, the patrol lost half its men but managed to take a handful of prisoners before it was pinned down by extremely heavy rifle and machine-gun fire. Corporal York assumed command of the patrol. While the rest of the survivors took up defensive positions and stood guard over the prisoners, York attacked alone. Firing rapidly and with deadly accuracy at the enemy gunners, York killed more than two dozen of them, which prompted the others to surrender. En route back to the American lines, he captured still more Germans, to a total of 132. York was promoted to the rank of sergeant, and later he received the Congressional Medal of Honor and similar honours from France and other countries. After the war, York returned to Tennessee, where he lived on a farm given to him by that state. There he helped establish an industrial institute and a Bible school for the education of rural youth.

armistice and of the evacuation be determined unilaterally by its own and the Allies' military advisers. Furthermore, that the "arbitrary power" of the German regime be removed in order that the forthcoming negotiations could be conducted with a government more representative of the German people.

By this time, the German supreme command had become more cheerful, even optimistic about outcomes on the Western Front, as it saw that the piercing of the Hindenburg Line had not been followed by an actual Allied breakthrough. More encouragement came from reports of a slackening in the force of the Allies' attacks, largely because they had advanced too far ahead of their

supply lines. However, Ludendorff still wanted an armistice, but only to give his troops a rest as a prelude to further resistance and to ensure a secure withdrawal to a shortened defensive line on the frontier. By October 17 he even felt that his troops could do without a rest. It was less that the situation had changed than that his impression of it had been revised; it had never been quite so bad as he had pictured it on September 29. But his dismal first impression had now spread throughout German political circles and the public. Although they had endured increasing privations and were half-starved due to the Allied blockade by mid-1918, the German people had retained their morale surprisingly well as long as they believed Germany had a prospect of achieving victory on the Western Front. When this hope collapsed in October 1918, many, and perhaps even most, Germans wished only that the war would end, even if it might mean their nation would have to accept unfavourable peace terms. German public opinion, having been more suddenly disillusioned, was now far more radically defeatist than the supreme command.

A third German note to the United States, sent on October 20, agreed to the unilateral settlement of conditions for the armistice and for the evacuation, in the express belief that Wilson would allow no affront to Germany's honour. The answering U.S. note of October 23 conceded Wilson's readiness to propose an armistice to the Allies, but added that the terms must be such as to make Germany incapable of renewing hostilities. Ludendorff saw this, militarily, as a demand for unconditional surrender and continued resistance. However, the situation had passed beyond his control. He was made to resign by the emperor on October 26, on Prince Max's advice. On October 27, Germany acknowledged the U.S. note.

Wilson now began to persuade the Allies to agree to an armistice and negotiations according to the U.S.-German correspondence. They agreed, but with two reservations: they would not subscribe to the second of the Fourteen Points (on the freedom of the seas); and they wanted "compensation . . . for damage done to the civilian population . . .

and their property by the aggression of Germany." Wilson's note on November 5 apprised the Germans of these reservations and stated that Foch would communicate armistice terms to Germany's accredited representatives. On November 8 a German delegation, led by Matthias Erzberger, arrived at Rethondes, in the Forest of Compiègne, where the Germans met face to face with Foch and his party. There they were informed of the Allies' peace terms.

Meanwhile, revolution was shaking Germany. The unrest began with a sailors' mutiny at Kiel on October 29 in reaction to the naval command's order for the High Seas Fleet to go out into the North Sea for a conclusive battle. Though the U-boat crews remained loyal, the mutiny of the surface-ship crews spread to other units of the fleet, developed into armed insurrection on November 3, and progressed to open revolution the next day. There were disturbances in Hamburg and in Bremen; "councils of soldiers and workers," like the Russian soviets, were formed in inland industrial centres; and in the night of November 7–8 a "democratic and socialist Republic of Bavaria" was proclaimed. The Social Democrats of the Reichstag withdrew their support from Prince Max's government in order to be free to contend against the Communists for the leadership of the revolution. While William II, at Spa, was still wondering whether he could abdicate his imperial German title but remain king of Prussia, Prince Max, in Berlin on November 9, announced William's abdication of both titles on his own initative. The Hohenzollern monarchy thus came to an end, joining those of the Habsburgs and the Romanovs. Prince Max handed his powers as chancellor over to Friedrich Ebert, a Majority Social Democrat, who formed a provisional government. A member of this government, Philipp Scheidemann, hastily proclaimed a republic. On November 10 William II took refuge in the neutral Netherlands, where on November 28, he signed his own abdication of his sovereign rights.

THE ARMISTICE

When finally presented in the railway carriage at Rethondes, the Allies' armistice terms were stiff. Germany was required to evacuate not only Belgium, France, and Alsace-Lorraine, but also all the rest of the left (west) bank of the Rhine; it also had to neutralize that river's right bank between the Netherlands and Switzerland. The German troops in East Africa were to surrender; the German armies in eastern Europe were to withdraw to the prewar German frontier; and the treaties of Brest-Litovsk and Bucharest were to be annulled. Lastly, the Germans were to repatriate all prisoners of war and hand over to the Allies a large quantity of war materials, including 5,000 pieces of artillery, 25,000 machine guns, 1,700 aircraft, 5,000 locomotives, and 150,000 railroad cars. Meanwhile, the Allies' blockade of Germany was to continue.

Pleading the danger of Bolshevism in a nation on the verge of collapse, the German delegation obtained some mitigation of these terms. They suggested that the blockade might be relaxed. They also asked for a reduction in the quantity of armaments to be handed over, and permission for the German forces in eastern Europe to stay put for the time being. The Germans might have held out longer for further concessions if the fact of revolution on their home front had not been coupled with the imminence of a new military blow from the west.

Though the Allied advance was continuing and seemed in some sectors even to be accelerating, the main German forces had managed to retreat ahead of it. The Germans' destruction of roads and railways along the routes of their evacuation made it impossible for supplies to keep pace with the advancing Allied troops. Therefore, pause in the advance would occur while Allied communications were being repaired, and that would give the Germans a breathing space in which to rally their resistance. By November 11, the Allied advance on the northern sectors of the front had come more or less to a standstill on a line running from Pont-à-Mousson through Sedan, Mézières, and Mons to Ghent. Foch, however, now had a Franco-U.S. force of 28 divisions and 600 tanks in the south ready to strike through Metz into northeastern Lorraine. Since Foch's general offensive had absorbed the Germans' reserves, this new offensive would fall on their bared left flank and held the promise outflanking their whole new line of defense (from Antwerp to the line of the

Meuse) and of intercepting any German retreat. By this time the number of U.S. divisions in France had risen to 42. In addition, the British were about to bomb Berlin on a scale hitherto unattempted in air warfare.

Whether the Allies' projected final offensive, intended for November 14, would have achieved a breakthrough can never be known. At 5:00 AM on Nov. 11, 1918, the armistice document was signed in Foch's railway carriage at Rethondes. At 11:00 AM on the same day, World War I came to an end.

The fact that Matthias Erzberger, who was a civilian politician rather than a soldier, headed the German armistice delegation became an integral part of the cultural legend of the "stab in the back" (*Dolchstoss im Rücken*). This legend's theme was that the German army was "undefeated in the field" (*unbesiegt im Felde*) and had been "stabbed in the back"—i.e., had been denied support at the crucial moment by a weary and defeatist civilian population and their leaders. This theme was adopted soon after the war's end by Ludendorff himself and by

A large crowd of soldiers and civilians celebrating the signing of the armistice by the German leadership, signaling the end of the war, Nov. 11, 1918. Time & Life Pictures/Getty Images

IN FOCUS: WILFRED OWEN

(b. March 18, 1893, Oswestry, Shropshire, Eng.—killed in action Nov. 4, 1918, France), English poet Wilfred Owen was noted for his anger at the cruelty and waste of war and his pity for its victims. He also is significant for his technical experiments in assonance, which were particularly influential in the 1930s.

Owen was educated at the Birkenhead Institute and matriculated at the University of London; but after an illness in 1913 he lived in France. He had already begun to write and, while working as a tutor near Bordeaux, was preparing a book of "Minor Poems—in Minor Keys—by a Minor," which was never published. These early poems are consciously modeled on those of John Keats; often ambitious, they show enjoyment of poetry as a craft.

In 1915 Owen enlisted in the British army. The experience of trench warfare brought him to rapid maturity; the poems written after January 1917 are full of anger at war's brutality, an elegiac pity for "those who die as cattle," and a rare descriptive power. In June 1917 he was wounded and sent home. While in a hospital near Edinburgh he met the poet Siegfried Sassoon, who shared his feelings about the war and who became interested in his work. Reading Sassoon's poems and discussing his work with Sassoon revolutionized Owen's style and his conception of poetry. Despite the plans of well-wishers to find him a staff job, he returned to France in August 1918 as a company commander. He was awarded the Military Cross in October and was killed a week before Armistice Day.

Published posthumously by Sassoon, Owen's single volume of poems contains the most poignant English poetry of the war. His collected poems, edited by C. Day-Lewis, were published in 1964; his collected letters, edited by his younger brother Harold Owen and John Bell, were published in 1967.

other German generals who were unwilling to admit the hopelessness of Germany's military situation in November 1918 and who wanted to vindicate the honour of German arms. The "stab in the back" legend soon found its way into German historiography and was picked up by German right-wing political agitators who claimed that Allied propaganda in Germany in the last stages of the war had undermined civilian morale. They also claimed that traitors among the politicians had been at hand ready to do the Allies' bidding by signing the Armistice. Adolf Hitler eventually became the foremost of these political agitators, branding Erzberger and the leaders of the Social Democrats as the "November criminals." Thus, Hitler advocated militaristic and expansionist policies by which Germany could redeem its defeat in the war, gain vengeance upon its enemies, and become the pre-eminent power in Europe.

CHAPTER 6

POLITICAL LEADERS

The following brief biographies of the major political leaders of the combatants concentrate on their actions during World War I.

AUSTRO-HUNGARIAN EMPIRE

FRANCIS JOSEPH
(b. Aug. 18, 1830, Schloss Schönbrunn, near Vienna—d. Nov. 21, 1916, Schloss Schönbrunn)

Francis Joseph was both emperor of Austria (1848–1916) and king of Hungary (1867–1916). He divided his empire into the Dual Monarchy, allowing Austria and Hungary to coexist as equal partners. In 1879 he formed an alliance with Prussian-led Germany. In 1914 his ultimatum to Serbia led Austria and Germany into World War I.

From 1908–14 Francis Joseph held fast to his peace policy despite warnings by the chief of the general staff, Franz, Graf Conrad von Hötzendorf, who repeatedly advocated a preventive war against Serbia or Italy. Yet, without fully considering the consequences, he was in July 1914, persuaded by Leopold, Graf von Berchtold, the foreign minister, to issue the intransigent ultimatum to Serbia that led to Austria and Germany's involvement in World War I.

CHARLES I
(b. Aug. 17, 1887, Persenbeug Castle, Austria—d. April 1, 1922, Quinta do Monte, Madeira)

Charles I was emperor (kaiser) of Austria and, as Charles IV, king of Hungary, the last ruler of the Austro-Hungarian monarchy (Nov. 21, 1916–Nov. 11, 1918).

A grandnephew of the emperor Francis Joseph I, Charles became heir presumptive to the Habsburg throne upon the assassination of his uncle, Francis Ferdinand (June 28, 1914), whose children were barred from succession because of his morganatic marriage. After his accession, Charles, a peace-loving man, attempted to remove Austria-Hungary from World War I by way of secret overtures to the Allied powers, the most promising being through his brother-in-law, Prince Sixtus von Bourbon-Parma. However, all attempts failed, largely at the emperor's refusal to cede any territories to Italy. Because he had also supported French claims to Alsace-Lorraine, his reputation both in Germany and at home suffered as these efforts were made public.

World War I accelerated the centrifugal forces of nationalism in Charles's multinational empire. In October 1918, he announced his solution to transform the Western part of the empire into a federated state. This, however, lacked sufficiency and the necessary time, and ultimately failed. On Nov. 11, 1918, following the collapse of the Austro-Hungarian armies on the Italian front, Charles renounced all participation in state affairs but did not abdicate. He was exiled to Switzerland in March 1919, he was deposed by the Austrian parliament that April. He twice tried to regain his Hungarian throne, but failed and was once again exiled to Madeira, where he lived impoverished and eventually died of pneumonia.

BRITAIN

DAVID LLOYD GEORGE
(b. Jan. 17, 1863, Manchester, Eng.—d. March 26, 1945, Ty-newydd, near Llanystumdwy, Caernarvonshire, Wales)

As British prime minister (1916–22), David Lloyd George dominated the British political scene in the latter part of World War I. He was raised to the peerage in the year of his death.

When concerns of entry into the war pressed the Cabinet in late July and early August 1914, Lloyd George initially seemed inclined to the isolationist section, and for a brief moment contemplated retirement. But the tide of events swept him to the other side. As chancellor, he plunged into the financial problems posed by the war.

Throughout the remainder of 1914 and into 1915, Lloyd George was a vigorous advocate of increased munitions production. Though this was opposed by Lord Kitchener in the War Office, Admiral Fisher's 1915 resignation forced Asquith

A portrait of David Lloyd George, British prime minister and delegate to the Versaille Peace Conference, 1919. Hulton Archive/Getty Images

to reconstruct the government on a coalition basis, and admit the Conservatives. In the new administration, Lloyd George became minister of munitions. In this capacity, he made one of the most notable contributions to the Allied victory. His methods were unorthodox and shocked the civil service, but his energy was immense. He imported able assistants from big business and used his eloquence to induce the cooperation of organized labour. When, in the summer of 1916, the great Battle of the Somme began, supplies were forthcoming.

Lloyd George formulated definite views on war strategy at an early stage.

He doubted the possibility of breaking through on the Western Front and instead advocated a flank attack from the Near East. He was thus at loggerheads with the view of the official military hierarchy, cogently pressed by Sir Douglas Haig and Sir William Robertson, that the war could only be won in the West. On June 5, 1916, Kitchener drowned on his way to Russia, when his ship struck a German mine. A last-minute accident—acute developments in the Irish situation—had prevented Lloyd George from travelling with him. After some hesitation, Asquith appointed Lloyd George to the vacant position at the War Office.

Lloyd George held the post for five months, but Robertson as chief of the imperial general staff possessed nearly all the important powers of the war minister. Lloyd George chafed under these restrictions, mostly because he disagreed with Robertson on issues of strategy. Thus frustrated, he began to survey the whole direction of the war with increasing skepticism. He did not conceal his doubts from friends who, by the end of November, were convinced that Asquith should delegate the day-to-day running of the war to a small committee chaired by Lloyd George. There was widespread uneasiness at Asquith's conduct of affairs, particularly in the Conservative Party. Asquith was forced into resignation on December 5, and was replaced two days later by Lloyd George. Although he was supported by the leading Conservatives, the most prominent Liberal ministers had resigned with Asquith.

One of Lloyd George's most notable achievements was in combating the submarine menace, which, in early 1917, threatened to starve Britain into submission. He accomplished this by forcing the adoption of the convoy system upon a reluctant Admiralty. The food shortage resulting from the submarine war was acute. Drastic action had to be taken to step up agricultural production, and eventually a system of food rationing had to be introduced (1918). In these matters Lloyd George was at his best—contemptuous of red tape, determined to take action and to make his will prevail.

It was in the field of grand strategy that he was least successful. Lloyd George remained profoundly skeptical of the ability of the British high command to conduct even a Western strategy successfully. Without warning Haig or Robertson in advance, he confronted them at the Calais Conference of February 1917 with a plan to place the British army under French command for General Robert Nivelle's forthcoming offensive. Haig and Robertson deeply distrusted Lloyd George from that moment onward. The Nivelle offensive was a total failure, and Lloyd George was, as a result, on shaky ground when he endeavoured to resist Haig's proposals for a major British campaign in Flanders in the summer. After much hesitation, he gave way, and on July 31, 1917, the ill-fated Passchendaele offensive began. Although it may have forestalled a possible German attack on the French, Passchendaele, with enormous loss of life, achieved none of its main objectives. Lloyd George was now convinced of the incompetence of the British high command.

He still dared not take action against them openly. Instead, he began what Sir Winston Churchill called "a series of extremely laborious and mystifying maneuvers," aimed to create a unified command under someone other than Haig. In February 1918 Robertson offered his resignation. Though Lloyd George accepted it, Haig remained commander in chief. Lloyd George continued to distrust Haig, so much that, during the winter of 1917–18, he deliberately kept him short of troops for fear that he might renew the attack. The result was that the German commander, General Erich Ludendorff, came near to launching a successful offensive against the British sector in March 1918. The emergency caused a unified command under Marshal Ferdinand Foch to be established (April), and by May the situation had stabilized.

The tide then turned, and the Western Allies launched a series of successful attacks upon the exhausted Germans. The Armistice of November 1918 presented Lloyd George with a dilemma. Should he allow a return to peacetime party politics or continue the coalition? There was little doubt of the answer. The leader of the Conservatives, Bonar Law, was willing to cooperate. A somewhat perfunctory offer to include Asquith was declined. The ensuing election in December gave the coalitionists an overwhelming victory. The rift between Lloyd George and Asquith's supporters became wider than ever, however, and Lloyd George was now largely dependent on Conservative support.

As one of the three great statesmen at Versailles, Lloyd George bore a major responsibility for the peace settlement. He pursued an intermediary course between Georges Clemenceau and Woodrow Wilson, but was pressured to pursue the more draconian policy of Clemenceau. It is to his credit that the final settlement was not far worse than actually occurred. The treaty was well received in Britain, and in August 1919 the king conferred on Lloyd George the Order of Merit.

FRANCE

Raymond Poincaré
(b. Aug. 20, 1860, Bar-le-Duc, France—d. Oct. 15, 1934, Paris)

Raymond Poincaré was the French prime minister in 1912 who largely determined the policy that led to France's involvement in World War I. During this period, he also served as president of the Third Republic.

In January 1912, Poincaré became prime minister, serving simultaneously as foreign minister until January 1913. In the face of new threats from Germany, he conducted diplomacy with new decisiveness and determination. In August 1912 he assured the Russian government that his government would stand by the Franco-Russian alliance. In November he concluded an agreement with Britain stating that both countries should consult in the event of an international crisis as well as to discuss joint military plans. Although his support of Russian activities in the Balkans and his uncompromising attitude toward Germany have been cited as evidence of warmongering revanchism, Poincaré believed that in contemporary Europe, war was inevitable and that only a strong alliance guaranteed security. His greatest fear was that France might once again become isolated as it had been in 1870, and fall easy prey for a militarily superior Germany.

Poincaré ran for the office of president; despite the opposition of the left, under Georges Clemenceau, a lifelong enemy, he was elected on Jan. 17, 1913. Although the presidency was a position with little real power, he hoped to infuse new vitality into it and make it the base of a *union sacrée* of right, left, and centre. Throughout World War I (1914–18) he strove to preserve national unity, even confiding the government to Clemenceau, the man best qualified to lead the country to victory.

Georges Clemenceau
(b. Sept. 28, 1841, Mouilleron-en-Pareds, France—d. Nov. 24, 1929, Paris)

Georges Clemenceau was a dominant figure in the French Third Republic and, as premier (1917–20), a major contributor to the Allied victory in World War I and a framer of the postwar Treaty of Versailles.

British Prime Minister David Lloyd George (left), *French Prime Minister Georges Clemenceau* (centre), *and American President Woodrow Wilson* (right) *walk together to the signing of the Treaty of Versailles, 1919.* Hulton Archive/Getty Images

In 1911 Clemenceau became both a member of the French Senate's commissions for foreign affairs as well as the army. He was convinced that Germany was intent upon war, and, haunted by the fear that France might again be caught unprepared, he enquired diligently into the state of France's armaments. In order to publicize his views on rearmament, he founded in May 1913 a new daily paper, *L'Homme Libre*, and acted as its editor. When World War I erupted in July 1914, the partisan in him gave way to the patriot, who called upon every Frenchman to join the fray. *L'Homme Libre* suffered at

the hands of the censors for Clemenceau's plain speaking and, in September 1914, was suppressed. Two days later, however, it reappeared entitled *L'Homme Enchaîné.*

Meanwhile, in the Senate Clemenceau agitated for more guns, munitions, and soldiers, for judicious use of the available manpower, and for a better organized and equipped medical service. Deeply concerned about the attitude of the United States to the war, he sent urgent appeals to the American public and to President Woodrow Wilson and was overjoyed at the United States' entry into the war in April 1917.

Above all, Clemenceau strove to create an indomitable "will to victory." As the war dragged on, weariness, slackness, and pacifism began to appear. He was the first to draw public attention to such insidious perils. In these difficult conditions, President Poincaré, in November 1917, called upon Clemenceau to form a government. Though he was 76 years of age, he formed his Cabinet and appointed himself minister of war as well as premier. Clemenceau's primary desire was to win the war; to this aim all other interests were subordinated. For traitors and defeatists he had no clemency. The hope of victory urged him on. He was obsessed over the need for a unified military command and was ultimately able to convert to his viewpoint the Allied governments and military leaders. In March 1918, Ferdinand Foch was designated sole commander. Despite disasters in May 1918, Clemenceau's resolve remained unshaken, and he declared that he would wage war "to the last quarter hour, for the last quarter hour will be ours."

The armistice signed by the defeated Germans on Nov. 11, 1918, proved him right and brought him, the last survivor of those who had protested at Bordeaux in 1871 against the harsh terms imposed on France, the satisfaction of seeing Alsace-Lorraine returned to France. Clemenceau found that building the peace was a more arduous task than winning the war. He wanted the wartime alliance to be followed by an indefectible peacetime alliance. He presided with authority over the difficult sessions of the Paris Peace Conference (1919).

The Treaty of Versailles was in preparation, and this necessitated strenuous days of work and delicate negotiations. Clemenceau made it his responsibility to reconcile the interests of France with those of Great Britain and the United States. He defended the French cause with enthusiasm and conviction, forcing his view alternately on the British prime minister, David Lloyd George, and the United States president, Woodrow Wilson. He also took care to see that Germany was disarmed. With his desire for poetic justice, he insisted that the Treaty of Versailles be signed (June 28, 1919) in the Hall of Mirrors of the Versailles palace where, in 1871, William I had himself proclaimed the German emperor.

GERMANY

WILLIAM II

(b. Jan. 27, 1859, Potsdam, near Berlin [Germany]—d. June 4, 1941, Doorn, Neth.)

William II was German emperor (kaiser) and king of Prussia from 1888 to the end of World War I in 1918. He was known for his frequently militaristic manner as well as for his vacillating policies.

What began as an attempt to save Austria-Hungary from collapse, was

William II, emperor of Germany, wearing his military uniform, c. 1915. Imagno/Hulton Archive/Getty Images

transformed into a world conflict by Germany. William, having encouraged the Austrians to adopt an uncompromising line, took fright when he found war looming, but was not able to halt the implementation of the mobilization measures that he had allowed his generals to prepare. During the war, although nominally supreme commander, William did not attempt to resist his generals when they kept its conduct in their own hands. He encouraged, instead of challenging, the grandiose war aims of the many generals and politicians that ruled out all chance of a compromised peace. By the autumn of 1918 he realized that Germany had lost the war, and he his throne. Refusing to abdicate, he was finally forced into resignation on November 9, 1918, then persuaded to seek asylum in The Netherlands. He avoided captivity and perhaps death, but asylum also made it impossible for William to retain his position of emperor of Germany. Subsequently, he lived quietly as a country gentleman in the Netherlands until his death in 1941.

ITALY

ANTONIO SALANDRA
(b. Aug. 13, 1853, Troia, Puglia, Kingdom of the Two Sicilies [Italy]—d. Dec. 9, 1931, Rome)

Antonio Salandra was premier of Italy at the beginning of World War I (1914–16).

Salandra became premier in March 1914 and so was confronted with a critical decision on the outbreak of World War I. Despite the generation-old Triple Alliance of Germany, Austria-Hungary, and Italy, Salandra chose neutrality, taking for legal ground the Austrians' failure to consult the Italian government before attacking Serbia. Salandra then used Italy's strong position to bargain with both sides, eventually bringing his country into the war, in May 1915, on the Allied side, on the basis of definite promises of the completion of Italian unification by acquisition of territory from Austria-Hungary.

In 1916 Salandra was forced to resign as a result of Italy's growing military difficulties. After the war his authoritarian conservatism led him to support Benito Mussolini and fascism, but, when the extreme course of the new regime became clear, he modified his support. Nevertheless, Mussolini made him a senator in 1928.

PAOLO BOSELLI
(b. June 8, 1838, Savona, Piedmont, kingdom of Sardinia [now in Italy]— d. March 10, 1932, Rome)

Paolo Boselli headed the Italian government that declared war on Germany in World War I.

The first professor of financial science at the University of Rome, Boselli served as a parliamentary deputy from 1870 to 1921. He later became a senator in 1921. He was minister of education in the government of Francesco Crispi in 1888, reorganized the Bank of Italy as minister of the treasury under Premier Luigi Pelloux in 1899, and was a minister in the government of Sidney Sonnino in 1906.

Favouring Italy's entry into World War I against Austria-Hungary (1915), he made an important speech in the chamber in support of a bill granting full powers to Premier Antonio Salandra. When Salandra's government fell after the Austrian offensive of May–July 1916, the 78-year-old Paolo Boselli became premier, forming a coalition government. After recovering territory lost in the Austrian offensive, Boselli's government declared war on Germany on Aug. 28, 1916. Italy's disastrous defeat at Caporetto brought about Boselli's resignation on Oct. 30, 1917.

Vittorio Emanuele Orlando
(b. May 19, 1860, Palermo, Italy—d. Dec. 1, 1952, Rome)

Vittorio Emanuele Orlando was the Italian prime minister during the concluding years of World War I and head of his country's delegation to the Versailles Peace Conference.

Having been educated at Palermo, Orlando first made a name for himself with writings concerning electoral reform and government administration. He was elected to the Chamber of Deputies in 1897. He served as minister of education in 1903–05 and of justice in 1907–09, resuming the same portfolio in 1914. He

favoured Italy's entrance into the war (May 1915), and in October 1917, in the crisis following the defeat of Italy's forces at the Battle of Caporetto by the Austrians, he became prime minister, successfully rallying the country to a renewed effort.

OTTOMAN EMPIRE

Said Halim Paşa
(b. 1863, Cairo, Egypt—d. Dec. 6, 1921, Rome, Italy)

Said Halim Paşa served as grand vizier (chief minister) of the Ottoman Empire from 1913 to 1916.

The grandson of Muḥammad ʿAlī Pasha, a famous viceroy of Egypt, Said was educated in Turkey and later in Switzerland. In 1888 he was appointed a member of the state judicial council. In 1911 he became the foreign minister in Mahmud Şevket's Cabinet. After Mahmud Şevket's death Said was made grand vizier. Although he signed the treaty of alliance with Germany in 1914, he was known to oppose Ottoman participation in World War I. While he was prepared to resign at the outset of war, he remained at his post at the insistence of the ruling Committee of Union and Progress. In 1916, however, he did resign, and then he became a member of the Senate. After the armistice signed at Mudros (Oct. 30, 1918), he was banished to Malta by British authorities. On his release he went to Rome, where he was assassinated by an Armenian.

RUSSIA

NICHOLAS II

(b. May 6 [May 18, New Style], 1868,
Tsarskoye Selo [now Pushkin], near St.
Petersburg, Russia—d. July 16/17, 1918,
Yekaterinburg)

Nicholas II was the last Russian emperor
(1894–1917). With his wife, Alexandra, and
their children, he was killed by the
Bolsheviks after the October Revolution.

After its ambitions in the Far East
were checked by Japan, Russia turned its
attention to the Balkans. Nicholas sym-
pathized with the national aspirations of
the Slavs and was anxious to win control
of the Turkish straits, but tempered his
expansionist inclinations with a sincere
desire to preserve peace among the Great
Powers. After the assassination of the
Austrian archduke Francis Ferdinand at
Sarajevo, he tried hard to avert the
impending war by diplomatic action.
Until July 30, 1914, he resisted the pressure of the military for general, rather
than partial, mobilization.

The outbreak of World War I temporarily strengthened the monarchy, but
Nicholas did little to maintain his people's
confidence. The Duma was slighted, and
voluntary patriotic organizations were
hampered in their efforts; the gulf
between the ruling group and public
opinion grew steadily wider. Alexandra
turned Nicholas's mind against the popular commander in chief, his father's cousin
the grand duke Nicholas, and on Sept. 5,

1915, the emperor dismissed him and
assumed supreme command himself.
Since the emperor had no experience of
war, almost all his ministers protested
against this step, as it was likely to impair
the army's morale. They were overruled,
however, and soon dismissed.

When riots broke out in Petrograd
(St. Petersburg) on March 8, 1917, Nicholas
instructed the city commandant to take
firm measures, sending troops to restore
order. It was too late, however, and the

*A portrait of Tsar Nicholas II of Russia,
c. 1910.* W. & D. Downey/Hulton Archive/
Getty Images

government resigned. The Duma, supported by the army, called on the emperor to abdicate. At Pskov on March 15, with fatalistic composure, Nicholas renounced the throne—not, as he had originally intended, in favour of his son, Alexis, but in favour of his brother Michael, who then refused the crown.

Nicholas was detained at Tsarskoye Selo by Prince Lvov's provisional government. It was planned that he and his family would be sent to England; but instead, mainly because of the opposition of the Petrograd Soviet, the revolutionary Workers' and Soldiers' Council, they were removed to Tobolsk in Western Siberia. This step sealed their doom. In April 1918 they were taken to Yekaterinburg in the Urals.

When anti-Bolshevik "White" Russian forces approached the area, the local authorities were ordered to prevent the prisoners' rescue. On the night of July 16–17, all of the prisoners were all slaughtered in the cellar of the house where they had been confined. The bodies were burned, cast into an abandoned mine shaft, and then hastily buried elsewhere.

Vladimir Ilich Lenin
(b. April 10 [April 22, New Style], 1870, Simbirsk, Russia—d. Jan. 21, 1924, Gorki [later Gorki Leninskiye], near Moscow)

Vladimir Lenin was the founder of the Russian Communist Party (Bolsheviks), inspirer and leader of the Bolshevik Revolution (1917), and the architect, builder, and first head (1917–24) of the Soviet state. He was the founder of the organization known as Comintern (Communist International) and the posthumous source of "Leninism," the doctrine codified and conjoined with Marx's works by Lenin's successors to form Marxism-Leninism, which became the Communist worldview.

When war broke out, in August 1914, Socialist parties throughout Europe were obliged by prewar congresses of the Second International to resist or even overthrow their respective governments should they plunge their countries into an imperialist war.

Lenin succeeded in reaching neutral Switzerland in September 1914, there joining a small group of antiwar Bolshevik and Menshevik émigrés. The war virtually cut them off from all contact with Russia and with like-minded Socialists in other countries. Nevertheless, in 1915 and 1916, antiwar Socialists in various countries managed to hold two antiwar conferences in Zimmerwald and Kienthal, Switzerland.

By 1917 it seemed to Lenin that the war would never end and that the prospect of revolution was rapidly receding. But in the week of March 8–15, the starving, freezing, war-weary workers and soldiers of Petrograd (until 1914, St. Petersburg) succeeded in deposing the tsar. Lenin and his closest lieutenants hastened home after the German authorities agreed to permit their passage through Germany to neutral Sweden.

Berlin hoped that the return of antiwar Socialists to Russia would undermine the Russian war effort.

Lenin arrived in Petrograd on April 16, 1917, one month after the tsar had been forced to abdicate. Out of the revolution was born the Provisional Government, formed by a group of leaders of the bourgeois liberal parties. This government's accession to power was made possible only by the assent of the Petrograd Soviet, a council of workers' deputies elected in the factories of the capital. Similar soviets of workers' deputies sprang up in all the major cities and towns throughout the country, as did soviets of soldiers' deputies and of peasants' deputies. Although the Petrograd Soviet had been the sole political power recognized by the revolutionary workers and soldiers in March 1917, its leaders had hastily turned full power over to the Provisional Government. The Petrograd Soviet was headed by a majority composed of Menshevik and Socialist Revolutionary (SR), or peasant party, leaders who regarded the March (February, Old Style) Revolution as bourgeois; hence, they believed that the new regime should be headed by leaders of the bourgeois parties.

On his return to Russia, Lenin electrified his own comrades, most of whom accepted the authority of the Provisional Government. Lenin called this government, despite its democratic pretensions, thoroughly imperialist and undeserving of support by Socialists. It was incapable of satisfying the most profound desires of the workers, soldiers, and peasants for immediate peace and division of landed estates among the peasants.

Initially, Lenin's fellow Bolsheviks thought that he was temporarily disoriented by the complexity of the situation; moderate Socialists thought him mad. It required several weeks of sedulous persuasion by Lenin before he won the Bolshevik Party Central Committee to his view. The April Party Conference endorsed his program: that the party must withhold support from the Provisional Government and win a majority in the soviets in favour of soviet power. A soviet government, once established, should begin immediate negotiations for a general peace on all fronts. The soviets should forthwith confiscate landlords' estates without compensation, nationalize all land, and divide it among the peasants. The government should establish tight controls over privately owned industry to the benefit of labour.

From March to September 1917, the Bolsheviks remained a minority in the soviets. By autumn, however, the Provisional Government (since July headed by the moderate Socialist Aleksandr Kerensky, who was supported by the moderate Socialist leadership of the soviets) had lost popular support. Increasing war-weariness and the breakdown of the economy overtaxed the patience of the workers, peasants, and soldiers, who demanded immediate and fundamental change. Lenin capitalized on the growing disillusionment of the people with Kerensky's ability and willingness to complete the revolution. Kerensky, in turn, claimed that only a freely elected constituent assembly would have the power to decide Russia's political future—but that must await the return of order. Meanwhile, Lenin and the party demanded peace, land, and bread—immediately, without further delay. The Bolshevik line won increasing support among the workers, soldiers, and peasants. By September they voted in a Bolshevik majority in the Petrograd Soviet and in the soviets of the major cities and towns throughout the country.

Lenin, who had gone underground in July after he had been accused as a "German agent" by Kerensky's government, now decided that the time was ripe to seize power. The party must immediately begin preparations for an armed uprising to depose the Provisional Government and transfer state power to the soviets, now headed by a Bolshevik majority.

Until 1917 all revolutionary Socialists rightly believed, Lenin wrote, that a parliamentary republic could serve a Socialist system as well as a capitalist. But the Russian Revolution had brought forth something new, the soviets. Created by workers, soldiers, and peasants and excluding the propertied classes, the soviets infinitely surpassed the most democratic of parliaments in democracy, because parliaments everywhere virtually excluded workers and peasants. The choice before Russia in early September

1917, as Lenin saw it, was either a soviet republic—a dictatorship of the quite vast propertyless majority—or a parliamentary republic—as he saw it, a dictatorship of the propertied minority.

From late September, Lenin, a fugitive in Finland, sent a stream of articles and letters to Petrograd feverishly exhorting the Party Central Committee to immediately organize an armed uprising, as the opportune moment might be lost. For nearly a month Lenin's forceful urgings from afar were unsuccessful. In April, Lenin again found himself in the party minority, and resorted to a desperate stratagem.

In disguise and at considerable personal risk, Lenin slipped into Petrograd and attended a secret meeting of the Bolshevik Central Committee held on the evening of October 23. Only after a heated 10-hour debate did he finally win a majority in favour of preparing an armed takeover. Consequently, these steps included enlisting the support of soldiers and sailors, and training the Red Guards, the Bolshevik-led workers' militia, for an armed takeover proceeded openly under the guise of self-defense of the Petrograd Soviet.

On November 7 and 8, the Bolshevik-led Red Guards and revolutionary soldiers and sailors, meeting only slight resistance, deposed the Provisional Government and proclaimed that state power had passed into the hands of the Soviets. By this time the Bolsheviks, with their leftist allies, constituted an absolute majority of the Second All-Russian Congress of Soviets. The delegates therefore voted overwhelmingly to accept full power and elected Lenin as chairman of the Council of People's Commissars, the new Soviet Government, and approved his Peace and Land Decrees. Overnight, Lenin had vaulted from his hideout as a fugitive to head the Revolutionary government of the largest country in the world.

The Allies refused to recognize the Soviet government; consequently it entered alone into peace negotiations with the Central Powers (Germany and its allies Austro-Hungary and Turkey) at the town of Brest-Litovsk. They imposed ruinous conditions that would strip away from Soviet Russia the western tier of non-Russian nations of the old Russian Empire. Left Communists fanatically opposed acceptance and preached a revolutionary war, even if it imperilled the Soviet government. Lenin insisted that the terms, however ruinous and humiliating, must be accepted or he would resign from the government. He sensed that peace was the deepest yearning of the people; in any case, the shattered army could not raise effective resistance to the invader. Finally, in March 1918, after a still larger part had been carved out of old Russia by the enemy, Lenin succeeded in winning the Central Committee's acceptance of the Treaty of Brest-Litovsk. At last Russia was at peace.

Brest-Litovsk, however, intensified the determination of counterrevolutionary forces and the Allies who supported them to bring about the overthrow of the Soviet government. That determination hardened when, in 1918, Lenin's government repudiated repayments of all foreign loans obtained by the tsarist and provisional governments and nationalized foreign properties in Russia without compensation. From 1918 to 1920 Russia was torn by a civil war, which cost millions of lives and untold destruction. One of the earliest victims was Lenin himself. In August 1918 an assassin fired two bullets into Lenin as he left a factory in which he had just delivered a speech. Because of his robust constitution, he recovered rapidly.

The Soviet government faced tremendous odds. The anti-Soviet forces, or Whites, headed mainly by former tsarist generals and admirals, fought desperately to overthrow the Red regime. Moreover, the Whites were lavishly supplied by the Allies with materiel, money, and support troops that secured White bases. Yet, the Whites failed.

From the moment Lenin came to power, his abiding aims in international relations were twofold: to prevent the formation of an imperialist united front against Soviet Russia; but, even more important, to stimulate proletarian revolutions abroad.

UNITED STATES

WOODROW WILSON
(b. Dec. 28, 1856, Staunton, Va., U.S.—
d. Feb. 3, 1924, Washington, D.C.)

Woodrow Wilson was the 28th president of the United States (1913–21). An American scholar and statesman, Wilson is best remembered for his legislative accomplishments and his high-minded idealism. Wilson led his country into World War I and became the creator and leading advocate of the League of Nations, for which he was awarded the 1919 Nobel Prize for Peace. During his second term the Nineteenth Amendment to the U.S. Constitution, giving women the right to vote, was passed and ratified. He suffered a paralytic stroke while seeking American public support for the Treaty of Versailles (October 1919), and his incapacity, which lasted for the rest of his term of office, caused the worst crisis of presidential disability in U.S. history.

The outbreak of World War I in August 1914, which coincided with his wife's death, tried Wilson's mind and soul. Almost no one questioned American neutrality in the beginning, but both the British blockade of maritime trade and German U-boat attacks soon made neutrality painful. On May 7, 1915, when a U-boat sank the British liner *Lusitania*, killing more than 1,100 people, including 128 Americans, the war came home with a vengeance. Wilson at first urged his countrymen to show restraint, declaring, "There is such a thing as a man being too proud to fight," but he also pressed the Germans to rein in their submarines and decided to build up the armed forces. A combination of patience and firmness on the president's part paid off when the

Germans, for military reasons of their own, pledged to curtail submarine warfare in April 1916. For the rest of that year the threat of war receded, while relations with Great Britain worsened because of their ever-tightening blockade and their brutal suppression of the Easter Rising, the armed revolt in Ireland that eventually led to independence.

Wilson prevailed in the 1916 election, becoming the first Democrat to win a second consecutive term since Andrew Jackson. His narrow victory by 277 to 254 electoral votes over Charles Evans Hughes, the nominee of the reunited and resurgent Republicans, was a great political feat. The campaign cry "He kept us out of war" helped, but Wilson's domestic record on progressive and labour issues played the biggest part in his achieving a healthy plurality in the popular vote and a small electoral margin.

His reelection assured, Wilson mounted a peace offensive in December 1916 and January 1917 aimed at ending the world war. First he made a public diplomatic appeal to the belligerent nations to state their peace terms and accept American mediation, and then on January 22 he gave a stirring speech in which he called for a "peace without victory" and pledged to establish a league of nations to prevent future wars.

Unfortunately, the Germans rendered Wilson's peace efforts moot by unleashing their submarines on February 1. For the next two months Wilson agonized over how to respond. Public opinion remained divided and uncertain, even

DRAWING BY I. KLEIN

PATHS OF GLORY LEAD BUT ...

Antiwar cartoon by I. Klein from The Masses. Library of Congress, Washington, D.C.

after publication of the Zimmermann Telegram, a secret communication by the German foreign secretary that offered Texas, New Mexico, and Arizona to Mexico in return for going to war against the United States. Wilson finally decided to intervene, seeing no alternative and hoping to use American belligerency as a means to build a just, lasting peace. On April 2, 1917, he went before Congress to ask for a declaration of war to fulfill his injunction that "the world must be made safe for democracy."

Wilson proved to be a surprisingly effective war president. Recognizing what he did not know, he delegated military decisions to professional soldiers, particularly General John J. Pershing, who commanded the American Expeditionary Force in France, and economic

(Left to right) *The "Big Four": David Lloyd George of Britain, Vittorio Orlando of Italy, Georges Clemenceau of France, and Woodrow Wilson of the United States, the principal architects of the Treaty of Versailles.* National Archives, Washington, D.C.

mobilization to such men as Bernard Baruch, William Gibbs McAdoo, and Herbert Hoover. Careful planning also ensured the success of the Selective Service Act, which became law in May. This helped to raise the strength of the armed forces to 5 million men and women, 2 million of whom reached France by the war's end. The boost given to the Allies by American money, supplies, and manpower tipped the scales against the Germans, who sued for peace and laid down their arms with the Armistice of Nov. 11, 1918.

A less happy side to Wilson's delegation of war-making tasks came at home, where some of his cabinet members, most notably U.S. Attorney General A. Mitchell Palmer, brutally suppressed dissent. The overzealous hounding of radical groups, aliens, and dissidents both during the war and in the Red Scare of 1919–20 was justified on grounds of national security but was condemned by civil libertarians and ultimately discredited. Diplomacy was the one job that Wilson kept to himself. He seized the initiative on war aims with his Fourteen Points speech of Jan. 8, 1918, in which he promised a liberal, nonpunitive peace and a league of nations. Determined to keep those promises, Wilson made the controversial decision to go in person to the Paris Peace Conference, where he spent seven months in wearying, often acrimonious negotiations with the British, French, and Italians. The final product, the Treaty of Versailles, was signed on June 28, 1919. The treaty's

financial and territorial terms severely compromised Wilson's aims, but those were offset by its inclusion of the Covenant of the League of Nations, which he believed would adjust international differences and maintain peace.

Wilson returned from the peace conference exhausted, in failing health, and in no shape to face the biggest fight of his career. Republican senators, led by Henry Cabot Lodge, sought either to reject the treaty or to attach reservations that would gravely limit America's commitments to the League of Nations. In September 1919, after two months of frustrating talks with senators, Wilson took his case to the people with the hope of shaping public opinion on this important issue of the day. A master of the English language and public oratory, he threw himself into a whirlwind cross-country tour, giving 39 speeches in three weeks.

The mental and physical strain was too much for him. He had a near breakdown on September 25, after which his doctor canceled the rest of the tour and rushed him back to Washington. On Oct. 2, 1919, Wilson suffered a massive stroke that left him partially paralyzed on his left side. His intellectual capacity was not affected, but his emotional balance and judgment were badly impaired.

This was the worst crisis of presidential disability in U.S. history, and it was handled poorly. No one seriously suggested that Wilson resign. His wife, Edith, controlled access to him, made decisions by default, and engineered a cover-up of his condition, by releasing misleadingly optimistic reports from his doctors. Although he gradually recovered from the worst effects of the stroke, Wilson never again fully functioned as president.

The peace treaty went down to defeat in the Senate. As a consequence of Wilson's stroke-induced rigidity, he demanded that Democratic senators spurn all efforts at compromise with Lodge and the Republicans. Twice, on Nov. 19, 1919, and March 19, 1920, the Treaty of Versailles failed to gain the two-thirds vote necessary for ratification. Later, under Warren G. Harding, Wilson's Republican successor, the United States made a separate peace with Germany, something Wilson had believed "would place ineffable stain upon the gallantry and honor of the United States." The United States never joined the League of Nations.

CHAPTER 7

MILITARY COMMANDERS

The following brief biographies of military commanders for the Entente and Central powers concentrate on their actions during World War I.

ENTENTE POWERS

ARAB

ḤUSAYN IBN ʿALĪ
(b. c. 1854, Constantinople, Turkey, Ottoman Empire [now Istanbul, Turkey]—d. 1931, Amman, Transjordan [now Jordan])

Ḥusayn ibn ʿAlī was emir of Mecca from 1908 to 1916 and king of Hejaz from 1916 to 1924.

Ḥusayn was born into the line of Hāshimites to which the Meccan emirate had passed in the early 19th century. He became emir in 1908 and was a leader in the Arab revolt against Ottoman rule during World War I. In October 1916 he proclaimed himself "king of the Arab countries," though the Allies formally recognized him only as king of the Hejaz. Ḥusayn was represented at the Versailles peace conference by his third son, Fayṣal, but refused to ratify the Versailles Peace Treaty (1919) as a protest against the mandatory regimes imposed on Syria, Palestine, and Iraq by France and Great Britain. Subsequently his domestic policy was marked by ever-increasing avarice and conservatism, while he sowed the seeds of future trouble by deliberately courting the enmity of Ibn Sa'ūd. In March 1924 he proclaimed himself caliph, but war with Ibn Sa'ūd was imminent, and the Wahhābīyah attack on aṭ-Ṭā'if in September found him unprepared. On October 5 he abdicated. The British conveyed him to Cyprus, where he lived until 1930.

Australia

Sir John Monash
(b. June 27, 1865, West Melbourne, Austl.—d. Oct. 8, 1931, Melbourne)

John Monash, a civil engineer and soldier, is best known for his role as commander of the Australian army corps in France during World War I.

Monash attended Scotch College and Melbourne University, obtaining degrees in the arts, civil engineering, and law. Active in the prewar militia, he commanded an infantry brigade at the Battle of Gallipoli during the Dardanelles Campaign in Turkey. From 1916–17, he commanded a division on the Western Front. Monash was not a frontline general, but his extensive and successful business experience led him to emphasize planning and organization. He favoured using technical and mechanical resources—tanks, artillery, and aircraft—to relieve the infantry as much as possible of the burden of fighting its way forward.

In March 1918 he took command of the Australian Corps, and on July 4 he tested his theory of the semimobile managed battle in a small-scale attack at Le Hamel, France. Its outstanding success led Monash to develop a more comprehensive plan for a sustained offensive, which shaped the general British plan as well. From August 8 until its withdrawal from the line in October, the Australian Corps was in almost continuous combat as the spearhead of the British Expeditionary Force's advance to victory.

Monash is generally considered among the best corps commanders of World War I, though his capacities at higher levels remained untested.

Britain

Edmund Henry Hynman Allenby
(b. April 23, 1861, Brackenhurst, near Southwell, Nottinghamshire, Eng.— d. May 14, 1936, London)

Edmund Allenby, a field marshal and the last great British leader of mounted cavalry, directed the Palestine campaign in World War I.

Educated at the Royal Military Academy, Sandhurst, Allenby joined the Inniskilling Dragoons in 1882 and saw active service in the Bechuanaland expedition (1884–85), in Zululand (1888), and in the South African War (1899–1902). He was inspector general of cavalry from 1910 to 1914, and upon the outbreak of World War I he took a cavalry division to France. After periods in command of the British cavalry and the 5th Corps, he became commander of the 3rd Army (October 1915) and was prominently engaged at the Battle of Arras (April 1917).

Allenby's service in the Middle East proved more distinguished. In June 1917 he took command of the Egyptian Expeditionary Force. The strength of his personality created a new spirit in his army, and after careful preparation and reorganization he won a decisive victory over the Turks at Gaza (November 1917), which led to the capture of Jerusalem (Dec. 9, 1917). Further advances were checked by calls from France for his troops, but after receiving reinforcements he won a decisive victory at Megiddo (Sept. 19, 1918), which, followed by his capture of Damascus and Aleppo, ended Ottoman power in Syria. Allenby's success in these campaigns was attributable partly to his skillful and innovative use of cavalry and other mobile forces in positional warfare. As high commissioner for Egypt (1919–25) Allenby steered that country firmly but impartially through political disturbances and saw it recognized as a sovereign state in 1922.

He was created 1st Viscount Allenby of Megiddo and of Felixstowe in October 1919.

A portrait of Gen. Edmund Allenby, c. 1917. Hulton Archive/Getty Images

DAVID BEATTY
(b. Jan. 17, 1871, Howbeck Lodge, Stapeley, near Nantwich, Cheshire, Eng.—d. March 11, 1936, London)

David Beatty was a British admiral of the fleet and commander of Britain's battle cruisers in the Battle of Jutland (1916).

Beatty was the son of Captain David Longfield Beatty. He began training as a naval cadet in 1884. From 1896 to 1898 he served in Egypt and the Sudan and then in 1900 in China during the Boxer Rebellion. He was promoted to captain at the early age of 29. In 1911, as a rear admiral, he became naval secretary to the first lord of the Admiralty, then Winston

Churchill, and in 1913 was appointed to command the battle cruiser squadron.

Soon after the outbreak of World War I in August 1914, Beatty's naval force made a raid into the Helgoland Bight and sank three cruisers and one destroyer without loss. A few months later he intercepted the German squadron under Admiral von Hipper in its third attempt on the English coastal towns. In a running fight, the rear German battle cruiser "Blücher" was sunk by British gunfire. This action was known as the Battle of the Dogger Bank.

In the Battle of Jutland on May 31, 1916, the battle cruiser fleet under Beatty was heavily engaged in a running fight with the German battle cruisers in the van under Hipper. Although Beatty's battle cruisers were superior in number, they proved unable to sustain the gunfire of the German ships, with the result that the "Indefatigable" and "Queen Mary" were sunk. Nevertheless, Beatty succeeded in his main object of drawing the combined German high sea fleet to the northward, whence Admiral Jellicoe, with the whole British grand fleet, was hastening to meet and engage it. The resulting engagement, the Battle of Jutland, proved indecisive. In December 1916, on Jellicoe's being appointed first sea lord, Beatty became commander in chief of the grand fleet.

Julian Hedworth George Byng
(b. Sept. 11, 1862, Wrotham Park, Middlesex, Eng.—d. June 6, 1935, Thorpe Hall, Essex)

Julian Byng was a British field marshal during World War I.

A career soldier from 1883, Byng was promoted to major general in 1909. As commander of the Canadian Corps in France (from May 1916), he was responsible for one of the most famous Canadian victories in either world war, the capture of Vimy Ridge, north of Arras (April 9, 1917). As commander of the British 3rd Army (from June 1917) he conducted the first large scale attack by tanks in history (at Cambrai, Nov. 20, 1917). His army broke the German Hindenburg Line on Sept. 27, 1918.

Byng was promoted to full general in 1917 and was made a field marshal in 1932. After World War I he served as governor-general of Canada (1921–26) and commissioner of London police (1928–31). He was created a baron in 1919 and a viscount in 1928.

Sir Arthur William Currie
(b. Dec. 5, 1875, Napperton, Ont., Can.—d. Nov. 30, 1933, Montreal, Que.)

From 1917, Arthur Currie was the first Canadian commander of Canada's overseas forces in World War I.

Currie taught school before going into business in Victoria, B.C. He enlisted in the militia and rose from the ranks to become lieutenant colonel of artillery. In spite of this minimum of professional training, he was given command of a battalion in the first Canadian contingent sent to assist Britain in 1914. He advanced steadily, winning distinction at the battles of Ypres and Saint-Julien in Belgium and at the battle of Vimy Ridge in France. Within three years he became lieutenant general and commander of the four divisions of the Canadian Corps, succeeding the British general Sir Julian Byng. He was one of the most successful and effective corps commanders in any army during the war's final months. Currie was knighted in 1918. After the war Currie served as inspector general of the Canadian militia and became the first general in the Canadian Army. In 1920 he accepted the position of principal and vice chancellor of McGill University, Montreal, and retained this post until his death.

JOHN FRENCH
(b. Sept. 28, 1852, Ripple, Kent, Eng.— d. May 22, 1925, Deal, Kent)

John French commanded the British army on the Western Front between August 1914, when World War I began, and Dec. 17, 1915, when he resigned under pressure and was succeeded by General (afterward Field Marshal) Douglas Haig.

The battles fought under French's direction at Ypres, Belg., and elsewhere were noteworthy in Britain for high numbers of British losses—e.g., more than 117,000 casualties in the first two battles of Ypres. He was considered unable to adapt himself to unfamiliar conditions of war or to work harmoniously with the British government, his own subordinates, or the French and Belgian generals with whom he was supposed to cooperate.

A soldier from 1874, French became a public figure with his successful leadership of British cavalry against the Boers in the South African War (1899–1902). He was appointed inspector general in 1907 and chief of the Imperial General Staff in 1913.

On Aug. 23, 1914, near Mons, Belg., French directed the first major engagement of British troops in the war. Although superior German strength forced him to retreat, he had intended merely to cover the withdrawal of the French 5th Army, and as a delaying action the battle was a success. He was criticized, however, for his failure to coordinate the movement of his two corps or even to remain in touch with their commanders. After a costly battle at Le Cateau, France, on August 26, he seemed to lose his nerve and planned to withdraw south of the Seine River and perhaps from France altogether. Lord Kitchener, the British secretary of state for war, induced him to remain in action and to work more closely with the French and Belgian armies.

On Oct. 19, 1914, French ordered his force, increased by that time to three corps, to start a two-branched offensive eastward from Ypres. The British collided with German armies that began an offensive of their own the next day. The bitter resistance of French's army helped prevent the German forces from advancing; however, no movement was made by the Allies either. By November 22 the battle had ended in a stalemate. In 1915, the battles of Neuve-Chapelle (from March 10), Ypres again (from April 22), and Loos (from September 25) also produced no Allied advance. French's indecisive use of his reserves at Loos led to his removal.

French was created a viscount in 1916 and an earl in 1922. He was commander in chief in the United Kingdom and then (1918–21) lord lieutenant of Ireland.

SIR HUBERT GOUGH
(b. Aug. 12, 1870, London, Eng.—d. March 18, 1963, London)

Hubert Gough was the World War I commander of the British 5th Army, which bore the brunt of the great German offensive in March 1918.

He joined the 16th Lancers in 1889 and served in the Tirah Expedition in India (1897) and in the South African War (1899–1902). He commanded the 3rd Cavalry Brigade in 1914 and opposed the use of force at the Curragh to compel Ulster to accept Home Rule.

In France, Gough became commander of the 5th Army on its formation (1916) and took part in the battles of the Somme (1916) and Ypres (1917), where he earned a reputation as a poor administrator and a hard driver—indifferent to the casualties his men suffered. In March 1918 his army was compelled to withdraw with considerable loss under heavy German pressure. Although his skillful handling of the battle led to the eventual stemming of the German advance, the government blamed him for temporary German successes and insisted on his removal. He retired in 1922 with the rank

of general and received the award of the Knight Grand Cross of the Bath in 1937.

DOUGLAS HAIG
(b. June 19, 1861, Edinburgh, Scot.—d. Jan. 29, 1928, London, Eng.)

Douglas Haig was a British field marshal and commander in chief of the British forces in France during most of World War I. His strategy of attrition (tautly summarized as "kill more Germans") made him a subject of controversy, and resulted in enormous numbers of British casualties but little immediate gain in 1916–17.

On the outbreak of World War I in August 1914, Haig led I Corps of the British Expeditionary Force (BEF) to northern France, and, early in 1915, he became commander of the 1st Army. On December 17 of that year, he succeeded Sir John French (afterward 1st Earl of Ypres) as commander in chief of the BEF. In July–November 1916, he committed great masses of troops to an unsuccessful offensive on the Somme River, resulting in 420,000 British casualties. The next year, when the French decided to stand on the defensive until forces from the United States (which had entered the war April 6) could arrive in quantity, Haig resolved to try to defeat the Germans by a purely British offensive in French and Belgian Flanders. In the resulting Third Battle of Ypres (July–November 1917), also called the Passchendaele Campaign, the number of casualties shocked the

A portrait of Gen. Douglas Haig, c. 1918. Hulton Archive/Getty Images

Allied commander on the western front. In March 1918, Haig secured the appointment of another French general, Ferdinand Foch, as Allied generalissimo. The two men worked well together, and Haig exercised full tactical command of the British armies, which had not been the case under Nivelle. After helping to stop the last German offensive of the war (March–July 1918), Haig showed perhaps his best generalship in leading the victorious Allied assault beginning August 8.

After the war, Haig organized the British Legion and traveled throughout the British Empire collecting money for needy former servicemen. He was created an earl in 1919.

Sir Ian Hamilton
(b. Jan. 16, 1853, Corfu, Ionian Islands [Greece]—d. Oct. 12, 1947, London, Eng.)

Ian Hamilton was the commander in chief of the British Mediterranean Expeditionary Force in the unsuccessful campaign against Turkey in the Gallipoli Peninsula during World War I.

Hamilton served in various campaigns in India and Africa, beginning in the 1870s, and was Lord Kitchener's chief of staff during the South African War (1899–1902). He was knighted in 1902. In 1910, he became British commander in chief in the Mediterranean.

On March 12, 1915, Hamilton was placed in charge of the expeditionary force intended to seize control of the Dardanelles Strait and to capture

British public, as the Somme death toll had done. Although he failed to reach his objective—the Belgian coast—he did weaken the German forces and helped prepare the way for their defeat in 1918.

Promoted to field marshal late in 1916, Haig was steadfastly supported by King George V, but not by David Lloyd George, prime minister from December of that year. From that month to May 1917, Haig was an unwilling subordinate of the French general Robert Nivelle, supreme

Constantinople. During the next six months, he conducted operations against the Turks at Gallipoli but suffered heavy casualties and made little headway. He remained unrealistically optimistic, and, when the British cabinet had begun to favour the evacuation of his force, he inopportunely reiterated his belief in the ultimate success of the campaign. He was recalled on Oct. 16, 1915, and was given no further command.

JOHN RUSHWORTH JELLICOE
(b. Dec. 5, 1859, Southampton, Hampshire, Eng.—d. Nov. 20, 1935, Kensington, London)

John Jellicoe was the British admiral of the fleet who commanded at the crucial Battle of Jutland (May 31, 1916) during World War I.

On the eve of World War I, Jellicoe was sent to join the home fleet at Scapa as second in command under Admiral Sir George Callaghan. He was soon appointed commander in chief with acting rank of admiral. He was confirmed in his rank in March 1915 and for two years organized and trained the grand fleet, keeping it ready for action. His command was put to the test at the Battle of Jutland. Although his tactics were severely criticized at the time, it is now accepted that he achieved a strategic victory that left the German high seas fleet ineffective during the remainder of the war. Toward the end of 1916 Jellicoe left his last command afloat to become first sea lord of the Admiralty.

During the next year his efforts to combat the new German submarine campaign were ineffective until the convoy system was adopted at the insistence of the prime minister, David Lloyd George, who was responsible for Jellicoe's retirement from the Admiralty at the end of 1917. After the armistice, Jellicoe was sent on a special mission to visit the dominions and advise on the postwar organization of their navies. Promoted to admiral of the fleet in 1919, he became governor of New Zealand in 1920.

For his services in World War I, Jellicoe was raised to the peerage as Viscount Jellicoe of Scapa in 1918. On his return from New Zealand and in recognition of his services as governor, he was created an earl and Viscount Brocas of Southampton in 1925.

ROGER JOHN BROWNLOW KEYES
(b. Oct. 4, 1872, Tundiani Fort, India—d. Dec. 26, 1945, Buckingham, Buckinghamshire, Eng.)

Roger Keyes was the British admiral who planned and directed the World War I raid on the German base at Zeebrugge, Belg., April 22–23, 1918, and thus helped to close the Strait of Dover to German submarines.

Keyes entered the Royal Navy in 1885. For bold action during the Boxer Rebellion in China in 1900, he was promoted to commander. As commodore in charge of submarines (1910–14), he was partly responsible for the British victory in the

Battle of Helgoland Bight (Aug. 28, 1914). In 1915, he was chief of staff for the unsuccessful Dardanelles expedition.

Appointed director of plans at the Admiralty in 1917, Keyes began to prepare operations to block the entrances to Zeebrugge and Ostend. On the first attempt, the mission at Zeebrugge succeeded, but the blockships could not find the Ostend entrance. Two weeks later, Keyes sent the *Vindictive* to Ostend, where its volunteer crew sank the ship at the harbour entrance, thus discouraging most German U-boat operations in Dover Command waters.

After the Armistice Keyes was made a baronet and received a government grant of £10,000. He held a number of commands, attaining the rank of admiral of the fleet from 1930. He sat in Parliament from 1934 until his elevation to the peerage in 1943. Briefly, in May 1940, he returned to prominence in an attack on Neville Chamberlain's conduct of World War II.

T. E. LAWRENCE
(b. Aug. 15, 1888, Tremadoc, Caernarvonshire, Wales—d. May 19, 1935, Clouds Hill, Dorset, Eng.)

T. E. Lawrence was a British archaeological scholar, military strategist, and author, who is best known for his legendary war activities in the Middle East during World War I and for his account of those activities in *The Seven Pillars of Wisdom* (1926).

As a protégé of the Oxford archaeologist D. G. Hogarth, Lawrence acquired a demyship (travelling fellowship) from Magdalen College and joined an expedition excavating the Hittite settlement of Carchemish on the Euphrates. He worked there from 1911 to 1914, first under Hogarth and then under Sir Leonard Woolley, and used his free time to travel on his own and get to know the language and the people. Early in 1914 he and Woolley, and Capt. S. F. Newcombe, explored northern Sinai, on the Turkish frontier east of Suez. Supposedly a scientific expedition, and in fact sponsored by the Palestine Exploration Fund, it was more a map-making reconnaissance from Gaza to Aqaba, destined to be of almost immediate strategic value. The cover study was nevertheless of authentic scholarly significance; written by Lawrence and Woolley together, it was published as *The Wilderness of Zin* in 1915.

The month the war began, Lawrence became a civilian employee of the Map Department of the War Office in London, charged with preparing a militarily useful map of Sinai. By December 1914 he was a lieutenant in Cairo. Experts on Arab affairs—especially those who had travelled in the Turkish-held Arab lands—were rare, and he was assigned to intelligence, where he spent more than a year interviewing prisoners, drawing maps, receiving and processing data from agents behind enemy lines, and producing a handbook on the Turkish Army. When, in mid-1915, his brothers Will and

Frank were killed in action in France, T. E. was reminded cruelly of the more active front in the West. Egypt was, at the time, the staging area for Middle Eastern military operations of prodigious inefficiency; a trip to Arabia convinced Lawrence of an alternative method of undermining Germany's Turkish ally. In October 1916 he had accompanied the diplomat Sir Ronald Storrs on a mission to Arabia, where Ḥusayn ibn ʿAlī, amīr of Mecca, had proclaimed a revolt against the Turks the previous June. Storrs and Lawrence consulted with Ḥusayn's son Abdullah, and Lawrence received permission to go on to consult further with another son, Fayṣal, who was then commanding an Arab force southwest of Medina. Back in Cairo in November, Lawrence urged his superiors to abet the efforts at rebellion with arms and gold and to make use of the dissident shaykhs by meshing their aspirations for independence with general military strategy. He rejoined Fayṣal's army as political and liaison officer.

Lawrence was not the only officer to become involved in the incipient Arab rising. However, from his own small corner of the Arabian Peninsula he quickly became—especially from his own accounts—its brains, its organizing force, its liaison with Cairo, and its military technician. His small but irritating second front behind the Turkish lines was a hit-and-run guerrilla operation, focused upon the mining of bridges and supply trains, and obscuring the location of Arab units first in one place and then another.

In doing so, he tied down enemy forces that otherwise would have been deployed elsewhere, and kept the Damascus-to-Medina railway largely inoperable, with potential Turkish reinforcements thus helpless to crush the uprising. In such fashion Lawrence—"Amīr Dynamite" to the admiring Bedouins—committed the cynical, self-serving shaykhs for the moment to his king-maker's vision of an Arab nation. He goaded them with examples of his own self-punishing personal valour when their spirits flagged, and bribed them with promises of enemy booty and English gold sovereigns.

Aqaba—at the northernmost tip of the Red Sea—was the first major victory for the Arab guerrilla forces; they seized it after a two-month march on July 6, 1917. Thenceforth, Lawrence attempted to coordinate Arab movements with the campaign of General Sir Edmund Allenby, who was advancing toward Jerusalem, a tactic only partly successful. In November Lawrence was captured at Darʿā by the Turks while reconnoitring the area in Arab dress and was apparently recognized and homosexually brutalized before he was able to escape. The experience, variously reported or disguised by him afterward, left physical and emotional scars from which he never recovered. The next month, nevertheless, he took part in the victory parade in Jerusalem before returning to increasingly successful actions in which Fayṣal's forces nibbled their way north, and Lawrence rose to the rank of lieutenant colonel with the Distinguished Service Order (DSO).

By the time the motley Arab army reached Damascus in October 1918, Lawrence was physically and emotionally exhausted, having forced body and spirit to the breaking point too often. He had been wounded numerous times, captured, and tortured; had endured extremities of hunger, weather, and disease; had been driven by military necessity to commit atrocities upon the enemy. His aspirations were defeated as he witnessed the chaos of Damascus. In the very moment of their triumph, their seemingly incurable factionalism rendered them incapable of becoming a nation. (Anglo-French duplicity, made official in the Sykes-Picot Agreement, Lawrence knew, had already betrayed them in a cynical wartime division of expected spoils.) Distinguished and disillusioned, Lawrence left for home just before the Armistice and politely refused, at a royal audience on Oct. 30, 1918, the Order of the Bath and the DSO, leaving the shocked king George V (in his words) "holding the box in my hand." He was demobilized as a lieutenant colonel on July 31, 1919.

LOUIS ALEXANDER MOUNTBATTEN
(b. May 24, 1854, Graz, Austria—d. Sept. 11, 1921, London, Eng.)

Louis Mountbatten, a British admiral of the fleet and first sea lord, was responsible, with Winston Churchill, for the total mobilization of the fleet prior to World War I.

The eldest son of Prince Alexander of Hesse, he was naturalized as a British subject in 1868, when he entered the Royal Navy. He took part in the British invasion of Egypt in 1882, which included the bombardment of Alexandria (July 11). After serving as director of naval intelligence, he was promoted to the rank of rear admiral in 1904 and vice admiral in 1908. He commanded the Atlantic Fleet from 1908 to 1910 and became first sea lord in 1912. As such he was charged with readying the fleet for war. After a test mobilization in July 1914, he ordered (with instructions from Churchill, first lord of the Admiralty) the reserve ships to remain in full commission; thus, the fleet was wholly mobilized on Aug. 3, 1914, the day before Great Britain entered World War I.

Despite this and other services, he was forced to resign as first sea lord (Oct. 29, 1914) because of his German birth. In 1917, at the request of King George V, he relinquished his German titles, assumed the surname of Mountbatten, and on July 17 of that year was created marquess of Milford Haven.

SIR WILLIAM ROBERT ROBERTSON
(b. Jan. 29, 1860, Welbourn, Lincolnshire, Eng.—d. Feb. 12, 1933, London)

William Robertson was chief of the British Imperial General Staff during most of World War I. He supported Sir Douglas Haig, the British commander in chief in France, in urging concentration of

Britain's manpower and matériel on the Western Front.

After serving as an enlisted man for 11 years, Robertson was commissioned in 1888. He served in India until 1896 and then became the first officer from the ranks to pass through the Staff College at Camberley, Surrey (1897). During the South African War (1899–1902) he was on the intelligence staff. He was appointed commandant of the Staff College (1910) and director of military training (1913) in the War Office. Robertson was widely regarded as "the cleverest man in the army."

From the beginning of World War I, Robertson was quartermaster general of the British expeditionary force in France. In January 1915 he was appointed chief of staff to Sir John French, and in December of that year he became chief of the Imperial General Staff.

In this capacity Robertson held most of the powers of the secretary of state for war. The holder of that office in the latter part of 1915, David Lloyd George, disagreed with Robertson and Haig that the war could and should be won in the west and advocated an Allied attack originating in the Middle East. The mutual distrust between the two generals on one side, and their civilian superior on the other, grew after Lloyd George became prime minister in December 1916. Finally, in February 1918, Robertson resigned as chief of the Imperial General Staff and was given a command in England. In 1919 and 1920, he commanded the British army of occupation on the Rhine.

Hugh Montague Trenchard
(b. Feb. 3, 1873, Taunton, Somerset, Eng.—d. Feb. 10, 1956, London)

Hugh Trenchard was the British officer and air marshal who helped lay the foundations of the Royal Air Force (RAF).

Trenchard entered the army in 1893 and served in the South African War and later in Nigeria. After being invalided home in 1912, he learned to fly and in 1913, he became assistant commandant of the Central Flying School, Upavon, Wiltshire. In 1915, during World War I, he assumed command in France of the Royal Flying Corps, which was then a branch of the British army. His policy of launching persistent attacks in order to establish dominance of the air became the standard doctrine of Britain's air force. In January 1918 he became Britain's first chief of air staff, though he resigned the post in April of that year. Subsequently that year, he organized the Inter-Allied Independent Bomber Force, a force of RAF heavy bombers to raid targets in Germany.

In 1919 Trenchard was appointed by War Minister Winston Churchill to be the chief of staff of the RAF. In this capacity he strengthened the RAF by founding colleges for air officer cadets and staff officers and by introducing a system of short-service commissions, thereby building a reserve of trained officers. He held the post of chief of air staff until he became the first marshal of the RAF in 1927. He retired from the service in 1929.

SIR HENRY HUGHES WILSON
(b. May 5, 1864, near Edgeworthstown, County Longford, Ire.—d. June 22, 1922, London, Eng.)

Henry Wilson was the chief of the British Imperial General Staff and the main military adviser to Prime Minister David Lloyd George in the last year of World War I. While director of military operations in the War Office (1910–14), he determined that Great Britain should support France in a war against Germany on the basis of French requirements. It was a policy not favoured by many British leaders.

A soldier from the early 1880s, Wilson rose to the command of the Staff College at Camberley, Surrey (1907–10). During this period he cultivated the friendship of his counterpart at the French war college, General (afterward Marshal) Ferdinand Foch—an association that may account for Wilson's readiness to involve Great Britain in French strategy. He also played a dubious part in the Curragh incident (March 1914), surreptitiously encouraging some British army officers who had refused to lead troops against Ulster opponents of Irish Home Rule.

On the outbreak of World War I, the British government chose Wilson's policy of fighting in France alongside French armies as opposed to attacking the German invaders in Belgium, the preferred strategy of the commander in chief, Field Marshal Earl Roberts. Wilson agreed with Roberts, however, on the necessity of military conscription (not instituted until 1916). The smooth mobilization of the standing army and its rapid movement to France in August 1914 may be credited largely to Wilson's prewar planning.

Wilson soon went to France as assistant chief of the general staff. His only field command in the war (December 1915–December 1916) was marked by the loss to the Germans of a sector of Vimy Ridge, near Arras, by his IV Corps. In September 1917 he took over the Eastern Command, a position that enabled him to live in London and ingratiate himself with Lloyd George. As chief of the imperial general staff (from Feb. 18, 1918), he aided the prime minister in securing Foch's appointment as supreme commander of the Allied armies on the Western Front.

CANADA

WILLIAM AVERY BISHOP

(b. Feb. 8, 1894, Owen Sound, Ont., Can.—d. Sept. 11, 1956, West Palm Beach, Fla., U.S.)

William ("Billy") Bishop was a Canadian fighter ace who shot down 72 German aircraft during World War I.

Bishop was educated at the Royal Military College, Kingston, and went overseas during World War I with the Canadian cavalry. In 1915 he transferred to the Royal Flying Corps, joining the

60th Squadron in France in 1917. He soon became highly skilled in aerial combat and shot down a total of 72 enemy aircraft, including 25 in one 10-day period. He was awarded the Victoria Cross and several other decorations, and in March 1918 he was promoted to the rank of major, assuming command of the 85th Squadron.

Once promoted to lieutenant colonel, Bishop was appointed to the staff of the British Air Ministry in August 1918, and in this capacity he helped to form the Royal Canadian Air Force (RCAF) as a separate service.

France

Ferdinand Foch
(b. Oct. 2, 1851, Tarbes, France—
d. March 20, 1929, Paris)

Ferdinand Foch was marshal of France and commander of Allied forces during the closing months of World War I. He is generally considered the leader most responsible for the Allied victory.

After commanding a division in 1911 and briefly commanding an army corps, he was, in August 1913, put in command of the XX Army Corps in Nancy, protecting the Lorraine frontier. It seemed to be the crowning point of Foch's career because he would reach retirement age in only three years.

When war broke out on Aug. 2, 1914, Foch first fought on the right flank, in Lorraine. On August 28 a dangerous gap appeared in the centre, and the commander in chief, Joseph Joffre, called Foch to command the army detachment—which later became the IX Army—that was being formed there. The enemy tried to break through, but Foch held on. His tenacity made it possible for Joffre to win at the First Battle of the Marne. The same was true at the battles of the Yser and of Ypres, where he had been sent by Joffre to coordinate the efforts of the English, the French, and the Belgians, who were being severely attacked.

For two thankless years—1915 and 1916—Foch, commanding the Northern Army Group, vainly tried to break through the German line in Artois and at the Somme, but was unable to compensate for the lack of equipment and supplies. In May 1917 he was appointed chief of the war minister's general staff, a position that made him adviser to the Allied armies. However, advising was not commanding. Russia was about to collapse, thus allowing Germany to bring all its forces back to the Western Front, where the Belgians, English, and French were lined up under separate commands. Foch predicted that when the Germans struck this poorly consolidated front, each force would think only of its own fate, and that the front would be broken up. He advocated establishing a single command, but the British Prime Minister David Lloyd George and Clemenceau (again appointed premier in November) refused to listen to Foch.

Events, however, were to prove Foch right. On March 21, 1918, the British front in Picardy collapsed under the impact of the German attack. By March 24, British commander Field Marshal Douglas Haig was thinking about his embarkation ports, and French commander General Philippe Pétain was thinking about Paris. The severance of the two armies had begun. The Germans, who quickly perceived the situation, were already crying victory.

Lloyd George and Clemenceau realized that Foch was the only person who could fill the void. By early May, Foch had been made commander in chief of all Allied armies on the Western and Italian fronts. The battle of two wills began: Erich Ludendorff, who was in virtual command of the German forces, versus Foch. Ludendorff, who had the initiative and superiority in numbers, redoubled his attacks. Foch resorted to parrying while waiting for the arrival of the American armies. He urged his men on to the limits of their endurance and succeeded in stopping Ludendorff in Picardy as well as Flanders. However, in order to support the English, who were being pushed back to the sea by Ludendorff, Foch withdrew troops from the French front. Ludendorff took advantage of this. On May 27 he broke through that front, and his troops spread as far as the Marne. On June 9 a new gap appeared at the Oise: Foch stopped it up again. Ludendorff then decided to gamble everything he had before the Americans joined the battle. On July 15 he made a massive attack in Champagne. Two days later he was stopped; he had lost.

It was now Foch's turn to strike. In two offensives on July 18 and on August 8, Foch drove Ludendorff back to a defensive position. The honour of marshal of France was conferred on Foch on August 6, just as he was intensifying his offensive on the Germans, giving no respite to the enemy nor to his own troops. Finally, the German army, already exhausted and dwindling in numbers, was threatened with disintegration by the revolution in Germany and was abandoned by its allies. Germany was forced to ask for an armistice, the conditions of which were dictated by Marshal Foch in the name of the Allies on Nov. 11, 1918, at Rethondes. On November 26 Foch returned to Metz, having succeeded in his lifelong goal of giving Alsace and Lorraine back to France.

After the war Foch was showered with honours, including being made marshal of Great Britain and of Poland. He was buried near Napoleon under the dome of the Church of Saint-Louis, in the Invalides in Paris.

LOUIS FRANCHET D'ESPÈREY
(b. May 25, 1856, Mostaganem, Alg.— d. July 8, 1942, Albi, France)

Louis d'Espèrey was a marshal of France and one of the most effective French military leaders of World War I. He was responsible for driving Bulgaria out of the war, thereby opening the road to Vienna for the Allies.

Trained at Saint-Cyr, d'Espèrey served during the prewar period in Algeria and Tunisia. At the outbreak of World War I, he was a corps commander at Lille. His successful leadership resulted in his being promoted to command the eastern army group (March 1916) and later the northern army group (January 1917). After a defeat by the Germans on the Chemin des Dames (a road between the Aisne and Ailette rivers in the Aisne district of northern France) in May 1918, d'Espèrey was sent to command the polyglot Allied armies in Macedonia. There he achieved the decisive victory (Sept. 15–29, 1918) that forced Bulgaria out of the war. He then led a bold thrust to the Danube, resulting in the collapse of demoralized German divisions hurriedly sent back from Russia and the surrender of Hungary. He was created a marshal of France in 1921 and was elected to the French Academy in 1934.

JOSEPH GALLIENI
(b. April 24, 1849, Saint-Béat, France—d. May 27, 1916, Versailles)

Joseph Gallieni, a French army officer, successfully directed the pacification of the French Sudan and Madagascar and the integration of those African territories into the French colonial empire.

After training at the military academy of Saint-Cyr and serving in the Franco-German War (1870–71), Gallieni was sent to Africa in the mid-1870s. As a captain in 1881 he was captured by the forces of the amīr Ahmadou in the Upper Niger region, but within a year he had extracted exclusive privileges for France in that area.

After serving in Martinique, Gallieni was named governor of the French Sudan, where he successfully combatted rebel Sudanese forces. In 1892–96 he served in French Indochina and was then sent to Madagascar. There he suppressed the revolt of monarchist forces and served as governor general until 1905, winning a reputation as a judicious, flexible, and humane colonial master. He was characterized by both a paternalistic regard for the indigenous people and an overriding sense of duty to France.

Gallieni was the logical choice for supreme commander of the French Army in 1911, but advanced age and poor health led him to decline in favour of General Joseph Joffre. Gallieni retired in April 1914 only to be recalled in August, just before the outbreak of World War I, as military commander of Paris. Rather than remain a passive figure, he launched an important counterattack against the German armies as they crossed the Marne in September. He became minister of war in October 1915 and served with distinction until ill health forced his retirement in March 1916.

JOSEPH JOFFRE
(b. Jan. 12, 1852, Rivesaltes, France— d. Jan. 3, 1931, Paris)

Joseph Joffre was commander in chief (1914–16) of the French armies on the Western Front in World War I. He won fame as "the Victor of the Marne."

After graduating from the École Polytechnique, he took part as a subaltern in the siege of Paris (1870–71) and later served in Indochina, West Africa, and

Madagascar. Promoted to general of division in 1905, he was appointed chief of the French general staff in 1911 and thereby commander in chief in the event of war. Joffre was responsible for the French Army's calamitous plan of campaign with which it began operations in 1914 against Germany, calling for mass attacks across the Franco-German frontier. The plan's futility became apparent when a massive German encircling movement through Belgium caught Joffre and the rest of the French high command unawares and threatened to outflank the Allied forces and capture Paris. Once convinced of the developing German threat on the French left flank, Joffre shifted his forces and created a new French army, the 6th, under his direct authority, to counter the threat of German envelopment. In this moment of supreme trial his best qualities came to the fore; his imperturbability, his force of character, and his courage saved the situation. Constantly threatened by greatly superior German forces wheeling in a great northern arc on Paris, the French retreated steadily until their left flank was fighting just outside the city on September 5. Joffre then issued the order that on September 6 launched the Allied counterstrike, the first of the battles of the Marne. The encounter resulted in the partial repulse of the German advance and the ruin of German hopes for a swift victory on the Western Front.

By the end of 1914 the Western Front had settled into the heavily entrenched lines that existed until 1918. Throughout 1915 the French armies under Joffre attempted to burst through the German positions at ruinous cost, and failed. Joffre's prestige began to wane, and the evident lack of French preparation for the German attack on Verdun in 1916, for which he was held responsible, prepared his downfall. After being stripped of the power of direct command, Joffre resigned on Dec. 26, 1916, and created a marshal of France on that same day.

CHARLES LANREZAC
(b. July 31, 1852, Pointe-à-Pitre, Guad.— d. Jan. 18, 1925, Neuilly-sur-Seine, France)

Charles Lanrezac was a French army commander during the first part of World War I. Though a capable tactician, he proved unable to stop the German advance in northern France and was consequently replaced.

Rising steadily in the French army, Lanrezac had by 1914 become a member of the Conseil Supérieur de la Guerre (Supreme War Council) and commander of the 5th Army. Poised on the left flank of the French force that was expected to sweep eastward into Germany through Alsace and Lorraine at the outbreak of World War I, he was compelled to swing his army northward to face the German armies advancing through Belgium. Forced to retreat south under pressure from Gen. Karl von Bülow's German 2nd Army, he became increasingly pessimistic about the outcome of the campaign. On orders of the French commander in chief, General Joseph Joffre, he nevertheless supported the British expeditionary force east of Paris, winning a brilliant tactical victory at Guise (Aug. 29, 1914). His continued retreat, however, led Joffre to replace him on September 3.

ROBERT NIVELLE
(b. Oct. 15, 1856, Tulle, France—d. March 23, 1924, Paris)

Robert Nivelle was commander in chief of the French armies on the Western Front for five months in World War I. His career was wrecked by the failure of his offensive in the spring of 1917.

Nivelle graduated from the École Polytechnique in 1878, served in Indochina, Algeria, and China as an artillery officer, and was made a general of brigade in October 1914 after World War I began. In 1915 he rose to command a division and then the 3rd Corps, which helped stem the German offensive at the Battle of Verdun early in 1916. In May 1916 he succeeded General Philippe Pétain as commander of the 2nd Army at Verdun. His use of creeping artillery barrages in two dazzlingly successful French counterattacks there (October, December 1916) enabled the French to retake nearly all the ground gained by the Germans over the previous six months.

That December, Nivelle was promoted over many senior officers to succeed General Joseph-Jacques Joffre as commander in chief of the French armies. He then proclaimed that his methods at Verdun could win the war.

David Lloyd George, the British prime minister, heartily subscribed to Nivelle's advocacy of frontal assaults carried out in close coordination with massive artillery bombardments, and he placed the British armies in France under Nivelle's command for his great offensive. Nivelle, however, steadily lost the confidence of his own chief subordinates, and his final offensive on the Aisne front (April 1917) failed to break through German lines and cost France 120,000 casualties. The next month there were widespread mutinies in the French armies. On May 15, 1917, Nivelle was replaced by Pétain as commander in chief, and in December 1917 he was transferred to North Africa.

PHILIPPE PÉTAIN
(b. April 24, 1856, Cauchy-à-la-Tour, France—d. July 23, 1951, Île d'Yeu)

Philippe Pétain was a French general. He became a national hero for his victory at the Battle of Verdun in World War I but was discredited as chief of state of the French government at Vichy in World War II. He died under sentence in a prison fortress.

His advancement until the outbreak of World War I in 1914—he was 58 when he finally became a general—was slow because as a professor at the War College he had propounded tactical theories opposed to those held by the high command. While the latter favoured the offensive at all costs, Pétain held that a well-organized defensive was sometimes called for and that before any attack the commander must be sure of the superiority of his fire power.

After successively commanding a brigade, a corps, and an army, in 1916, Pétain was charged with stopping the German attack on the fortress city of Verdun. Though the situation was practically hopeless, he masterfully reorganized both the front and the transport systems, made prudent use of the artillery, and was able to inspire in his troops a heroism that has become historic. He became a popular hero, and, when serious mutinies erupted in the French army following the ill-considered offensives of Gen. Robert Nivelle, Pétain was named his successor as French commander in chief.

He reestablished discipline with a minimum of repression by personally explaining his intentions to the soldiers and improving their living conditions. Under Pétain the French armies participated in the victorious offensive of 1918, led by Marshal Ferdinand Foch, generalissimo of the Allied armies. Pétain was made a marshal of France in November 1918 and was subsequently appointed to the highest military offices (vice president of the Supreme War Council and inspector general of the army).

An undated portrait of General Henri Pétain. Library of Congress Prints and Photographs Division

ITALY

LUIGI CADORNA
(b. Sept. 4, 1850, Pallanza, Piedmont, Kingdom of Sardinia [Italy]—d. Dec. 21, 1928, Bordighera, Italy)

Luigi Cadorna completely reorganized Italy's ill-prepared army on the eve of World War I and was chief of staff during the first 30 months of that conflict.

Cadorna was commissioned a second lieutenant in the Italian army in 1868. Rising through the ranks for half a century, he was appointed chief of the Italian general staff in July 1914. When Italy entered World War I by declaring war on Austria-Hungary in May 1915, Cadorna was given command on the Austro-Italian frontier. While maintaining a defensive posture in the Trentino, he mounted a series of offensives along the Isonzo River that incurred heavy casualties and gained little ground. Cadorna's principal military successes were the blunting of the Austrian offensive in the Trentino (spring 1916), the capture of Gorizia (August 1916), and the victory at Baensezza (1917).

The entry of Germany into the Austro-Italian theatre in 1917 turned the balance of forces decisively against Italy. After the overwhelming defeat of the Italian army on the Isonzo front at the Battle of Caporetto (Oct. 24, 1917), Cadorna was removed as chief of staff and transferred to the Allied military council at Versailles. However, the official inquiry into the defeat at Caporetto forced his recall from Versailles. Nevertheless, he was named a field marshal in 1924.

Armando Diaz
(b. Dec. 5, 1861, Naples, Italy—d. Feb. 29, 1928, Rome)

Armando Diaz was chief of staff of the Italian army during World War I.

A graduate of the military colleges of Naples and Turin, Armando Diaz served with distinction in the Italo-Turkish War (1911–12). Appointed major general in 1914, he collaborated with Gen. Luigi Cadorna in the reorganization of the Italian Army in preparation for World War I. When Italy entered the war in May 1915, he was chief of operations under Cadorna and contributed as a staff officer, then as a division and corps commander, to the Italian victories at Carso and Gorizia (August 1916). When the Italians were overwhelmingly defeated by the Austrians at Caporetto (October 1917), Diaz replaced Cadorna as chief of staff. Diaz succeeded in sufficiently stabilizing the Italian Army enough to mount a strong counteroffensive after repelling the Austrian offensive in June 1918. Diaz' decisive victory at Vittorio Veneto (Oct. 24–Nov. 3, 1918) signalled the defeat of the Austrian forces.

As a reward for his military successes, he was named *duca della vittoria* (Italian: "duke of victory") in 1921 and appointed marshal in 1924. He served as minister of war in the first Fascist Cabinet (1922–24). Poor health, however, forced him to resign and to retire to private life.

Russia

Nicholas
(b. Nov. 18 [Nov. 6, Old Style], 1856, St. Petersburg, Russia—d. Jan. 5, 1929, Antibes, France)

Nicholas was a Russian grand duke and army officer. He served as commander in chief against the Germans and Austro-Hungarians in the first year of World War I and was subsequently (until March 1917) Emperor Nicholas II's viceroy in the Caucasus and commander in chief against the Turks.

The son of the emperor Alexander II's brother, the grand duke Nikolay

Armando Diaz, 1921. Encyclopædia Britannica, Inc.

lead the Russian armies himself and appointed the grand duke Nicholas commander in chief. Despite their early successes, the Russians were outgeneralled by the German chief of staff, Erich Ludendorff, and eventually were immobilized by munitions shortages. The grand duke is considered to have done as well as possible, considering he was obliged to follow the general staff's plans.

On Sept. 5 (Aug. 23, Old Style), 1915, the emperor assumed supreme military command. He sent the grand duke to the Caucasus, where he remained until the overthrow of the monarchy in 1917. The emperor's last official act was to appoint the grand duke commander in chief once more. However, his appointment was canceled almost immediately by Prince Georgy Y. Lvov, head of the provisional government. Two years later, after the war, Grand Duke Nicholas sailed from Russia in a British warship. He lived in France until his death, heading an organization that sought to unite all anticommunist Russian émigrés.

SERBIA

RADOMIR PUTNIK
(b. Jan. 24, 1847, Kragujevac, Serbia—
d. May 17, 1917, Nice, France)

Radomir Putnik was a Serbian army commander. He was victorious against the Austrians in 1914, but a year later, he was defeated and relieved of his command.

Educated at the artillery school, Putnik was commissioned in 1866. He

Nikolayevich "the Elder," Nicholas was educated at the general staff college and commissioned in 1872. He served in the Russo-Turkish War of 1877–78 and as inspector general of cavalry (1895–1905), introducing major reforms in training and equipment. He was made commander of the St. Petersburg military district in 1905 and also was appointed first president of the short-lived imperial committee of national defense.

When World War I began, Emperor Nicholas II abandoned his intention to

graduated from the staff college in 1889 and became a general in 1903. Except for three periods when he was war minister (1904–05, 1906–08, 1912), he was chief of staff from 1903 to 1916. The skill, good equipment, and fighting spirit of the Serbian army during the war were mainly due to Putnik's leadership.

Putnik headed a brigade in the two wars against Turkey (1876, 1877–78) and headed a divisional staff in the war against Bulgaria (1885). He was commander in chief in the two Balkan Wars (1912–13), routing the Turks at Kumanovo (October 1912) and—as field marshal—at Monastir, Tur. (now Bitola, Macedonia; November 1912). Largely because of him, the Bulgarians were defeated at Bregalnica (June–July 1913). When World War I began, Putnik, then in Austria, was escorted to Romania. In poor health, he resumed the post of commander in chief and routed overwhelming Austrian forces on Cer Mountain (August 1914), the first Allied victory in the war, and on the Kolubara River (November–December 1914). A year later, Putnik, carried in a sedan chair, shared in the retreat of his army across Albania. Relieved of his command, he retired to Nice.

United States

Hunter Liggett

(b. March 21, 1857, Reading, Pa., U.S.— d. Dec. 30, 1935, San Francisco, Calif.)

Hunter Liggett served as an American corps and army commander in World War I.

After graduating from West Point in 1879, Liggett served in frontier posts and in the Philippines. He attended the Army War College (1909–10) and then served on the General Staff, earning wide respect for his ability and character. By 1913 he was a brigadier general and president of the War College. Arriving in France with the American Expeditionary Force (AEF) in October 1917, Liggett took command of the U.S. Army's I Corps on Jan. 20, 1918. This appointment was a sign of the high esteem that the AEF commanding general, John J. Pershing, had for him, in spite of Liggett's strong dissent from Pershing's commitment to open-order tactics (as opposed to rigid formations), as well as Liggett's arthritic, overweight, and generally unprepossessing appearance.

Liggett took the I Corps to war on July 4, 1918, commanding it in the Second Battle of the Marne (July 15–18, 1918), in which the corps crossed the Ourcq and Vesle rivers while suffering heavy casualties. In the Saint-Mihiel offensive that began on September 12, the corps took its objectives ahead of schedule, and as a result it was assigned to one of the best-defended sectors in the battles of the Meuse-Argonne (Sept. 26–Nov. 11, 1918). By October 10, I Corps had cleared most of the Argonne Forest against stubborn German resistance, and on October 16, Pershing appointed Liggett commander of the First U.S. Army. Liggett spent two weeks reorganizing chaotic administrative and replacement systems, then he resumed the offensive successfully until the November 11 armistice.

Liggett commanded the American occupation forces in Germany until July 1919, and he retired in 1921. The AEF's best senior field commander, Liggett justified his own aphorism that fat around the waist was less dangerous than fat above the collar.

WILLIAM MITCHELL
(b. Dec. 29, 1879, Nice, France—d. Feb. 19, 1936, New York, N.Y., U.S.)

William ("Billy") Mitchell was an American army officer and early advocate of a separate U.S. air force and greater preparedness in military aviation. He was court-martialed for his outspoken views and did not live to see the fulfillment during World War II of many of his prophecies concerning the importance of military aviation in wartime, including strategic bombing, mass airborne operations, and the eclipse of the battleship by the bomb-carrying airplane.

After serving as a private in the infantry during the Spanish-American War (1898), Mitchell received a commission as a second lieutenant in the signal corps. He served in Cuba, the Philippines, and Alaska and in 1909 graduated from the Army Staff College at Fort Leavenworth, Kan. In 1915 he was assigned to the aviation section of the signal corps. During World War I Mitchell became the outstanding U.S. combat air commander, advancing to the rank of brigadier general. In September 1918 he commanded a French-U.S. air armada of almost 1,500 planes—the largest concentration of air

Col. William "Billy" Mitchell, advocate for a U.S. air force, 1925. Library of Congress Prints and Photographs Division

power up to that time. In the Meuse-Argonne campaign he used formations of up to 200 planes for mass bombing of enemy targets.

After the war Mitchell was appointed assistant chief of the air service. He became a strong proponent of an independent air force and of unified control of air power, both of which were opposed by the army general staff and the navy. As a result, he became increasingly outspoken in his criticism of the military hierarchy, and, when his term ended in April 1925, he was sent to the remote post of San Antonio, Texas. The climax of his conflict with military leadership came in September 1925, when the loss of the navy dirigible *Shenandoah* in a storm inspired him publicly to accuse the War and Navy departments of "incompetency, criminal negligence, and almost treasonable administration of the national defense." In December an army court-martial convicted him of insubordination. Sentenced to suspension from rank and duty for five years, he resigned from the army (Feb. 1, 1926).

JOHN J. PERSHING
(b. Sept. 13, 1860, Laclede, Mo., U.S.—d. July 15, 1948, Washington, D.C.)

John J. Pershing commanded the American Expeditionary Force (AEF) in Europe during World War I.

Gen. John Pershing (centre) *inspects British troops, Brest, France, 1918.* Hulton Archive/Getty Images

Graduating from the U.S. Military Academy at West Point, N.Y., in 1886, Pershing served in several Indian wars, in the Spanish-American War (1898), as brigadier general in the Philippine Islands (1906–13), and as commander of a punitive raid against the Mexican revolutionary Pancho Villa (1916). He also was a military instructor at the University of Nebraska, Lincoln, and at West Point.

After the United States declared war on Germany (April 1917), President Woodrow Wilson selected Pershing to command the American troops being sent to Europe. In June he submitted a "General Organization Report" recommending an army of 1,000,000 men by 1918 and 3,000,000 by 1919. Though early U.S. planning had not included such a large force, Pershing's recommendations prevailed.

Pershing was determined to preserve the integrity of the AEF as an independent army, despite pressure from the Allied high command to use U.S. troops as replacement units in European divisions, many of which were exhausted from the setbacks of 1917. Pershing largely resisted these pressures, although, during the March-June 1918 German offensive threatening Paris, he was finally persuaded to release his troops temporarily to the inter-Allied commander Marshal Ferdinand Foch.

Although Pershing's army never became entirely self-sufficient, it conducted two significant operations. In September 1918, the AEF assaulted the Saint-Mihiel salient successfully. Then, at Foch's request, Pershing quickly regrouped his forces for the Meuse-Argonne offensive later that month, despite his original plans to advance toward Metz. Though incomplete preparations and inexperience slowed the Meuse-Argonne operations, the inter-Allied offensive in France destroyed German resistance in early October and led to the Armistice the next month.

Pershing was criticized for operational and logistic errors, but his creation of the AEF was a remarkable achievement. He returned home with a sound reputation and, in 1919, was given the rank of general of the armies of the United States. Pershing's nickname, "Black Jack," was originally derived from his service with an African American regiment early in his career. However, it came to signify his stern bearing and rigid discipline. Eschewing politics, Pershing remained in the army and served as chief of staff from 1921 until his retirement three years later.

EDWARD VERNON RICKENBACKER
(b. Oct. 8, 1890, Columbus, Ohio, U.S.—d. July 23, 1973, Zürich, Switz.)

Edward ("Eddie") Rickenbacker was a pilot, industrialist, and the most celebrated U.S. air ace of World War I.

U.S. Army Air Corps pilot and flying ace Eddie Rickenbacker, c. 1916. Topical Press Agency/Hulton Archive/Getty Images

Rickenbacker developed an early interest in internal-combustion engines and automobiles, and, by the time the United States entered World War I, he was one of the country's top three racing drivers. He entered the army in 1917 as a driver attached to General John J. Pershing's staff and drove a car for Colonel William ("Billy") Mitchell, the noted advocate of tactical air power.

With Mitchell's help, he became a fighter pilot and was assigned to the 94th Aero Pursuit Squadron. He accumulated 26 air victories and numerous decorations, including the Medal of Honor.

CENTRAL POWERS

Austro-Hungarian Empire

Franz Conrad von Hötzendorf
(b. Nov. 11, 1852, Penzing, Austria—d. Aug. 25, 1925, Mergentheim, Ger.)

Franz von Hötzendorf was a controversial military strategist and one of the most influential conservative propagandists of Austria-Hungary. He planned the Habsburg monarchy's campaigns during World War I.

Advancing rapidly in the Austro-Hungarian army, Conrad became chief of staff in 1906 on the recommendation of the heir to the throne, archduke Francis Ferdinand, whose military views he shared. A staunch conservative, Conrad distrusted the expansionist tendencies of Serbia and Austria's ally Italy, advocating preventive wars against both. His vociferously aggressive stance toward Italy in 1911 caused his temporary dismissal, but he returned to head the General Staff in 1912. He devised two plans for an eventual war in the East. If Russia remained neutral, he would throw preponderant forces against Serbia. However, if Russia became involved, Austria would concentrate its strength on that front.

Upon Russia's entry into World War I, most Austrian troops were sent to face that enemy. As a result, Conrad's invasion of Serbia failed; that country was not finally subdued until the end of 1915, and then only with German aid. His offensives on the Russian front also were repulsed, in part because of his late redeployment of Austria's strategic reserve to the East, but more so because of Conrad's insistence on attacking a numerically superior enemy. Only German intervention saved Austria from total disaster. The Austro-German offensive of 1915, planned by Conrad, succeeded, but by this time the Austrian army had become increasingly subordinated to the German general staff and had virtually lost its independence. His Italian offensive of 1916 also came close to success, but troop withdrawals from the Italian frontier to the threatened Russian front again cost him victory. When the new emperor, Charles I, took over command in 1916, he dismissed the strong-willed Conrad, who commanded an army group on the Italian front until the summer of 1918.

Germany

Georg Bruchmüller
(b. Dec. 11, 1863, Berlin [Ger.]—d. Jan. 26, 1948, Garmisch-Partenkirchen, W. Ger.)

Georg Bruchmüller, a German artillery officer, revolutionized techniques of fire support during World War I.

Bruchmüller's peacetime career was undistinguished, and he was retired as a lieutenant colonel on medical grounds in 1913. However, he was recalled to active duty in 1914, serving on the Eastern Front, where in 1915–16 he recognized the limitations of long artillery preparations and massive barrages. Instead, Bruchmüller advocated combined operations in which intense bombardments, lasting only a few hours, would stun the defenders just before attacking infantry could reach them. He also favoured heavy use of gas and smoke shells, which immobilized and disrupted targets without destroying the intervening ground. Systematic preparation of the attack front, accompanied by surprise and secrecy, were essential tactical requirements. The core of Bruchmüller's system, however, was the functional, flexible organization of artillery under central control for specific purposes such as deep interdiction, counterbattery, and close support.

First tested at the attack on Riga, Russia, in September 1917, Bruchmüller's methods proved so successful that, despite intense opposition within some military quarters, they were adopted for the March 1918 Western offensive. Bruchmüller was responsible for fire support in five separate attacks. While unable to compensate for the army's lack of tanks as compared to the Allied forces, the German artillery was so successful at breaking open Allied defenses that its commander received the nickname *Durchbruchmüller* ("Breakthrough Müller"). Inscribed on his tombstone, the nickname epitomizes Bruchmüller's status as the father of modern artillery methods.

ERICH VON FALKENHAYN
(b. Nov. 11, 1861, near Graudenz, West Prussia—d. April 8, 1922, near Potsdam, Ger.)

Erich von Falkenhayn was the Prussian minister of war and chief of the imperial

A portrait of Gen. Eric von Falkenhayn, c. 1905. Hulton Archive/Getty Images

German general staff early in World War I.

Falkenhayn gained military experience as an instructor to the Chinese army and as a member of the Prussian General Staff in the international expedition of 1900 against the Boxers in China. He served as Prussian minister of war from July 1913 to January 1915 an office for which he was responsible for the armament and equipment of the German army. Within Germany he greatly improved the system of munitions supply and transportation of troops by rail. He ignored some recommendations of Gen. Helmuth von Moltke, chief of the General Staff, who for that reason considered him responsible for the army's failure in France in 1914. On Sept. 14, 1914, after the German retreat from the Marne, William II chose Falkenhayn as Moltke's successor.

Falkenhayn was convinced that the war had to be won in France, chiefly by Germany's standing on the defensive and exhausting its enemies. He did not believe Russia could be defeated militarily. Thus, he opposed the plan of Field Marshal Paul von Hindenburg and Gen. Erich Ludendorff for an eastern offensive and was reluctant to provide troops for a theatre he believed "gave nothing back." Instead, he began concentrating resources for an attack on Verdun that he believed would wear out the French army. On Aug. 29, 1916, following a long and unsuccessful German assault on that French fortress-city, Falkenhayn was dismissed as chief of the General Staff by the emperor in favour of the more aggressive Hindenburg.

After leading a German army against Romania for 10 months, Falkenhayn took command of the Central Powers forces (mainly Turkish) in Palestine (July 9, 1917). There he was unable to stop the advance of the British under Gen. Edmund Allenby. Having been succeeded in Palestine by Gen. Otto Liman von Sanders, Falkenhayn commanded an army in Lithuania from March 4, 1918, until the end of the war a few months later.

WILHELM COLMAR
(b. Aug. 12, 1843, near Labiau, East Prussia [now Polessk, Russia]—d. April 19, 1916, Baghdad, Iraq, Ottoman Empire [now in Iraq])

Wilhelm Colmar was the imperial German field marshal who reorganized the Turkish army (1883–96) and served as commander in chief of Turkish forces against the British in Mesopotamia (Iraq) during World War I. Despite his advanced age, he successfully conducted the 143-day-long siege of General Sir Charles Townshend's British contingent at Kut (1915–16).

In August 1914, the first month of World War I, Colmar was appointed governor-general of German-occupied Belgium. In November of that year, he became aide-de-camp to the Ottoman sultan Mehmed V. Placed in command of the Turkish First Army in Mesopotamia, he halted Townshend's Anglo-Indian army at Ctesiphon on Nov. 22, 1915, and then, on December 8, trapped Townshend inside Kut. After Colmar's troops had repulsed a large British relief force, Townshend surrendered on April 29, 1916. According to the official report, Colmar had died of typhus, but it also has been said that he was poisoned by the revolutionary Young Turks.

GUSTAV RÜDIGER
(b. Dec. 8, 1865, Züllichau, Brandenburg, Prussia [now Sulechów, Pol.]—d. Nov. 4, 1946, Kinsegg, Allgäu, W. Ger.)

Gustav Rüdiger was a German army officer who, at the end of World War I, tried unsuccessfully to build a German-controlled *Baltikum* in Latvia in order to prevent domination of that country by Soviet Russia.

A general commanding an infantry division in France, Rüdiger was transferred to Finland in March 1918 to help the Finnish national army against the Finnish-Russian Red Army. Entering Helsinki on April 13, his division successfully held the city until after the armistice of Nov. 11, 1918. In January 1919 the German high command appointed him "governor" of Liepāja (Libau), Latvia, where Prime Minister Kārlis Ulmanis' Latvian government had taken refuge from the Red Army occupying Riga. Arriving at Liepāja on February 3, he took command of the German-Latvian VI Reserve Corps, which, on May 22, captured Riga. There, he attempted to set up a pro-German civil government. In a battle near Cesis (Wenden) on June 19–22, however, he was defeated by an Estonian-Latvian force under Estonian General Johan Laidoner and forced to abandon Riga, to which the Ulmanis government returned.

On July 19, British General Sir Hubert de la Poer Gough, head of the Allied military mission to the Baltic countries, ordered Rüdiger and his troops to return to Germany. Rüdiger declined to obey his orders for five months, using such stratagems as the pretense that his army comprised anti-Communist White Russians rather than Germans. Finally, on Dec. 18, 1919, he retreated into East Prussia.

PAUL VON HINDENBURG
(b. Oct. 2, 1847, Posen, Prussia [now Poznań, Pol.]—d. Aug. 2, 1934, Neudeck, Ger. [now in Poland])

Paul von Hindenburg served as a German field marshal during World War I and as second president of the Weimar Republic (1925–34). His presidential terms were wracked by political instability, economic depression, and the rise to power of Adolf Hitler, whom he appointed chancellor in 1933.

Hindenburg was the son of a Prussian officer of old Junker (aristocratic) stock. His mother, however, was from a middle-class family—a fact he preferred to ignore. A cadet at the age of 11, he served in the Austro-Prussian (Seven Weeks') War of 1866 and in the Franco-German War of 1870–71. He retired as a general in 1911 after an honourable but not especially distinguished career.

Hindenburg was called back into service in August 1914 to be the nominal superior of Maj. Gen. Erich Ludendorff. Acclaimed as one of the army's best strategists, Ludendorff was to drive a Russian invasion force from East Prussia. For this achievement, the rocklike Hindenburg, rather than Ludendorff, received the nation's applause. Soon Hindenburg's popular standing overshadowed that of Emperor William II. He was promoted to the rank of field marshal, and in 1916 the emperor was pressured into giving him command of all German land forces, with Ludendorff his co-responsible chief aide. Unable to win the war on land, the duo tried starving Britain into surrender by unrestricted submarine warfare. However, Germany's policy of unrestricted submarine attacks eventually drew the United States into the war, and caused Germany's ultimate defeat. When they conceded defeat, Hindenburg let Ludendorff take the blame.

After the overthrow of William II, Hindenburg collaborated briefly with the new republican government. He directed the withdrawal of German forces from France and Belgium and had his staff organize the suppression of left-radical risings in Germany. With both tasks accomplished (and the old officer corps preserved in the process), he retired once more in June 1919. Living quietly in Hanover, he occasionally expressed antirepublican views but, on the whole, cultivated his image of a nonpartisan national hero.

MAX HOFFMANN
(b. Jan. 25, 1869, Homberg an der Efze, Hesse [Germany]—d. July 8, 1927, Bad Reichenhall, Ger.)

Max Hoffmann was primarily responsible for several striking German victories on the Eastern Front in World War I.

Hoffmann joined the German army in 1887, studied at the Berlin War Academy, and eventually became the General Staff's expert on the eastern sector (Russia and Japan). In August 1914, as a colonel and chief staff officer of the German 8th Army, he tried to persuade the 8th Army's commanding officer, General Max von Prittwitz, not to withdraw the army behind the Vistula River and so abandon East Prussia to the Russian forces. Prittwitz was soon recalled in disgrace, and his replacements, generals Paul von Hindenburg and Erich Ludendorff, accepted Hoffmann's plans for the 8th Army to attack the uncoordinated Russian armies in the area. The result of the consequent Battle of Tannenberg on August 26–30 was Germany's first great military victory on the Eastern Front.

Hoffmann planned the Battle of the Masurian Lakes (February 1915), another German victory. In August 1916, a year and a half later, he was promoted to colonel and appointed chief of staff to the new German commander of the Eastern Front. At the Brest-Litovsk peace talks (December 1917–March 1918), Hoffmann, as the senior representative of the German High Command, and Richard von Kühlmann, the foreign minister, attempted to negotiate German treaties with Ukraine and Russia. When the Bolsheviks showed reluctance to sign a treaty, however, Hoffmann denounced (Feb. 16, 1918) the Russo-German armistice and two days later launched a massive German offensive against Russia. With this offensive, Hoffman captured a great deal of territory and thus forced the Bolshevik government to agree to peace terms with Germany on March 1.

ALEXANDER VON KLUCK
(b. May 20, 1846, Münster, Prussian Westphalia [Germany]—d. Oct. 19, 1934, Berlin)

Alexander von Kluck commanded the German 1st Army in the offensive against Paris at the beginning of World War I.

Although Kluck is best known for his service in World War I, he first saw service in the Seven Weeks' War (1866) and in the Franco-German War (1870–71). In 1906 he became a general of infantry and in 1913 an inspector general. On the outbreak of war in 1914 he assumed his war appointment as commander of the 1st Army on the extreme right flank of the German force that would penetrate into northern France. His task was to roll up the left flank of the French armies, encircle Paris, and thus bring the war in the West to a rapid conclusion. However, partly because of lack of control by supreme headquarters, these plans miscarried and Kluck's army prematurely executed a wheel to the west of Paris, a maneuver that opened up a gap in the German lines which afforded an opportunity for a counteroffensive by French and British forces. Kluck almost succeeded in reaching Paris but was defeated only 13 miles (21 km) from the city by Anglo-French forces in the First Battle of the Marne, Sept. 6–9, 1914. By October 1914 the German advance had been halted and trench warfare had begun. Kluck was wounded in March 1915 and retired the next year.

PAUL VON LETTOW-VORBECK
(b. March 20, 1870, Saarlouis, Rhine Province, Prussia [now in Germany]— d. March 9, 1964, Hamburg, W. Ger.)

Paul von Lettow-Vorbeck commanded Germany's small African force during World War I. He was a determined and resourceful leader who favoured guerilla tactics and hoped to influence the war in Europe by pinning down a disproportionately large number of Allied troops in his area.

Lettow-Vorbeck served on the expedition to put down the Herero and Hottentot rebellion (1904–07) in German South West Africa (now Namibia), during which he gained experience in bush fighting. Appointed military commander of German East Africa in 1914, he repelled a British landing at Tanga (Tanzania) in November of that year. For four years, with a force that never exceeded about 14,000 men (3,000 Germans and 11,000 askaris, or native Africans), he held in check a much larger force (estimates range to more than 300,000) of British, Belgian, and Portuguese troops.

On his return to Germany in January 1919, Lettow-Vorbeck was welcomed as a hero. In July 1919 he led a corps of right-wing volunteers that occupied Hamburg to prevent its take-over by the left-wing Spartacists. He was a deputy to the Reichstag (parliament) from May 1929 to July 1930. Though a member of the right wing, he was not a Nazi and unsuccessfully tried to organize a conservative opposition to Hitler.

OTTO LIMAN VON SANDERS
(b. Feb. 17, 1855, Stolp, Pomerania— d. Aug. 22, 1929, Munich)

German General Otto Liman von Sanders was largely responsible for making the Ottoman army an effective fighting force in World War I, especially in the defeat of the Allies at Gallipoli.

Liman began his military career in 1874 and rose to the rank of lieutenant general. In 1913 he was appointed director of a German military mission charged with reorganizing the Turkish army. Up to the outbreak of World War I, he did much to improve its fighting capabilities, which had been impaired by reverses during the Balkan Wars.

In March 1915 Liman was given command of the 5th Turkish Army at Gallipoli. Assisted by Turkish commanders, he succeeded in forcing the British and Australian invasion force to evacuate the Dardanelles, thus preventing an Allied seizure of Constantinople (now Istanbul). In March 1918 he headed the 4th, 7th, and 8th Turkish armies in Syria and Palestine. For a time he held up the British advance but was forced to withdraw to Aleppo. After the armistice, he organized the repatriation of German soldiers who had served in Turkey during the war.

ERICH LUDENDORFF
(b. April 9, 1865, Kruszewnia, near Poznań, Prussian Poland—d. Dec. 20, 1937, Munich, Ger.)

A portrait of Gen. Erich Ludendorff, c. 1916. Hulton Archive/Getty Images

Erich Ludendorff was mainly responsible for Germany's military policy and strategy in the latter years of World War I. After the war he became a leader of reactionary political movements, for a while joining the Nazi Party and subsequently taking an independent, idiosyncratic right-radical line.

In 1908, Ludendorff was put in charge of the 2nd (German) department in the army general staff, the institution generally known as the "great general staff," which was responsible for preparing contingency deployment and mobilization plans. Under the chief of the general staff, General Helmuth von Moltke, Ludendorff played a significant part in the revision of the Schlieffen Plan. This plan envisaged a gigantic outflanking movement involving the infringement of Belgian neutrality with the aim of crushing France with one blow. Moltke and Ludendorff decided to secure more firmly the extended southern flank between Switzerland and Lorraine. They also discarded the idea of forcing a way through southern Holland. Instead, they made preparations for the surprise capture of Liège, the most important fortress in eastern Belgium, often characterized as "impregnable."

The excessively active departmental chief irritated the military authorities, and in 1913 Ludendorff was transferred to the infantry as regimental commander. Consequently, when war broke out in 1914, he was appointed quartermaster in chief (supply and administration) of the 2nd Army in the west.

It was not until two Russian armies threatened to overrun the German 8th Army in East Prussia that Ludendorff was appointed chief of staff of the 8th Army. Serving under the elderly General Paul von Hindenburg, who was renowned for his iron nerves, Ludendorff was considered dynamic but occasionally harsh and, in times of crisis, often nervous. However, Ludendorff regarded the problems with which he and his commander in chief were faced as difficult but never insoluble.

The spectacular victory of Hindenburg and Ludendorff over the Russians in August 1914 at Tannenberg, in East Prussia, a battle that brought Hindenburg worldwide renown, was followed by the German defeat on the Marne in the west that signaled the failure of Ludendorff's revised Schlieffen Plan. Hindenburg and Ludendorff fought off the Russians in the east for two years. Ludendorff's plan of a general offensive against Russia by means of a temporary reduction of the German forces in the west did not receive approval by the supreme army command in the summer of 1915.

Only in August 1916, after the failure of the German offensive at Verdun and in view of the Allied onslaught on both the eastern and western fronts, did the emperor finally appoint the two generals to assume supreme military control. They attempted to conduct a sort of total war by mobilizing the entire forces of the home front, which was already suffering from the effects of the British blockade. Ludendorff staked everything on a single card, the stubborn pursuit of a "victorious peace" that was to secure German territorial gains in east and west. In 1917 he approved the unrestricted submarine warfare against the British that led to the entry of the United States into the war against Germany but not to England's collapse. After the tsar had been deposed in March 1917, Ludendorff gave his blessing to the return of the Russian Bolshevik emigrants (including the as yet unknown V. I. Lenin), in the hope of persuading the

Russians to conclude peace. Hindenburg and Ludendorff, who now exercised a sort of military semidictatorship, also brought about the dismissal of Chancellor Theobald von Bethmann Hollweg in the vain hope that "a strong man" could be found to assume the leadership of the Reich.

On March 21, 1918, Ludendorff opened a general offensive on the Western Front with the object of smashing the Anglo-French armies and forcing a decision in Europe before the Americans arrived in force. However, he had overestimated the strength of the German armies. The offensive failed, and when, in the autumn of 1918, the collapse of the German allies—Austria-Hungary, Bulgaria, and Turkey—was imminent, Ludendorff demanded immediate negotiations for an armistice. For a while, the nerves of the hopelessly overworked general gave way, and a psychiatrist had to be summoned to supreme headquarters. When Ludendorff realized the severity of the armistice conditions, he instead insisted that the war be carried on. Then, when he saw that the political leaders were not prepared to do this, he offered his resignation, which William II accepted on Oct. 26, 1918. At the same time, the emperor, much to Ludendorff's distaste, ordered Hindenburg to remain at his post. A titan of willpower and energy who had attempted the impossible was suddenly torn away from his sphere of activity; the shock was immense. Ludendorff met the revolution that broke out in November 1918 with complete resignation and went into exile in Sweden for several months.

While, according to Prussian custom, general staff officers accepted joint responsibility for all decisions made, they had to preserve strict anonymity. Ludendorff, however, whose ambition was as immense as his strategic gifts, at the close of the lost war claimed to have been the sole real "commander" of World War I. He asserted that he had been deprived of victory by sinister forces that had been operating behind the scenes. By propagating the legend that the German army, undefeated in the field, was sabotaged by the "home front," he did a great deal to poison public life against the government in the Weimar Republic.

AUGUST VON MACKENSEN
(b. Dec. 6, 1849, Haus Leipnitz, Saxony [Germany]—d. Nov. 8, 1945, Celle, Ger.)

August von Mackensen was one of the most successful German commanders in World War I.

Beginning his army career in 1869, Mackensen served in various campaigns, received successive promotions, and, during World War I, took command of the combined German-Austrian 11th Army in western Galicia (Poland; April 1915). Then, ably assisted by his chief of staff, Hans von Seeckt, Mackensen achieved the great German breakthrough in the Gorlice-Tarnów area (Poland), for which he was promoted to field marshal (June 20, 1915). The breakthrough was the beginning of a series of victories for Mackensen: the defeat of the Russians at Brest-Litovsk and at Pinsk (August–September 1915), the overrunning of Serbia (October–November 1915), and the occupation of Romania (1916–17). After the Armistice, Mackensen was interned for a year. He retired from the army in 1920 and was made a Prussian state councillor in 1933 by Hermann Göring. Mackensen, a nationalist rather than a National Socialist, frequently appeared at Nazi functions wearing his imperial cavalry uniform; he became a major symbol of the integration of the Second and Third Reichs.

HELMUTH VON MOLTKE
(b. May 25, 1848, Gersdorff, Mecklenburg [Germany]—d. June 18, 1916, Berlin)

Helmuth von Moltke was chief of the German general staff at the outbreak of World War I. He modified the German attack plan in the west and as unable to retain control of his rapidly advancing armies, which significantly contributed to the halt of the German offensive on the Marne in September 1914 and the frustration of German efforts for a rapid, decisive victory.

Moltke rose rapidly in the German army, becoming adjutant in 1882 to his uncle and namesake, who was chief of the General Staff at the time. The personal favour of the emperors William I and William II, coupled with his great name, quickly elevated him to offices for which he was completely unqualified. In 1903 Moltke became quartermaster general; three years later he succeeded Alfred von Schlieffen as chief of the General Staff. He thus inherited Schlieffen's plan for a war on two fronts, which envisaged only light German forces facing Russia on the east until France on the west had been defeated. In the Schlieffen plan of campaign against France, the German left (southern) wing would hold Alsace-Lorraine defensively while an overwhelmingly strong right (northern) wing would advance rapidly through Belgium and northern France, outflanking and eventually helping encircle the French armies while also capturing Paris.

As chief of staff, however, Moltke's principal duty was to revise the Schlieffen Plan to meet modern conditions. But his task was a difficult one, and when war broke out in August 1914 Moltke did not measure up to its requirements. He allowed several army commanders on the German left wing to attack into France instead of remaining on the defensive. Moreover, he reinforced these attacks with divisions taken from the crucial right wing and then sent several more divisions to the Eastern Front to check the Russian advance into East Prussia. The German high command lost communication with the advancing armies of the right wing, and the movements of that wing's constituent units became disjointed. These and other factors culminated not only in the right wing failing to encircle the French left, but becoming itself the victim of a French and British flank attack that halted the entire German offensive at the Battle of the Marne (Sept. 6–12, 1914). Moltke's mood became more and more despairing during this time, and finally he abdicated responsibility completely. On Sept. 14, 1914, Emperor William II functually replaced Moltke as chief of staff, though Moltke retained nominal command until the end of the year. A speedy victory in the west had eluded Germany's grasp. In fact, within a few months of the Battle of the Marne the Western Front had settled down to the murderous and static trench warfare that was to persist unabated for almost three years. Moltke died a broken man less than two years later.

Manfred, baron von Richthofen
(b. May 2, 1892, Breslau, Ger. [now Wrocław, Pol.]—d. April 21, 1918, Vaux-sur-Somme, France)

Baron von Richthofen was Germany's top aviator and leading ace in World War I. He was known as the "Red Baron" for his red-painted Fokker triplane—an unusual and daring colour choice when most pilots opted instead for a colour with better camouflage characteristics.

Members of a prosperous family, both Richthofen and his younger brother Lothar followed their father into military careers. In 1912 Richthofen became a lieutenant in the 1st Uhlan Cavalry Regiment of the Prussian Army. As a member of this regiment, he fought in Russia after the outbreak of World War I and then participated in the invasion of Belgium and France. When trench warfare settled in and the cavalry became sidelined, Richthofen joined the infantry. In 1915 he transferred to the Imperial Air Service and in September 1916 entered combat as a fighter pilot. He became commander of Fighter Wing I (Jagdgeschwader 1), which, because of its frequent moves by rail and its fancifully decorated planes, came to be known as "Richthofen's Flying Circus." Richthofen personally was credited with shooting down 80 enemy aircraft. However, he was killed in his red Fokker triplane when caught in a barrage of Australian enemy ground fire during a battle near Amiens. According to another account, he was shot down by Captain A. Roy Brown, a Canadian in the Royal Air Force. His eventual successor as commander of the fighter group was Hermann Göring.

Reinhard Scheer
(b. Sept. 30, 1863, Obernkirchen, Hanover [Germany]—d. Nov. 26, 1928, Marktredwitz, Ger.)

Reinhard Scheer commanded the German High Seas Fleet at the Battle of Jutland (1916).

Scheer entered the German navy in 1879 as a cadet at the age of 15, and by 1907 had become the captain of a battleship. He became chief of staff of the High Seas Fleet under Henning von Holtzendorff in 1910 and commander of a battle squadron in 1913. After the outbreak of World War I, he advocated the use of submarines and gained fame as a submarine strategist. He planned subsurface raids off the English coast, which consisted of using surface units as bait for any British ships lured into the open sea, with submarines lying ready to ambush. Scheer received command of the fleet in January 1916; he hoped to precipitate a strategic division of the British Grand Fleet and catch it at a disadvantage. A combination of both planning and chance resulted in the two fleets converging at the Battle of Jutland (May 31–June 1, 1916), the only major fleet action of World War I and considered to be the largest naval battle in history. Although the Grand Fleet was not successfully divided and the British decisively outnumbered the Germans, Scheer's maneuvering ultimately saved the High Seas Fleet. The battle itself proved inconclusive, with both sides claiming victory.

On Aug. 8, 1918, Scheer succeeded Holtzendorff as chief of the admiralty staff, serving for five more months until his retirement.

ALFRED, COUNT VON SCHLIEFFEN
(b. Feb. 28, 1833, Berlin, Ger.—d. Jan. 4, 1913, Berlin)

Count von Schlieffen was head of the German general staff and responsible for the plan of attack (Schlieffen Plan) that the German armies used, with significant modifications, at the outbreak of World War I.

Schlieffen, the son of a Prussian general, entered the army in 1854. He soon moved to the general staff and participated in the Seven Weeks' War against Austria (1866) and the Franco-Prussian War (1870–71). By 1884 he had become head of the military-history section of the general staff and in 1891 replaced Alfred, Graf von Waldersee, as chief of the Great General Staff.

Germany, by this time, had to face the possibility of a two-front war—against France in the west and Russia in the east—decades before World War I actually began. In attempting to solve this problem, Schlieffen differed from his predecessors, Waldersee and Field Marshal Helmuth, Graf von Moltke, who had aimed the first strike against Russia. Taking into account the vast territorial expanse of Germany's eastern neighbour and its growing defensive strength, he proposed to aim a rapid, decisive opening blow on the Western front against France. Further, realizing that frontal assaults against mass armies would be costly and often indecisive, Schlieffen decided to strike at the enemy's flank. The plan that gradually emerged through the 1890s and the first years of the 20th century envisaged that only small numbers were to be left in the east to contain any threat by slowly mobilizing Russian forces, while the great bulk of Germany's armies were to be deployed in the west. Schlieffen predicted that a flanking movement would have greatest success in the north, through Belgium and possibly Holland, as the south was too mountainous to allow the rapid movement of large bodies of troops. Hence,

Schlieffen proposed to hold the southern portion of the Western Front with relatively few men, while concentrating a vast force in the north, which would sweep through Belgium and northern France, enveloping the French armies and eventually crushing them against Germany's southern wing. This, in essence, was the Schlieffen Plan as it was finalized in 1905, the year of its author's retirement.

The plan was not applied in its pure form at the beginning of World War I, however. Schlieffen's successor, Helmuth von Moltke, drastically reduced the strength of the attacking armies and thus, is often blamed for Germany's failure to win a quick, decisive victory.

MAXIMILIAN, COUNT VON SPEE
(b. June 22, 1861, Copenhagen, Den.—
d. Dec. 8, 1914, off Falkland Islands)

Count von Spee commanded the German naval forces in the battles of Coronel and the Falkland Islands early in World War I. He entered the German Navy in 1878, and in 1887–88 he commanded the port in German Cameroon. In 1908 he was made chief of staff of the German Ocean (North Sea) Command, and at the end of 1912 he was appointed commander of the Far Eastern Squadron.

When World War I began, Spee was in the Caroline Islands. Japan's declaration of war against Germany (Aug. 22, 1914) caused him to abandon plans for operations in Chinese waters and to head

for South America. After bombarding Tahiti on September 22, he destroyed a hastily assembled British cruiser squadron on Nov. 1, 1914, off Coronel, Chile.

Two battle cruisers under Vice Admiral Sir Frederick Doveton Sturdee were sent from England against Spee. They arrived at Port Stanley, Falkland Islands, on Dec. 7, 1914. Spee, who had left Chile on November 26, appeared off the Falklands on December 8, perhaps not knowing that the British squadron was there. The Germans were defeated; Spee's flagship, the armoured cruiser Scharnhorst, went down with all hands.

ALFRED VON TIRPITZ
(b. March 19, 1849, Küstrin, Prussia—
d. March 6, 1930, Ebenhausen, near
Munich, Ger.)

Alfred von Tirpitz was the chief builder of the German Navy in the 17 years preceding World War I and a dominant personality of Emperor William II's reign. He was ennobled in 1900 and attained the rank of admiral in 1903 and that of grand admiral in 1911; he retired in 1916.

In June 1897 Tirpitz became secretary of state of the Imperial Navy Department. His appointment marked the beginning of his two-decade buildup of the German fleet in close collaboration with Emperor William II. In 1898 Tirpitz introduced the First Fleet Act, for the reorganization of Germany's sea power. This law provided for an active navy consisting of 1 flagship, 16 battleships, 8 armoured coastal ships,

A portrait of Adm. Alfred von Tirpitz, c. 1910. Hulton Archive/Getty Images

and a force of 9 large and 26 small cruisers to be ready by 1904. Such a navy was regarded as strong enough for limited offensives in a war against France and Russia. While the 1898 act was designed to meet the need for a high-seas battle fleet, Tirpitz's Second Fleet Act of 1900 laid down a more ambitious program—to build a larger and more modern oceangoing fleet—that the navy was never able to practically fulfill. This law set 1917 as the year of completion for an active navy of 2 flagships, 36 battleships, 11 large cruisers, and 34 small cruisers. Tirpitz knew how to stimulate public interest in a bigger navy, and, as secretary of state from 1897, he displayed great skill as a parliamentarian. Tirpitz was ennobled in 1900 and awarded the Order of the Black Eagle, and in 1911 he rose to the rank of grand admiral.

In the meantime not even the 1900 navy law had evoked any significant political response in Britain. The reactions to the expansion of the German navy were late in coming: after the British formed their alliances of 1904 (with France) and 1907 (with Russia), they launched the *Dreadnought* (1906) in an effort to score an important technical advantage over Germany by constructing oversized capital ships. Their building program turned out to be a miscalculation, however, because not only all the other great powers but even many countries with small navies such as Chile and Turkey immediately followed suit. Nevertheless, because Britain had had a head start since 1905, it had an edge of seven capital ships over its principal rival, Germany. Because of rapidly increasing British and declining German construction, there were 49 British battleships either in service or being built in 1914, compared to 29 German vessels of the same type. Tirpitz's construction plan was never completed as he originally envisioned it.

As grand admiral, Tirpitz advocated for unrestricted submarine warfare against Great Britain. However, his vocal agitations to lift restrictions on German submarines put him out of favour with the emperor, who feared that the destruction of ships carrying American passengers would draw the ire of the U.S. government and people. Thus, Tirpitz was forced to resign from his post in March 1916—the same month that Germany resumed unrestricted U-boat attacks and a full year before the United States declared war on Germany.

OTTO WEDDIGEN
(b. Sept. 15, 1882, Herford, Westphalia, Ger.—d. March 18, 1915, at sea off the Moray Firth, Scot.)

Otto Weddigen's feat of sinking three British armoured cruisers in about an hour, during the second month of World War I, has made him one of the most famous of German submarine commanders.

Weddigen entered the German navy in 1901 and participated from the beginning in the development of the U-boat force, which he led by the beginning of the war in August 1914. Off the Dutch coast on Sept. 22, 1914, Weddigen's U-9 torpedoed first the *Aboukir* and then, when they stopped to rescue survivors, the *Hogue* and the *Cressy*, with a combined loss of 1,400 men. On Oct. 15, 1914, the U-9 also sank the cruiser *Hawke* off Scotland, costing the British 500 more lives. Afterward, Weddigen commanded a more modern submarine, the U-29, which was lost with all hands, including Weddigen, when it was rammed by the British battleship *Dreadnought* off the Moray Firth, Scotland, in March 1915.

OTTOMAN EMPIRE

KEMAL ATATÜRK
(b. 1881, Salonika [now Thessaloníki], Greece—d. Nov. 10, 1938, Istanbul, Tur.)

Kemal Atatürk was the founder and first president (1923–38) of the Republic of Turkey. He modernized the country's legal and educational systems and encouraged the adoption of a European way of life, with Turkish written in the Latin alphabet and with citizens adopting European-style names.

Mustafa Kemal (Atatürk), 1923. UPI/ Bettmann Newsphotos

In October 1912, while Mustafa Kemal was in Vienna, the First Balkan War broke out. He was assigned to the defense of the Gallipoli Peninsula, an area of strategic importance with respect to the Dardanelles. Within two months the Ottoman Empire lost most of its territory in Europe. The Second Balkan War, of short duration (June–July 1913), saw the Ottomans regain part of their lost territory. Furthermore, relations were renewed with Bulgaria. Mustafa Kemal's former schoolmate Ali Fethi was named ambassador to Bulgaria, and Mustafa Kemal accompanied him to Sofia as military attaché. There he was promoted to lieutenant colonel.

Mustafa Kemal complained of Enver Paşa's close ties to Germany and predicted German defeat in a hypothetical international conflict. Once World War I broke out, however, and the Ottoman Empire entered on the side of the Central Powers, he sought a military command. Enver made him wait in Sofia, but finally Mustafa Kemal was given command of the 19th Division being organized in the Gallipoli Peninsula. It was here on the peninsula that the Allies attempted their ill-fated landings, giving Mustafa Kemal the opportunity to throw them back and thwart their attempt to force the Dardanelles (February 1915–January 1916). His success at Gallipoli thrust his name and reputation onto the world scene. He was hailed as the "Saviour of Istanbul" and was promoted to colonel on June 1, 1915.

In 1916 Mustafa Kemal was assigned to the war's Russian front and promoted to general, acquiring the title of pasha. He was the only Turkish general to win any victories over the Russians on the Eastern Front. Later that year, he took over the command of the 2nd Army in southeastern Anatolia. There he met Colonel İsmet (İnönü), who would become his closest ally in building the Turkish republic at the end of the war.

Fighting was halted by the Armistice of Mudros (Oct. 30, 1918). Shortly afterward, Enver and other leaders of the Committee of Union and Progress fled to Germany, leaving the sultan to lead the government. To ensure the continuation of his rule, Mehmed VI was willing to cooperate with the Allies, who assumed control of the government.

However, the Allies did not wait for a peace treaty to begin claiming Ottoman territory. Early in December 1918, Allied troops occupied sections of Istanbul and set up an Allied military administration. The Allies made plans to incorporate the provinces of eastern Anatolia into an independent Armenian state. French troops advanced into Cilicia in the southeast. Greece and Italy put forward competing claims for southwestern Anatolia. The Italians occupied Marmaris, Antalya, and Burdur, and on May 15, 1919, Greek troops landed at Izmir and began a drive into the interior of Anatolia, killing Turkish inhabitants and ravaging the countryside. Allied statesmen seemed to be abandoning Woodrow Wilson's Fourteen Points in favour of the old imperialist views set down in covert treaties and contained in their own secret ambitions.

Meanwhile, Mustafa Kemal's armies had been disbanded. He returned to Istanbul on Nov. 13, 1919, just as ships of the Allied fleet sailed up the Bosporus. He was determined to oust them. In various parts of Anatolia, Turks had already taken matters into their own hands, calling themselves "associations for the defense of rights" and organizing paramilitary units. They began to come into armed conflict with local non-Muslims, and it appeared that they might soon do so against the occupying forces as well.

Fearing anarchy, the Allies urged the sultan to restore order in Anatolia. The grand vizier recommended Mustafa Kemal as a loyal officer who could be sent to Anatolia as inspector general of the 3rd Army. Mustafa Kemal contrived to get his orders written in such a way as to give him extraordinarily extensive powers. These included the authority to issue orders throughout Anatolia and to command obedience from provincial governors.

Modern Turkish history may be said to have begun on the morning of May 19, 1919, with Mustafa Kemal's landing at Samsun, on the Black Sea coast of Anatolia. There he told a cheering crowd that the sultan was the prisoner of the Allies and that he had come to prevent the nation from slipping through the fingers of its people. The Allies pressured the sultan to recall Mustafa Kemal, who ignored all communications from Istanbul. The sultan dismissed him and telegraphed all provincial governors, instructing them to ignore Mustafa

Kemal's orders. Imperial orders for his arrest were circulated.

Mustafa Kemal avoided outright dismissal from the army by officially resigning late on the evening of July 7. As a civilian, he pressed on with his retinue from Sivas to Erzurum, where General Kâzim Karabekir, commander of the 15th Army Corps of 18,000 men, was headquartered. At this critical moment, when Mustafa Kemal had no military support or official status, Kâzim threw in his lot with Mustafa Kemal, placing his troops at Mustafa Kemal's disposal. This was a crucial turning point in the struggle for Turkish independence.

Kâzim had called for a congress of all defense-of-rights associations to be held in Erzurum on July 23, 1919. Mustafa Kemal was elected head of the Erzurum Congress, thereby gaining an official status again. The congress drafted a document covering the six eastern provinces of the empire. Later known as the National Pact, it affirmed the inviolability of the Ottoman "frontiers"—that is, all the Ottoman lands inhabited by Turks when the Armistice of Mudros was signed. It also created a provisional government, revoked the special status arrangements for the minorities of the Ottoman Empire (the capitulations), and set up a steering committee, which then elected Mustafa Kemal as head.

Unconvinced of the sultan's ability to rid the country of the Allied occupation, Mustafa Kemal established the seat of his provisional government in Ankara,

300 miles from Istanbul. There he would be safer from both the sultan and the Allies. This proved a wise decision. On March 16, 1920, in Istanbul, the Allies arrested leading nationalist sympathizers and sent them to Malta.

Many prominent Turks escaped from Istanbul to Ankara, including İsmet and, after him, Fevzi (Çakmak), the sultan's war minister. Fevzi became Mustafa Kemal's chief of the general staff. New elections were held, and a parliament, called the Grand National Assembly (GNA), met in Ankara on April 23, 1920. The assembly elected Mustafa Kemal as its president.

In June 1920 the Allies handed the sultan the Treaty of Sèvres, which he signed on Aug. 10, 1920. By the provisions of this treaty, the Ottoman state was greatly reduced in size, with Greece one of the major beneficiaries. Armenia was declared independent. Mustafa Kemal repudiated the treaty. Having received military aid from the Soviet Union, he set out to drive the Greeks from Anatolia and Thrace and to subdue the new Armenian state.

With Anatolia rid of most of the Allies, the GNA, at the behest of Mustafa Kemal, voted on Nov. 1, 1922, to abolish the sultanate. This was soon followed by the flight into exile of Sultan Mehmed VI on November 17. The Allies then invited the Ankara government to discussions that resulted in the signing of the Treaty of Lausanne on July 24, 1923. This treaty fixed the European border of Turkey at the Maritsa River in eastern Thrace.

The nationalists occupied Istanbul on October 2. Ankara was named the capital, and on October 29 the Turkish republic was proclaimed. Turkey was now in complete control of its territory and sovereignty, and the Ottoman Empire was no longer.

ENVER PAŞA
(b. Nov. 22, 1881, Constantinople [now Istanbul], Tur.—d. Aug. 4, 1922, near Baldzhuan, Turkistan [now in Tajikistan])

Enver Paşa was an Ottoman general and commander in chief, a hero of the Young Turk Revolution of 1908, and a leading member of the Ottoman government from 1913 to 1918. He played a key role in the Ottoman entry into World War I on the side of Germany, and, after the Ottoman defeat in 1918, he attempted to organize the Turkic peoples of Central Asia against the Soviets.

An organizer of the Young Turk Revolution, Enver joined General Mahmud Şevket, under whose command an "Army of Deliverance" advanced to Constantinople to depose the Ottoman sultan Abdülhamid II. In 1911, when warfare broke out between Italy and the Ottoman Empire, he organized the Ottoman resistance in Libya, and in 1912 he was appointed the governor of Banghāzī (Benghazi; now in modern Libya).

Back in Constantinople, he participated in the politics of the Committee of Union and Progress, leading the coup

Enver Paşa. Encyclopædia Britannica, Inc.

When the Ottoman Empire entered World War I on the side of the Central Powers (November 1914), Enver cooperated closely with German officers serving in the Ottoman army. His military plans included Pan-Turkic (or Pan-Turanian) schemes for uniting the Turkic peoples of Russian Central Asia with the Ottoman Turks.

These plans resulted in the disastrous defeat in December 1914 at Sarıkamış, where he lost most of the 3rd Army. He recovered his prestige, however, when the Allied forces withdrew from the Dardanelles (1915–16). In 1918, following the Russian Revolution of 1917 and Russia's withdrawal from the war, he occupied Baku (now in Azerbaijan). However, after the Armistice in Europe, Enver fled to Germany (November 1918).

In Berlin he met the Bolshevik leader Karl Radek, and in 1920 he went to Moscow. He proposed the idea of overthrowing the regime of Mustafa Kemal (Atatürk) in Turkey with Soviet aid, but this plan received no support from Moscow. Though the Russian leaders became suspicious of him, Enver was nevertheless allowed to go to Turkistan with a plan for helping to organize the Central Asian republics. In 1921, however, the revolt of the Basmachi in Bukhara against the Soviet regime flared up, and Enver joined the insurgents. He was killed in action against the Red Army.

d'état of Jan. 23, 1913, which restored his party to power. In the Second Balkan War (1913), Enver was chief of the general staff of the Ottoman army. On July 22, 1913, he recaptured Edirne (Adrianople) from the Bulgars; and until 1918, the empire was dominated by the triumvirate of Enver, Talât Paşa, and Cemal Paşa.

In 1914, Enver, as minister of war, was instrumental in the signing of a defensive alliance with Germany against Russia.

CHAPTER 8

CASUALTIES OF WAR

The casualties suffered by the participants in World War I dwarfed those of previous wars: some 8,500,000 soldiers died as a result of fighting wounds and/or disease. The greatest number of casualties and wounds were inflicted by artillery, followed by small arms, and then by poisonous gases. The bayonet, which was relied on by the prewar French Army as the decisive weapon, actually produced few casualties in World War I. War was increasingly mechanized from 1914 and produced casualties even when nothing important to the outcome of the war was happening. On even a quiet day on the Western Front, many hundreds of Allied and German soldiers died. The heaviest loss of life for a single day occurred on July 1, 1916, during the Battle of the Somme, when the British Army suffered 57,470 casualties.

Sir Winston Churchill once described the battles of the Somme and Verdun, which were typical of trench warfare in their futile and indiscriminate slaughter, as being waged between double or triple walls of cannons fed by mountains of shells. In an open space, surrounded by masses of these guns, large numbers of infantry divisions collided. They fought in this dangerous position until battered into a state of uselessness. Then, they were replaced by other divisions. So many men were lost in the process, and shattered beyond recognition, that there is a French monument at Verdun to the 150,000 unlocated dead whose unidentifiable remains are assumed to be buried in the vicinity.

This kind of war made it difficult to prepare accurate casualty lists. There were revolutions in four of the warring countries in 1918, and the attention of the new governments quickly shifted away from the grim problem of war losses. A completely accurate table of losses of human life incurred during the war may never be compiled.

The best available estimates of World War I military casualties are assembled in the table on page 219.

Similar uncertainties exist about the number of civilian deaths attributable to the war. During World War I, there were no agencies established to keep records of these fatalities; however, it is clear that the displacement of peoples through the movement of the war in Europe and in Asia Minor, accompanied as it was in 1918 by the most destructive outbreak of influenza in history, led to the deaths of large number of civilians. It has been estimated that the number of civilian deaths attributable to the war was higher than the military casualties, around 13,000,000 people. These civilian deaths were largely caused by starvation, exposure, disease, military encounters, and massacres.

THE WAR GUILT QUESTION

THE SEARCH FOR CAUSES

Debate over the origins and causes of World War I was from the start partisan and moral in tone. Each of the belligerents published documentary collections selected to shift the blame and prove that they were fighting in self-defense. Serbia, as told by Serbians, was defending itself against Austrian aggression. On the other hand, Austria-Hungary claimed to be defending its very existence against terror plotted on foreign soil. Russia was defending Serbia and the Slavic cause against German imperialism. Germany was defending its lone reliable ally from attack and itself from entente encirclement. France, with most justification, was defending itself against unprovoked German attack. And Britain was fighting in defense of Belgium, international law, and the balance of European power.

In the Treaty of Versailles (1919), the victorious coalition justified its peace terms by forcing Germany and its allies to acknowledge guilt for the war. This tactic was historically dubious and politically disastrous, but it stemmed from the liberal conviction, as old as the Enlightenment, that peace was normal and war an aberration or crime for which clear responsibility—guilt—could be established. Almost at once, revisionist historians examined the thousands of documents that governments made available after 1920 and challenged the Versailles verdict. The German government had indeed issued the risky "blank check" and urged Vienna on an aggressive course. It had swept aside all proposals for mediation until events had gained irreversible momentum. It had, finally, surrendered its authority to a military plan that ensured the war could not

COUNTRY	TOTAL MOBILIZED FORCES	KILLED AND DIED	WOUNDED	PRISONERS AND MISSING	TOTAL CASUALTIES	PERCENTAGE OF MOBILIZED FORCES IN CASUALTIES
ARMED FORCES MOBILIZED AND CASUALTIES IN WORLD WAR I*						
ALLIED AND ASSOCIATED POWERS						
Russia	12,000,000	1,700,000	4,950,000	2,500,000	9,150,000	76.3
British Empire	8,904,467	908,371	2,090,212	191,652	3,190,235	35.8
France	8,410,000	1,357,800	4,266,000	537,000	6,160,800	73.3
Italy	5,615,000	650,000	947,000	600,000	2,197,000	39.1
United States	4,355,000	116,516	204,002	4,500	323,018	8.1
Japan	800,000	300	907	3	1,210	0.2
Romania	750,000	335,706	120,000	80,000	535,706	71.4
Serbia	707,343	45,000	133,148	152,958	331,106	46.8
Belgium	267,000	13,716	44,686	34,659	93,061	34.9
Greece	230,000	5,000	21,000	1,000	27,000	11.7
Portugal	100,000	7,222	13,751	12,318	33,291	33.3
Montenegro	50,000	3,000	10,000	7,000	20,000	40.0
Total	42,188,810	5,142,631	12,800,706	4,121,090	22,064,427	52.3
CENTRAL POWERS						
Germany	11,000,000	1,773,700	4,216,058	1,152,800	7,142,558	64.9
Austria-Hungary	7,800,000	1,200,000	3,620,000	2,200,000	7,020,000	90.0
Turkey	2,850,000	325,000	400,000	250,000	975,000	34.2
Bulgaria	1,200,000	87,500	152,390	27,029	266,919	22.2
Total	22,850,000	3,386,200	8,388,448	3,629,829	15,404,477	67.4
GRAND TOTAL	65,038,810	8,528,831	21,189,154	7,750,919	37,468,904	57.5

As reported by the U.S. War Department in February 1924. U.S. casualties as amended by the Statistical Services Center, Office of the Secretary of Defense, Nov. 7, 1957.

be localized. Indeed, the whole course of German foreign policy since 1890 had been restless and counterproductive, calling into existence the very ring of enemies it then took extreme risks to break. But, on the other hand, Russia's hasty mobilization expanded the crisis beyond the Balkans, initiated a round of military moves, and contributed to German panic. Given the military realities of the age, Sazonov's notion of Russian mobilization as a mere "application of pressure" was either disingenuous or foolish. France also could be faulted for not restraining Russia and for issuing its own "blank check." Even the British might have done more to preserve peace, either through more vigorous mediation or by making clear that they would not remain neutral in a continental war, thus deterring the German military aggression. Finally, what of the states at the heart of the crisis? Surely Belgrade's use of political terrorism in the name of Greater Serbia, and Austria-Hungary's determination to crush its tormentors, provoked the crisis in the first place. By the 1930s, moderate historians had concluded, as had Lloyd George, that no one country was to blame for the war: "We all stumbled into it."

Thus, the failure of documentary research to settle the war-guilt question led other historians to look behind the July 1914 crisis for long-range causes of the war. Surely, they reasoned, such profound events must have had profound origins. As early as 1928, the American Sidney B. Fay concluded that none of the

European leaders had wanted a great war, and identified as its deeper causes the alliance systems, militarism, imperialism, nationalism, and the newspaper press. (Marxists, of course, from the publication of Lenin's *Imperialism, the Highest Stage of Capitalism* in 1916, had held finance capitalism to be accountable for the war.) In this view, the polarization of Europe into alliance systems had made "chain-reaction" escalation of a local imbroglio almost assured. Militarism and imperialism had fed tensions and appetites among the Great Powers, while nationalism and sensationalist journalism had stoked popular resentments. How else could one explain the universal enthusiasm with which soldiers and civilians alike greeted the outbreak of war? Such evenhanded sentiments, along with the abstraction of the terms of analysis that exculpated individuals while blaming the system, were both appealing and prescriptive. In the 1930s, British statesmen in particular would strive to learn the lessons of 1914 and so prevent another war. But as another generation's hindsight would reveal, the lessons did not apply to the new situation.

After World War II and the Cold War had left the issues of 1914 passé, a committee of French and German historians agreed that World War I was an unwilled disaster for which all countries shared blame. Only a few years later, however, in 1961, that consensus shattered. The German historian Fritz Fischer published a massive study of German war aims during 1914–18 and held that Germany's

This painting by William Orpen commemorating the signing of the Treaty of Versailles in 1919 depicts Dr. Johannes Bell of Germany signing the treaty. He is surrounded by dignitaries from the United States, France, Great Britain, Canada, Japan, Portugal, Yugoslavia, India, Italy, Belgium, South Africa, and Australia. Hulton Archive/Getty Images

government, social elites, and even broad masses had consciously pursued a breakthrough to world power in the years before World War I. Thus, the German government, fully aware of the risks of world war and of British belligerency, had deliberately provoked the 1914 crisis. Fischer's thesis sparked bitter debate and a rash of new interpretations of World War I. Leftist historians made connections between Fischer's evidence and evidence that had been cited 30 years before by Eckhart Kehr, who had traced the social origins of the naval program to the cleavages in German society and the stalemate in the Reichstag. Other historians saw links to the Bismarckian technique of using foreign policy excursions to stifle domestic reform, a technique dubbed "social imperialism." To these historians, it appeared that Germany's rulers had resolved before 1914 to overthrow the world order in hopes of preserving the domestic order.

Traditionalist critics of Fischer pointed to the universality of imperialistic, social Darwinist, and militaristic behaviour, especially among the Great Powers, on the eve of the war. The kaiser, in his most nationalistic moods, only spoke and acted like many other influential figures among the Great Powers. Did not Sazonov and the Russian generals, in their unrecorded moments, yearn to erase the humiliation of 1905 and conquer the Dardanelles, or Poincaré and General J.-J.-C. Joffre wonder excitedly if the recovery of Alsace-Lorraine were finally at hand? And were not Primrose and

navy leagues thrilled at the prospect of a Nelsonian clash of dreadnoughts? The Germans were not the only people who grew weary of peace or harboured grandiose visions of empire. To this universalist view leftist historians like the American A. J. Mayer then applied the "primacy of domestic policy" thesis and hypothesized that all the European powers had courted war as a means of cowing or distracting their working classes and national minorities from domestic political unrest.

Such "new left" interpretations triggered a period of intense study of the connections between domestic and foreign policy, leading to the conclusion that a postulation of internal origins of the war, while obvious for Austria and plausible for Russia, failed in the cases of democratic Britain and France. If anything, internal discord made for reticence rather than assertion on the part of their foreign policy elites. The conservative historian Gerhard Ritter even challenged the Fischer thesis in the German case. The real problem, he argued, was not fear of the Social Democrats but the age-old tension between civilian and military influence in the Prussian-German government. Politicians, exemplified by Bethmann, did not share the eagerness or imprudence of the general staff but lost control of the ship of state in the atmosphere of deepening crisis leading up to 1914. Finally, a moderate German historian, Wolfgang J. Mommsen, dispensed with polemics altogether. Germany's rapid industrialization and the tardiness of modernization in Austria-Hungary

In Focus: League of Nations

During the war, influential groups in the United States and Britain had urged the creation of a supranational organization to solve disputes between countries, and U.S. President Woodrow Wilson strongly favoured the idea as a means of preventing another destructive world conflict. A league covenant, embodying the principles of collective security (joint action by league members against an aggressor), arbitration of international disputes, reduction of armaments, and open diplomacy, was formulated and subscribed to by the Allies at the Paris Peace Conference in 1919. The Covenant established the League of Nations' directing organs: an assembly composed of representatives of all members; a council composed of permanent representatives of the leading Allied Powers (with additional rotating members); and a secretariat (executive), presided over by a secretary-general. It also provided for a Permanent Court of International Justice and for a system whereby colonies in Asia and Africa would be distributed among the Allied Powers in the form of mandates.

During the 1920s the League of Nations, with its headquarters at Geneva, assimilated new members (neutral and enemy nations had been initially excluded), helped settle minor international disputes, and experienced no serious challenges to its authority. It was seriously weakened, however, by the nonadherence of the United States; the U.S. Congress failed to ratify the Treaty of Versailles (containing the covenant). One of the league's main purposes in preventing aggression was to preserve the status quo as established by the post–World War I peace treaties.

and Russia, he concluded, created instabilities in central and eastern Europe that found expression in desperate self-assertion. Echoing Joseph Schumpeter, Mommsen blamed the war on the survival of precapitalist regimes that simply proved "no longer adequate in the face of rapid social change and the steady advance of mass politics." This interpretation, however, amounted to an updated and elaborated version of the unsophisticated consensus that "we all stumbled into it." Were the world wars, then, as some historians claimed, beyond human control?

Thus, the search for long-range causes, while turning up a wealth of new information and insight, ran ultimately aground. After all, if "imperialism" or "capitalism" had caused the war, they had just as assuredly caused the unprecedented era of peace and growth that preceded it. Imperialist crises, though tense at times, had always been resolved, and even Germany's ambitions were on the verge of being served through a 1914 agreement with Britain on a planned partition of the Portuguese empire. Imperial politics were simply not a casus belli for anyone except Britain. Military preparedness was at a peak. However, armaments are responses to tensions, not the cause of them, and they had, perhaps, served to deter war in the numerous crises preceding 1914. Capitalist activity since the turn of the century tied the nations of Europe together as never before, and in 1914 most leading businessmen were advocates of peace. The alliance systems between the Great Powers themselves were defensive and deterrent by design and had served as such for decades. Nor were they inflexible. Italy opted out of its alliance, the tsar was not bound to risk his dynasty on behalf of Serbia, or the kaiser his on behalf of Austria-Hungary, while the French and British cabinets might never have persuaded their parliaments to take up arms had the Schlieffen Plan not forced the issue. Perhaps the 1914 crisis was, after all, a series of irreparable blunders, in which statesmen failed to perceive the effects their actions would have on the others.

THE CENTRALITY OF THE HABSBURG MONARCHY

Perhaps a long-range view that is still serviceable in explaining what caused the war is precisely the one derived from old-fashioned analysis of the balance-of-power system, forgotten amid the debates over national or class responsibility. This view, suggested by Paul Schroeder in 1972, asks not why war broke out in 1914, but why not before? What snapped in 1914? The answer, he argued, is that the keystone of European balance, the element of stability that allowed the other powers to chase imperial moonbeams at will, was Austria-Hungary itself. The

heedless policies of the other powers, however, gradually undermined the Habsburg monarchy until it was faced with a mortal choice. At that point, the most stable member of the system became the most disruptive, the girders of security (the alliances) generated destructive pressures of their own, and the European system collapsed. To be sure, Austria-Hungary was threatened with its own nationality problem, aggravated by Serbia. It could better have met that threat, however, if the Great Powers had worked to ameliorate pressures on it, just as they had carried the declining Ottoman Empire for a full century. Instead, the ambitions of Russia, France, and Britain, and the stifling friendship of Germany, only served to push Austria-Hungary to the brink. This was not their intention, but it was the effect.

The central fact of global politics from 1890 to 1914 was Britain's relative decline in power and influence. This occurred naturally, as industrial power diffused, but was aggravated by the particular challenge of Germany. Overextended, the British sought partners to share the burdens of a world empire and were obliged in return to look kindly on those partners' ambitions. However, the resulting Triple Entente was not the cause of Germany's frustrations in the conduct of *Weltpolitik*. Rather it was the cause of Germany's frustrations to pursue an imperial policy *à outrance*. Situated in the middle of Europe, with hostile armies on two sides, and committed to the defense of Austria-Hungary, Germany was unable to make headway in the overseas world despite its strength. By contrast, relatively weak France or hopelessly ramshackle Russia could engage in adventures at will, suffer setbacks, and return to the fray in a few years. Schroeder concluded: "The contradiction between what Germany wanted to do and what she dared to do and was obliged to do accounts in turn for the erratic, uncoordinated character of German world policy, its inability to settle on clear goals and carry them through, the constant initiatives leading nowhere, the frequent changes in mid-course." All Germany could do was bluff and hope to be paid for doing nothing: for remaining neutral in the Russo-Japanese War, for not building more dreadnoughts, for letting the French into Morocco, for not penetrating Persia. Of course, Germany could have launched an imperialist war in 1905 or 1911 under more favourable circumstances. It chose not to do so, and German might was such that prior to 1914 the other powers never considered a passage of arms with Germany.

Instead, Triple Entente diplomacy served to undermine the stability of Austria-Hungary. Everyone recognized that it was the "sick man of Europe" and that its demise would be inconvenient at very best and would almost certainly expose the ethnic mare's nest of southeastern Europe to civil war or Russian or German domination. Yet nothing was done about it. France could scarcely afford to intervene—its security was too tightly bound to Russia's—but France's policy of wooing Italy out of the Triple Alliance was a grave setback, not for Germany but for Austria-Hungary. Russia brazenly pushed the Slavic nationalities forward, thinking to make gains but never realizing that tsarism was as dependent on Habsburg survival as Austria-Hungary had been on Ottoman survival. Only Britain had the capacity to maneuver, to restrain the likes of Serbia and Russia and take some of the Austro-Hungarian burden off Germany's shoulders. And indeed it had done so before—in 1815–22, 1878, and 1888. But now the British chose vaguely to encourage Russia in the Balkans, letting Austria-Hungary, as it were, pay the price for distracting Russia from the frontiers of India. So, by 1914, Austria was encircled and Germany was left with the choice of watching its only ally collapse or risking a war against all Europe. Having chosen the risk, and lost, it is no surprise that the Germans (as well as the other powers) gave vent to all their prewar bitterness and pursued a thorough revision of world politics in their own favour.

GLOSSARY

ameliorate To make better; to improve.

aphorism A terse saying dealing with a general truth.

apotheosis Ideal example; epitome.

armistice A temporary suspension of hostilities by agreement of all warring parties.

assonance Poetic device in which the same vowel sounds are used with different consonants in the stressed syllables of the rhyming words.

attenuate To weaken or reduce in force or intensity.

attrition A reduction in numbers, size, or strength.

avarice Insatiable greed; miserly desire to gain or hoard wealth.

bellicosity Eagerness to fight; hostility.

cadre Key group of military officers necessary to train and establish a new military unit.

caliph A former leader of the Ottoman Empire.

chancellor The chief minister of state in certain parliamentary governments, as with Germany.

chassis The frame and wheels of a motor vehicle.

commodore In the navy, an officer next in rank below rear admiral.

conscription Compulsory enrollment in military services; draft.

cumbrous Cumbersome, difficult to carry.

dreadnought A type of battleship armed with big guns in all of its turrets.

emplacement The platform for a gun or battery and its accessories.

exculpate To clear of guilt or blame.

execrate To curse; denounce.

foxhole A small pit dug for shelter in a battle area.

fruition Realization of something desired; attainment.

generalissimo In certain countries, the name for the supreme commander of armed forces.

hegemony Leadership or predominant influence exercised by one power over another.

historiography The body of techniques, theories, and principles of historical research.

hubris Excessive pride.

ignominious Marked by humiliation and disgrace.

imbroglio Disagreement of a bitter nature, as between persons or nations.

immolate Sacrifice.

intelligentsia Intellectuals considered as a group or class.

interdiction Steady bombardment of enemy positions.

intransigent Uncompromising; inflexible.

kaiser A German or Austrian emperor.

laconic Expressing much in few words; concise.

nonpareil A person or thing without equal; peerless.

peerage The rank of any of the five degrees of nobility in Great Britain.

perfunctory Performed only as routine duty; hasty and superficial; lacking care or enthusiasm.

phalanx A body of troops in close order.

pincer A movement in which an enemy force is attacked from both sides and the front.

posthumously Arising or occurring after one's death.

prophylactic Defense against a disease or infection, as a drug.

pusillanimous Cowardly, lacking courage or resolution.

riposte A sharp return in speech or action; counterstroke.

salvo Simultaneous discharge of artillery shells.

sedulous Diligent; persevering, assiduous.

shaykh Also called a sheik, a spiritual guide.

sortie A rapid movement of troops from a defensive position to a place of attack.

union sacrée Political truce in France during World War I in which the left wing agreed not to oppose the government.

vanguard The front section of an advancing army.

viscount A nobleman below earl and above baron in rank.

BIBLIOGRAPHY

John Keegan, *The First World War* (1999), is a good dramatic overview. Comprehensive general accounts include Gerard J. De Groot, *The First World War* (2001), and Spencer Tucker, *The Great War 1914–1918* (1998). Hew Strachan (ed.), *The Oxford Illustrated History of the First World War* (1998), is a first-rate survey. Niall Ferguson, *The Pity of War* (1999), is best read as an extended interpretive essay. Hew Strachan, *The First World War* (2001), contains a superb analysis of the war's origins. A more detailed account is provided in Luigi Albertini, *The Origins of the War of 1914*, 3 vol. (1952–57, reprinted 1980; originally published in Italian, 1942–43). Peter Liddle and Hugh Cecil (eds.), *Facing Armageddon* (1996), includes a large number of excellent specialized essays covering the entire war. *Passchendaele in Perspective* (1997) and *At the Eleventh Hour* (1998), by the same editors, focus on the later years. Roger Chickering and Stig Foerster (eds.), *Great War, Total War* (2000), addresses the war as a total experience.

Jay Winter and Richard Wall (eds.), *The Upheaval of War* (1988), provides a comparative dimension on the home fronts. John Horne (ed.), *State, Society, and Mobilization in Europe during the First World War* (1997), offers case studies in responses to specific stresses. Gerd Hardach, *The First World War,* 1914–1918 (1987), is strong on economics and accessible to general readers.

Holger Herwig, *The First World War: Germany and Austria-Hungary, 1914–1918* (1997), tells the story of the Central Powers' war with flair and insight. Norman Stone, *The Eastern Front, 1914–1917* (1975), covers tsarist Russia's efforts. Jacques Becker, *The Great War and the French People* (1985), and Stephane Audoin-Rouzeau, *Men at War, 1914–1918: National Sentiment and Trench Journalism during the First World War* (1991), cover the war from a French perspective. Gerard J. De Groot, *Blighty: British Society in the Era of the Great War* (1996), challenges conventional wisdoms. David Kennedy, *Over Here* (1980), analyzes the U.S. experience.

Martin Middlebrook, *The First Day on the Somme* (1971), and Alistair Horne, *Verdun: The Price of Victory* (1962), are general-audience works. Robin Prior and Trevor Wilson, *Passchendaele: The Unknown Story* (1996), is an academic analysis. John Schindler, *Isonzo* (2001), takes a similar approach to the Italian front. Barbara Tuchman, *The Guns of August* (1962), is best read in conjunction with Sewall Tyng, *The Campaign of the Marne* (1935). Tony Ashworth, *Trench Warfare 1914–1918* (1980), and John Ellis, *Eye-Deep in Hell* (1989), present the routines of the Western Front. Bruce Gudmundsson, *Stormtroop Tactics*

(1989), discusses the German attempt to find a tactical solution to the war. T.E.H. Travers, *The Killing Ground* (1987) and *How the War Was Won* (1992), present the British approach to winning the war. Bill Rawling, *Surviving Trench Warfare* (1992), presents a Canadian perspective on the war. G. D. Sheffield, *Leadership in the Trenches* (2000), covers officer-enlisted man relations in the British army. Peter Simkins, *Kitchener's Army* (1986), analyzes the last great volunteer force. Douglas Porch, *The March to the Marne* (1981), is excellent on the French army's prewar matrix. Leonard Smith, *Between Mutiny and Obedience* (1984), interprets the mentality of the wartime force by focusing on one of its divisions. Edward M. Coffman, *The War to End All Wars* (1968), and James Hallas (ed.), *Doughboy War* (2000), combine to present the American Expeditionary Forces experience. Edward Erickson, *Ordered to Die* (2001), surveys the Ottoman army.

The five-volume history, Arthur Marder, *From the Dreadnought to Scapa Flow* (1961–70), is a detailed presentation from a British perspective. Paul Halpern, *A Naval History of World War I* (1994), is more comprehensive and less forbidding. John Morrow, *The Great War in the Air* (1993), and Lee Kennett, *The First Air War, 1914–1918* (1991), cover the new third element of conflict.

Modris Eksteins, *Rites of Spring* (1989), and Paul Fussell, *The Great War and Modern Memory* (1975), discuss the war's mentalities. John Horne and Arnold Kramer, *German Atrocities: A History of Denial* (1992), analyzes the psychology of atrocities. Jay Winter, *Sites of Memory, Sites of Mourning* (1995), deals with emotional legacies.

Manfred Boemke, Gerald Feldman, and Elisabeth Glaser (eds.), *The Treaty of Versailles: A Reassessment after 75 Years* (1998), makes a case that the Versailles treaties offered at least reasonable possibilities for reconstruction and reconciliation. Arno Mayer, *The Politics and Diplomacy of Peacemaking* (1969), stresses Western fear of radicalism in determining the peace processes.

INDEX